Violence and Reform in American History

Violence and Reform in American History

Rhodri Jeffreys-Jones

New Viewpoints
A Division of Franklin Watts
New York | London | 1978

New Viewpoints
A Division of Franklin Watts
730 Fifth Avenue
New York, New York 10019

Library of Congress Cataloging in Publication Data

Jeffreys-Jones, Rhodri.
  Violence and reform in American history.

  Bibliography: p.
  Includes index.
  1. Violence—United States—History.   I. Title.
HN90.V5J43   301.6′33′0973   78–4279
ISBN 0–531–05404–7
ISBN 0–531–05613–9 pbk.

FOR MY WIFE, JANETTA

Contents

Acknowledgments

AT THE CONCLUSION OF FOURTEEN YEARS OF RESEARCH AND WRITING, IT is a pleasure to acknowledge the help that made this book possible and to thank in the warmest possible terms the individuals concerned.

It was the late Sir Denis Brogan who encouraged my work on industrial violence, but the progress of this scheme owes much to Sidney Fine, who drew my attention to valuable archival sources, Oscar Handlin, under whose guidance I was extremely fortunate to find myself as a graduate student in 1965–1966, and William R. Brock, who skillfully supervised the presentation of my doctoral dissertation at Cambridge University.

A Twenty-Seven Foundation Award from the Institute of Historical Research, a Fulbright Travel Fellowship, a Fellowship at the Charles Warren Center for Studies in American History at Harvard University, and several grants from the University of Edinburgh made up the generous financial assistance that enabled me to pursue postdoctoral research. Dallas L. Jones allowed me to use the Walter Drew Papers, and John M. Whitcomb, the Rose Pastor Stokes Papers. C. W. Derek Peare of the Statistical Office of the European Communities, Luxembourg, gave me expert advice on quantitative data. Thomas J. Barron, Stuart M. Blumin, James V. Compton, and Jim Potter kindly subjected portions of the manuscript to critical readings. Bernard Bailyn and Donald Fleming edited and improved a long essay that formed the basis of several chapters of this book and first appeared as "Violence in American History: Plug Uglies in the Progressive Era" in *Perspectives in American History,* VIII (1974). The custodians of the libraries and archives listed on page 203 supplied me with generous and scholarly assistance.

I am deeply grateful to all the foregoing, and to my wife Janetta, whose support and encouragement allowed this study to come to fruition.

R. J.-J.

Violence and Reform in American History

Chapter 1

Introduction ─────────

MANY DISCUSSIONS OF U.S. AFFAIRS AND HISTORY ARE PREDICATED ON THE assumption that America is a violent country with a violent past. The assumption is based on the conduct of the Pilgrim Fathers, who fell upon the aborigines, and of their successors, through Regulation and Revolution, Civil War and Lynch Law, Big-Time Crime and Campus Revolt. This emphasis on American violence is heavy and persistent but not always well placed.

Violence has received disproportionate attention for several reasons. To begin with, it sells. News of disaster spreads with the speed of scandal. It is profitable to the commercial vendors of information, such as the press. Violence can also broadcast political messages. Whatever their slogan—the reactionaries' "Law and Order" or the insurgents' "Reform Before Revolution"—politicians are aware that on the wings of violence their views will be carried to the voters.

There have always been strong political motives for placing undue emphasis on violence. For example, President Woodrow Wilson's industrial investigation of 1912–1915 conveniently forecast class war as the alternative to reform; President Lyndon B. Johnson's investigation of violence in the 1960s similarly perceived a possibility of race revolution. The objectivity of such inquiries is easily questioned. The violence that they portrayed in reams of gripping prose cannot be taken for granted.

In challenging the traditional assessment of American violence, it would be futile to dispute the plain facts, exaggerated though these may have been. This book does not set out to prove that the Pilgrim Fathers were true to their Christian pacifist principles, though the Quakers, until the 1750s, frequently were. It does not seek to undermine the significance of the Second Amendment to the U.S. Constitution by dwelling unduly on the fact that the American right to bear arms had its documentary origin in the English Bill of Rights of 1689.[1] To find a lawyer for every Regulator, a bookworm for each student rocking a paddy wagon, is merely to replace one kind of selectivity with another. The object of this book is to chip away, in an unsensational manner, at an assumption that has too long been held. It is suggested here that periodic crises of order were often crises of the mind, that particular manifestations of disorder, even the anarchic propensity of America as a whole, seem the less for comparison.

The focus of this book is the problem of industrial violence in the Progressive period. The focus is narrowed, widened, lengthened, and shortened in a way designed to place the problem in perspective and to cast light on allied problems such as race riots. On the specific plane, there is an account of the widely misinterpreted "National Dynamite Campaign" conducted by the McNamara brothers on behalf of the International Association of Bridge, Structural and Ornamental Iron-workers (the Bridgemen's Union) between 1905 and 1910. More generally, there is a survey and discussion of industrial violence from ante-bellum days to the 1960s; this, in turn, is considered in the context of a wider framework of violence. While many forms of American violence are considered, the main subtheme of the book is racial violence —of the variety directed against whites by blacks, not vice-versa. For the book explores the relationship between violence and general-welfare reform, and in this sense the study of labor and black history is particularly fruitful, while the study of vigilantism, lynching, and white ethnic riots is less so.[2] Another form of violence with a definite, if controversial, relationship to reform is war. The vexed questions of Revolutionary and Civil War ideology are, however, left aside in this book; they have already engaged the attention of gifted historians and have less bearing on general-welfare legislation than the wars of the twentieth century, which, as we shall see, had a definite effect in this respect.[3]

The problem of industrial violence became acute in the Progressive period. In the Gilded Age, which preceded it, American capitalism had achieved triumphant expansion and reorganization, at considerable social and political cost. From the 1890s to the 1920s, Progressives tried to redress the social and political balance. But their role as social and political saviors was apparently threatened by the rival economic initiatives of the trade unions. From 1897, the membership of unions affiliated with the American Federation of Labor grew, never to suffer a serious reverse. At the same time, the rise of political socialism—the Socialist Party of America achieved almost a million votes in the Presidential election of 1912—comprised a political threat to Progressives from the left.

The success of trade unionism produced allegations of unfairness and prognostications of disaster. After 1900, writers of several different persuasions protested that industrial violence, of both unions and trusts, was becoming more and more prevalent. Even a union journal, *The Weekly Bulletin of the Clothing Trades,* could agree in 1905 that "notwithstanding the influence and authority of labor leaders . . . violence during strikes is on the increase." [4]

At an early stage of research, the present writer accepted the oft-repeated assumption that American industrial violence was exceptional in degree and that it reached a climax in the Progressive period. Yet it transpired that this was distortion, both external and internal. Externally compared, *industrial* violence as such was not remarkable; internally, industrial violence *in the Progressive period* was less notable for its exceptional intensity than for the ballyhoo that it occasioned. It was the latter that prompted *Nation* to descry in 1912 a "Vogue for Violence." [5]

This idea invites a new kind of inquiry: What occasioned the exaggeration of actual and potential violence? The question may be asked of the 1960s as well as of the Progressive period, and some, but not all, of the answers are similar. For example, public opinion began to focus after the Haymarket Bomb Affair of 1886 on an image of workers' violence given a glamorous notoriety by socialist theory; similarly, black nationalist ideology inspired distorted reactions in the John F. Kennedy–Lyndon B. Johnson years. Another parallel is the widespread willingness on the part of both labor and black leaders to exploit violence in spite of their generally nonrevolutionary outlook. The tendency contributed, along with other factors, to the distortions of both periods.

On the other hand, one short-term factor that gave to the harmlessly growing labor movement a menacing, insurrectionary appearance was never discernible in black history. Private detective agencies underwent mushroom-like growth and proliferation after 1900. "Pinkertonism" was an eponym by the 1890s, a fact that only obscures the presence of many commercial rivals to Pinkerton's National Detective Agency. The business of most of the new agencies, run by tough men like James Farley, was to play on fears of trade unionism. Enjoying their greatest prestige in the dozen years preceding the Great War, they invented threats of violent insurrection to frighten employers and then profited as company guards and labor spies. W. J. Burns, the prestigious founder of one of the leading agencies, went so far as to charge that organized labor, under the leadership of the AFL, was waging a "Masked War" on society.[6]

If America's peculiarly commercial detectives had a pecuniary motive for contributing to a rhetoric of violence, the nation's reformers believed they had good reasons for *using* it. This was particularly true of those intellectuals who flocked to the Progressive banner. Thinkers who accepted and elaborated upon the premise that class conflict was the probable alternative to Progressive reform included Theodore Roosevelt, for seven years President of the United States, Walter Lippmann, a young and able journalist, and John R. Commons, a sober labor economist from Wisconsin. Just as detectives aimed to frighten capitalists into engaging their services, so the ideological leaders of Progressivism wished to persuade the electorate to vote for reform from a fear of class conflagration.

The political heirs of those Progressives who had advocated a general-welfare state used the same tactics during the New Deal of the 1930s, the Fair Deal of the 1940s, and the Democratic administrations of the 1960s. During the politically successful New Deal, however, the rhetoric of conflict was muted, while in the Fair Deal it was largely directed toward the Russians (though it backfired domestically in the form of McCarthyism). The political rhetoric of violence reemerged in its most conspicuous form in the 1960s, when advocates of civil rights and social reform used black nationalist speeches and urban race riots in an attempt to prise legislation out of Congress. In 1968 reformers felt the sting of the political backlash that they themselves had helped to create when Republican Richard M. Nixon was elected President with the help of the "law-and-order" issue.

This book is not an attack on liberalism as such, but on one of the tactics used by liberals. Just as it is possible to question abolitionist tactics and motives without supporting slavery, so one may underscore the vitiating effects of liberal strategy without dismissing the case for Medicare. It is, of course, arguable that the abolitionists' failure to solve the problem of what to do with emancipated blacks reflected less their own ineptitude than the intractability of race relations. Similarly, one might dwell on the significance of John R. Commons' point that the American working class was a permanent minority, arguing that the social-reforming Progressives' resort to the issue of class violence was the consequence of an intractable problem, that of appealing to a majority of the voters.[7] It might be added that a comparable necessity later governed the tactical options of the champions of another minority, the black people.

This apparent defense may be bolstered by referring to the new character of twentieth-century liberalism. The historian Charles Forcey has suggested that liberals reached a "crossroad" in 1912: From then on they tried to use the power of the national state instead of opposing it.[8] But American society had remained pluralistic, different issues appealing to various groups and regions yet rarely to a majority of them. Unable to find a cohesive, campaign-winning issue that would yield them national power, perhaps the liberals of the Progressive period and 1960s thought they had to invent one. Necessary though such a tactic may have seemed, we shall see that it simply did not work in terms of permanent legislative achievement.

Chapter 2

The Anatomy of a Myth —

THE AMERICAN HAS GENERALLY BEEN A SOCIAL OPTIMIST. HE HAS SUC-
cumbed to social anxiety in many of its shapes and subtleties, but he
has not as a rule indulged in the European's forebodings of revolutionary conflict. It is all the more interesting, therefore, to observe two
departures from equanimity in the twentieth century. The first, which
we shall examine in this chapter, took place when a fear of class conflict
gripped the United States between 1903 and 1912, springing to life
again in the "Red Scare" of 1919. The second occurred in the 1960s,
when protesters against racism and the Vietnam War assumed the
fearsome role occupied fifty years earlier by militant workers.

Both scares in question were part of an international mood; both
were based on a distorted statistical appraisal of the violent propensi-
ties of rank-and-file workers or protesters; both scares were associated
with major initiatives in social reform. In the last respect, the scares
were distinctively American. The tendency to link violence with reform has been a tragic characteristic of twentieth-century American
politics.

The class conflict scare of 1903–1912 acquired unprecedented proportions. This, however, cannot be said of the "class violence" on
which it was based. A review of industrial violence from the 1830s to

8

the 1960s shows that the phenomenon was by no means limited to the Progressive Era of the early twentieth century.

Though Americans of various economic and political persuasions often used the term "class conflict" to describe collective disturbances from the Civil War to the 1920s, they were usually talking about industrial violence. As we shall see, they tried to quantify the extent of industrial violence and for this purpose used, in practice, a narrow and manageable definition of the phenomenon. Quantifiers of "class" or industrial violence included in their definition illegal, physical assaults on people and property, occurring in (1) work stoppages arising out of disputes between wage earners and their employers, (2) times of uneasy industrial peace, (3) periods of labor agitation and organization, and (4) open-shop offensives. This, then, must be the working definition for our analysis of the departure from social optimism that occurred in the Progressive period and of the background of actual industrial violence from the 1830s to the 1960s.

In the antebellum period there was little evidence of such conflict, because industrialization was not yet fully under way. Some industrial disturbances did occur, though they were not entirely distinct in character from preindustrial crowd disturbances. By the 1870s, industrial violence had reached a level that did not significantly abate until the very last years of the New Deal in the 1930s.

Collective bargaining by riot was a sporadic occurrence in the period from the 1830s to the close of the Civil War. New York City stonecutters rioted during a wage movement in 1834. In 1839 troops in Maryland shot ten casual laborers, and lesser disturbances of a similar nature took place as early railroads and canals were constructed. Mill girls in western Pennsylvania in 1846 proved themselves more disorderly than their Massachusetts counterparts when they dragged strikebreakers away from their machines during a major industrial dispute. But these various manifestations of force pale into insignificance in the context of an age marked by eye-gouging fights between gentlemen, when gangs known as Plug Uglies, Forty Thieves, Swamp Angels, and Slaughterhouse Boys terrorized metropolitan areas and policemen patrolled at their peril.[1]

With the growth of industry after the Civil War, mass confrontations between powerfully organized factions of labor and capital became commonplace. Between the 1870s and the 1920s diverse industries experienced clashes between organized workers and their employers: the railroads in 1877, 1886, and 1911; coal mines and metalliferous mines during each decade, and in some areas perennially; iron and steel on several occasions, notably at Homestead, Pennsylvania, in 1892 and at Gary, Indiana, in 1919.

Given these facts, it is possible to understand the alarm caused by the advent of a revolutionary movement in the United States. Anarchists who formed armed societies in the late 1870s and 1880s were regarded as eccentrics unlikely to harm society, but a succession of events beginning with the Haymarket Bomb Affair and culminating in the steel strike of 1919 and the formation of American Communist parties made the left increasingly suspect.

These developments forced trade unions to set a premium on respectability. If they nevertheless resorted to violence, they used discreet means. The handpicked walking delegate, the dynamite time bomb, and eventually the hired thug were preferred to the massed pickets whose actions embarrassed union leaders. As a result, labor violence had a tendency to become tied to specific goals. Some examples of riots fanned by mass hysteria can be found, however, even in the twentieth century.

Another characteristic of post-Appomattox industrialization was that employers were more successful in controlling violence. They used several techniques for protecting strikebreakers and property. Such traditional means as regulator or vigilante activity or the skillful control of the state militia continued to be at the disposal of capitalists. In Pennsylvania, coal and iron masters were able to employ their own police under the protection of the laws from 1866 to 1931. Other groups, such as the General Managers' Association in Chicago, organized mass posses of sheriffs or marshals. The Pinkerton Protective Patrol was established in 1866 and, until discredited by its involvement in the Homestead strike in 1892, openly supplied armed guards to employers. During the first decade of the twentieth century, the provision of armed guards became an important minor industry, as attested by the proliferation of detective agencies advertising that function. Yet, while industrial violence had become institutionalized, it had also leveled off. Strike mortalities from 1890 to 1909 were not increasing in number.

In the period from 1919 to 1939 private detective agencies lost some of their credibility, but employers assumed responsibility for anti-unionism, setting up company unions and in some cases amassing veritable arsenals in preparation for the day when it would be necessary to man the barricades. In the meantime, city and state police forces became, if less partisan, more efficient. The means for a small-scale battle existed. Although New Deal legislation seemed to remove the reasons for violence and the labor movement remained predominantly nonrevolutionary, the Great Depression sowed bitterness, and Franklin D. Roosevelt's Presidency saw a massive organizing drive by the Committee for Industrial Organization.

The killing of ten steel strikers on Memorial Day 1937 outside the South Chicago plant of the Republic Steel Corporation showed the potential of the 1930s for lawlessness; on the other side, the potential for violence on the part of unionists was revealed in bitter jurisdictional disputes. If the work of John Steuben is to be relied upon, 1934 was one of the most violent years in American history as measured by strike mortalities. Steuben's figures for total annual strike mortalities for the years from 1934 to 1949 are: 43, 32, 8, 20, 5, 8, 7, 9, 2, 0, 0, 1, 5, 1, 5, and 2 (according to Steuben, from 1941 his figures are incomplete).[2] The decline in strike mortalities, which coincided with the end of the New Deal and the outbreak of World War II, continued in peacetime and well into the era of the Taft-Hartley Act. According to Philip Taft and Philip Ross, the figures for the years from 1947 to 1962 were: 0, 4, 1, 2, 2, 0, 3, 0, 1, 0, 2, 3, 5, 1, 1, and 3.[3] On the available evidence, twentieth-century industrial violence as measured by strike mortalities was at its lowest ebb in the early 1960s.

In examining the reactions to actual industrial violence, middle-class sensitivity to the question is evident. In spite of the absence of any corresponding lower-class consciousness in American history, there has been a long-standing concern with class conflict. The sense of impending crisis that developed in the Progressive period was not instant panic but the outgrowth of a constant undercurrent of concern.

Industrial violence was a minor theme before the Civil War. Few were prepared to extol workingmen's violence. True, in 1830 Fanny Wright rejoiced that:

It is no longer nation pitched against nation for the good pleasure of and sport of Kings and great Captains, nor sect cutting the throats and roasting the carcasses of sect for the glory of God and satisfaction of priests. . . . No; it is now everywhere the oppressed

millions who are making common cause against oppression. . . .
And truly the struggle hath not come too soon.[4]

Yet most radicals of the 1830s were disposed, like Robert Owen, to believe in class harmony.

That class conflict was discussed is, however, worthy of note. The problem was acute enough to elicit definite responses from politicians, lawyers, and legislators. Statesmen like Hamilton had always been concerned over the danger of violence between domestic factions, and in a speech in the Senate in 1837 John C. Calhoun revived old fears: "There is and always has been in an advanced stage of wealth and civilization, a conflict between labor and capital. . . . We have, in fact, but just entered that condition of society where the strength and durability of our political institutions are to be tested." [5]

Opinions held by the legal fraternity may be determined from arguments delivered and verdicts rendered in criminal conspiracy cases. Curiously, the association of unions with violent practices appears to have been an accompaniment of legitimization. While the legitimacy of unions was in question, there was no need to criticize their methods. In a successful prosecution of New York cordwainers in 1809 for having conspired to raise their wages, the prosecution admitted that there had been "no personal violence, no outrage or disorder"; however, one journeyman who opted out of the alleged conspiracy was dismayed at his new role, for "to the real impoverishment which he must undergo, and to the evils heaped upon all who befriend him; to all this was added, the opprobrious epithet of scab." [6] If counsel was willing to abandon the charge of violence, the court was prepared to be lenient. Characteristically, light fines were imposed. The court's chief concern was to establish the principle of unlawful conspiracy.

A generation later, in *Commonwealth v. Hunt* (1840 and 1842), the conservative Whig chief justice of Massachusetts, Lemuel Shaw, upheld the legitimacy of trade unions that sought to establish the closed shop. Although not uniformly followed, this case was an important precedent. Future attacks on organized labor sought to curtail the functions of unions, rather than eliminate them altogether. In 1863 and 1864 laws prohibiting picketing and intimidation were considered or passed in Minnesota, New York, Massachusetts, and Illinois.[7]

What Calhoun had dreaded in the 1830s came to pass—industrialization produced depressed quarters and classes in American cities. Particularly after the Paris Commune of 1871, the poorer working classes by their very existence wrought terror in the hearts of many Americans. Reacting to the Commune, the social philanthropist Charles Loring Brace claimed that such associations as the Dead Rabbits and the Plug Uglies were identifiable with "The Prolétaires of New York." He wrote in *Dangerous Classes of New York* (1872) that ". . . certain small districts can be found in our metropolis with the unhappy fame of containing more human beings packed into the square yard, and stained with more acts of blood and riot within a given period, than is true of any other equal space of earth in the civilised world." [8]

Another typical reaction was that of *The New York Times:* "The Trade Unions of England have resorted to murder, assassination and arson in order to strike terror into the hearts of those who oppose them. This root of evil has been planted in American soil and in the mining regions of Pennsylvania we see its legitimate fruit. . . ." [9]

The larger context of such remarks was the emergence in post-Civil War America of middle- and upper-class consciousness of the conflict between labor and capital. A multitude of printed works testified to the growing disquiet over the "Labor Question." In the greatest of these, Henry George wrote in 1879 that the "association of poverty with progress is the great enigma of our times. . . . The reaction must come. The tower leans from its foundations, and every new story but hastens the final catastrophe." [10]

Expressions of concern over the labor problem took various forms. On the political level, the nation sought to inform itself. Between 1883 and 1885, the Senate Committee on Education and Labor investigated relations between labor and capital. The intellectual politicians and the political intellectuals offered numerous solutions to the problem of conflict, including the imperial expansion advocated by Henry Cabot Lodge and Brooks Adams. [11]

An acclaimed social solution of the nineteenth century was that of "nationalism" (the national administration of industry) as proposed in the novel *Looking Backward* (1888). Here, Edward Bellamy warned of a possibly "impending social cataclysm," in words more urgent than those of Henry George a decade earlier. [12] Within ten years, 425,000 copies of Bellamy's novels had reached the public. Ignatius Donnelly through scenes of horrible class warfare in his 1890 novel *Caesar's Column* was another purveyor of cataclysmic visions. Cataclysmic writers were not among the leading analysts of social conflict. Their writings were, however, symptomatic of a growing public disquietude.

Christian attitudes to social conflict, though not uniform, showed widespread concern. In 1895 the Reverend A. J. F. Behrends chastised the Brooklyn streetcar strikers, comparing their "insurrection" to the rebellion of the South, and quoting St. Paul in support of his view that state authority should not be challenged.[13] Such hostility to strikers' helping themselves was the hard edge of Behrends' philosophy expressed in *Socialism and Christianity* (1886), in which he attacked the laissez-faire doctrine and preached the conservative social gospel. In Behrends' Protestant Christian view, social clashes should be averted by introducing a new style of liberal reform.

Several Catholics also wished to liberalize society. One of their early steps was to tolerate and even encourage labor organizations that practiced nonviolent methods. In 1883 the grand secretary of the Knights of Labor had assured H. W. Blair, chairman of the Senate investigation, that members of the order never contemplated violence as a policy; this continued to be the position of Knights speaking in an official capacity.[14] By 1888 Cardinal Gibbons was able to bestow official sanction on the palpably nonrevolutionary and remedial order. Thereafter, such Catholics as Father Yorke of San Francisco and Ralph Easley of the National Civic Federation continued their individual efforts to liberalize society by acting in conjunction with trade unions.

In the first dozen years of the twentieth century, a full-blown debate developed around the theme of industrial violence. Some could not get away from the idea that labor was the aggressor. If paternally inclined, they might blame not the workers themselves but outside agitators, labor unionists, and socialists. On the other side, there were those who blamed employers. They included some of benevolent disposition who, instead of blaming employers directly, singled out the private detective for particular opprobrium. A further response of the Progressive generation was to attempt an objective explanation of labor violence.

Underlying these various reactions was the conviction that industrial violence had reached exceptional proportions. Yet, at the same time, lower-class consciousness had developed only in isolated and sporadic forms in the United States. The labor movement had, in the main, entered a conservative, institutional stage. Against this background, at least some writers tried to shed their prejudices, to be rational about the labor problem, and to quantify industrial violence.

The new concern for quantification signified no disbelief in class conflict. On the contrary, Upton Sinclair's *Jungle* (1906) was intended to reek of class violence as well as of decayed meat. In the same year, David M. Parry, president of the National Association of Manufacturers, published his *Scarlet Empire*, a novel about the terrors of life following a successful revolution by the AFL. Jack London's *War of the Classes* and *Iron Heel* appeared in 1905 and 1907 respectively, while the Haymarket Affair was given fictional form in 1909 in *The Bomb* by Frank Harris. Robert Hunter's *Violence and the Labor Movement* (1914) was an intelligent attempt to analyze class warfare, and two other serious treatments of the subject were prepared but never published. The political theorist Walter Weyl began a book on "The Class War" in 1911, and a federal investigator, Mrs. Inis Weed, prepared a manuscript on industrial violence on the eve of World War I.[15]

Newspaper editors presented stories of strike disorders beneath banner headlines. Such stories at times occupied the whole front page of a newspaper in an affected city, spreading also into the interior pages and editorial columns. In times of crisis these stories monopolized front pages for days, yielding only to news of an even more sensational nature, such as a train crash or the battles of the Russo-Japanese War (1904–1906).

Ray Stannard Baker's article in *McClure's* in January 1903 attacking the intimidation of nonunion men in the anthracite coal strike of 1902 helped to launch the muckraking era. A cluster of magazine articles appeared between 1900 and 1904, characterizing the period as one of great labor struggles.[16]

By 1904 the trade union movement had greatly expanded its membership, but from 1905 there was a lull in the industrial battle. One apologist for the employers acknowledged that following the defeat of the Chicago teamsters' strike in 1905, it was now safe for nonunion men to work all over the country.[17] Another complained that publishers would not print stories about union dynamite activities; on the contrary, some editors were now accepting articles exposing capitalists' frame-ups, strikebreaking tactics, and the utilization of private detectives.[18] On the other hand, A. Damon Runyon (who soaked up atmosphere, if nothing else, in a Long Island bar run by the union gangster Tom Slattery) belittled the dangers of class conflict in his satirical article on western mining strife, "Defense of Strikeville."[19]

The years following 1905 gained a retrospective reputation for vio-

lence in 1911. It was in December of that year, after an explosion in
the Los Angeles Times building resulting in twenty deaths, that John J.
McNamara of the Bridgemen's Union confessed to having organized
the widespread National Dynamite Campaign in the interests of his
union. (He actually admitted to having conspired to dynamite the
Llewellyn Iron Works in Los Angeles as part of this campaign but was
frequently associated with the more horrendous *Los Angeles Times*
explosion, in which his brother, James B., was implicated.) The Mc-
Namara affair reopened the discussion of labor violence in general.
C. P. Connolly, for instance, argued that although W. D. Haywood
and C. Moyer had been acquitted of having murdered the governor
of Idaho on behalf of the Western Federation of Miners, the similari-
ties between this case of 1905–1908 and that of the McNamaras were
too obvious to be ignored.[20] There was disagreement over the reasons
for the significance of the McNamara confession. The socialist H. M.
Tichenor thought the affair did not so much confirm people's suspicions
as shock them: the "Wave of Horror" reported in the press "disclosed
the fact that the world is not accustomed to tales of wholesale murder committed by members of the working class." [21] But no one
doubted the impact of the McNamara confession on public opinion.

Employers' allegations of union violence in the Progressive period
were the product of four factors. First, the legitimization of trade
unions meant that they could be attacked no longer as institutions but
only for their activities. To use the labor injunction effectively against
picketing, it was necessary to create in legal and political minds a con-
fusion between picketing and violence. Employers thus lobbied in
Washington against the proposed anti-injunction law and simultaneously
sought evidence of union violence.

Another factor underlying the vehemence of employers' charges was
the collectivization of their effort. The National Association of Manufacturers had been founded in the 1890s but grew in financial strength
and membership as a result of its anti-union campaign from 1903 on.
Other militantly open-shop organizations were the National Founders'
Association (established in 1898) and the National Metal Trades Association (1899). The Homestead victory of 1892, in which Andrew
Carnegie's deputy, Henry Clay Frick, successfully locked out the men
during a dispute, thereby abridging the power of the Amalgamated
Association of Iron, Steel and Tin Workers, had been a great encouragement to open-shop employers in the metal trades. In the 1900s it was

hoped that the building trades, the citadel of urban labor unionism, could be cracked open. The assault was made through the National Erectors' Association (NEA), whose members used steel to construct bridges and buildings. It would be possible to draw on the capital of firms based on steel to combat a labor force based on the walking delegate. To this end, Walter Drew was made commissioner of the NEA.

Drew was a corporation lawyer from Grand Rapids, Michigan, who directed the operations of the NEA against the plug-uglies and dynamiters of McNamara's Bridgemen's Union. He was a pro-injunction lobbyist in Washington, D.C., and an open-shop publicist. He maintained that labor organizations were threatening to achieve the closed shop through economic and physical force: "In its cruder aspects, it is force direct, physical, violent. Men seeking to bring their labor to market which a union desires for its own are threatened, assaulted, killed. This violence is one of the commonest features of all our strikes." [22] This opinion of Drew's was expressed in a pamphlet published for the NAM, which attempted to coordinate the activities and propaganda of other employers' organizations.

A third factor in the employers' choice of tactics was the tendency of public opinion to become calmer and to reflect on the virtues of the union side of the case. Many employers, in contrast, still believed unions to be immoral or economically disastrous or both. For this reason, employers allowed the intrusion into industrial relations of a final factor, the private detective. Since Drew, who used detectives, was obviously hot on the trail of the Bridgemen's dynamiters, it is understandable why the presidents of major steel companies, the railroads, and employers' associations such as the NAM should have been interested in financing anti-union sleuths.[23] In other less convincing cases, a multitude of private agents induced employers to proclaim, and possibly to believe, that unions throve on intimidation.

Characteristic of such proclamations was the colorful language employed. In his presidential address to the NAM in 1903, David M. Parry observed that "organized labor knows but one law, and that is the law of physical force—the law of the Huns and Vandals, the law of the savage. . . . Its history is stained with blood and ruin." John Kirby, Jr., brought the annual convention to its feet when he assured manufacturers that Mr. Parry would "lead them through" (Kirby was later president of the NAM).[24] Excitable employers were kept at fever pitch by association journals, such as the *Bulletin of the National Metal Trades Association* (which in 1905 became *Open Shop*) and the NAM's *American Industries.* The Citizens' Industrial Association of St. Louis chose the subtitle *A Journal of Law and Order* for their organ, *The Exponent.* The Citizens' Industrial Association of America, whose *Square Deal* had the progressive subtitle *For the Promotion of Industrial Peace,* assiduously chronicled strike violence.

Some employers tried to quantify or specify their charges. In 1904 the Colorado Mine Operators' Association published a pamphlet, known after its color as the "Red Book," charging a long and specific list of crimes committed in the West against the Western Federation of Miners, a list the union described as a catalogue of all crimes, whether by union men or not, since 1893.[25] In 1908 the National Founders' Association published their booklet, *A Policy of Lawlessness,* which consisted of a hundred pages closely printed with extracts from affidavits concerning various forms of riot, murder, and other coercion alleged to have occurred in strikes called by the Iron Molders' Union between 1904 and 1907.[26] Such publications were plausibly detailed. Similarly, there was some substance in the claim made by James C. Craig, president of the State Citizens' Alliance of Colorado (*American Industries,* May 16, 1904), that his organization was the result of encroachments in Colorado by socialist-anarchist unionism.[27] It required an additional flight of imagination, however, to accept Parry's possibility of a "Scarlet Empire" established by the AFL.

With employers attempting to discredit them for their tactics, trade unionists were defensive about violence. In the wake of Haywood's acquittal in 1907, the Chicago correspondent of the *Typographical Journal* regretted that the "Average American" associated strikes and violence with the very name of unionism.[28] The position of journal editorials is indicative of the same point. Trade-union journals were not daily newspapers and commented on the news mainly in editorials. Journal editors usually gave first prominence in their editorial columns to union grievances, but they did permit comment on news of industrial violence already reported in the city newspapers.

The *Coast Seamen's Journal,* official organ of the West Coast organization, the International Seamen's Union of America, is a convenient example in that its editorial columns contained a discussion of industrial violence throughout America over the period from 1890 to 1910. Under different editors, W. J. B. Mackay and N. Jortall, the average position of sixteen editorials on aspects of violence was about second out of an average of three editorials. Violence received a similarly middling prominence in the *American Federationist, The Railroad Trainmen's Journal,* and *The Teamsters.* Such caution was the result of a mounting attack on labor-union practices at a time when their members sought respectability. In the late 1880s and early 1890s, when employers' violence had been overt and their propaganda as disorganized as the workers themselves, the position of similar discussions in the *Journal of the Knights of Labor* had been higher. Thus, not every journal subscribed to the defensive pattern. Indeed, *The United Mine Workers' Journal* afforded great prominence to stories of violence as news items; otherwise, employers' terrorization in remote mining areas would have gone unnoticed. In summary, trade-union journals were constantly preoccupied with the question of industrial violence, but this preoccupation was usually manifested as a defensive editorial undercurrent. In the average trade union journal, there was little effort to foster a class spirit by affording prominence to overt manifestations of conflict.[29]

American socialists did not wish to be thought of as encouraging class conflict, but in effect they placed a more positive emphasis on violence than the trade unionists. In 1903 the Marxist A. M. Simons warned socialists to guard against the agent provocateur. Both employers and workers had organized into formidable combinations; during the inevitable next depression, the disorders of 1877, 1886, and 1894 would recur.[30] In 1911 Simons published *Social Forces in American History,* which included an economic interpretation of the American Constitution. In this widely acclaimed book, he denounced the use of violence as opportunistic, but cited it as evidence of social conflict in American history.

Contemporary reviews of *Social Forces* reveal that with respect to violence, the gulf between socialists and conservatives was perhaps narrower than that between trade unionists and either. A critic for the *Independent,* among others, accused Simons of basing his interpretation on "selected and unusual incidents." [31] A reviewer for the *Pittsburgh Gazette* doubted whether "the most rabid stump speaker of partisan politics" would dare treat in such an outrageous fashion the capitalist violence of 1877 and 1894, for fear of being taken for an inciter.[32] The interesting thing about these reviews is that, whereas Simons magnified present industrial conflict by comparing it too closely with past disorders, his political adversaries magnified it by forgetting that there had been such disorders. In the words of a reviewer for *Living Age,* "the book may be regarded as at once a symptom and a product of the prevailing industrial unrest." [33]

Whether based on reality or not, the cardinal ideological objection to socialists in America was that they aimed to change the social fabric by force and were therefore undemocratic. Socialists with differing views concerning revolutionary tactics only encouraged this objection when they imputed violence to each other, as well as to their common foes. Such attacks occurred following the assassination of President William McKinley in 1901 by Leon Czolgosz, a supposed anarchist. Simons delivered a "lecture" published on the front page of the *Chicago Workers' Call* in which he stated the position of the social democrats and attacked anarchism as a "fad of the radical bourgeoisie." [34] Daniel De Leon likewise attacked anarchism in his pamphlet *Socialism versus Anarchism,* thus dissociating the Socialist Labor Party, which he led, from anarchical violence.[35]

The launching in 1905 of an American syndicalist movement, the Industrial Workers of the World, provided many socialists with a new butt for attack. Increasingly after 1908, when the strictly nonviolent De Leon left the main IWW to form a rival organization, socialists denounced the former body. Spurred by the confession of McNamara in 1911, members of the Socialist Party criticized the use of violence by labor organizations, providing in 1912 for the expulsion from their party of its advocates. In 1914, Robert Hunter published his *Violence and the Labor Movement,* a conspicuous attack on the advocates of violence within the labor movement as well as on the lawlessness of private detectives hired by employers.

Just as academic societies in the 1960s asked for scholarly contributions on so-called Negro riots, so the American Economic Association in 1906 heard a paper from Thomas S. Adams on "Violence in Labor Disputes." Adams had collaborated with Richard T. Ely in bringing up to date the most popular pre-New Deal economic textbook, *Outlines of Economics* (1893, rev. ed., New York, 1908). He was a professor of political economy at the University of Wisconsin, a leading statistician, and destined to become, under the influence of Wisconsin's social economist John R. Commons, the architect of progressive taxation in America. Adams had already remarked in his *Labor Problems* (1905, published in conjunction with Helen Sumner) that "there can be little doubt at all about the prevalence of industrial violence. . . ." He concluded his contribution on strikes and lockouts with a powerful exhortation to unions to stop shielding the "scab-slugger" and "bomb-thrower." [36]

It is significant that in his paper of 1906 Adams acknowledged the aid of his colleagues at the University of Wisconsin, and of their close collaborators at the Wisconsin State Bureau of Industrial Research, for Adams' approach reflected three characteristics of economic thinking at Wisconsin.[37] In the first place, a concern for quantification led him to concede that, compared with other kinds of domestic homicide, "strike violence is as dust in the balance." [38] Second, he was influenced by the institutional approach to economics advocated by Commons, which comprised not merely the study of new associations like unions, but also a consideration of social expectations. Even if instances of violence were comparatively rare, Adams argued, the expectation of being slugged was effectively intimidation. Similarly, laws that were excellent in principle but had no chance of being implemented because they were divorced from reality or laws that bore more heavily on the union than the employers' side would meet with Adams' censure. Finally, Adams urged the adoption of a solution tried successfully in other fields at Wisconsin. Commissions should be set up to enforce the laws and provide a permanent arbitration service; this would reduce the number of strikes and, therefore, the incidence of violence.[39]

The Wisconsin professors strongly influenced political and economic thought in America. Their expertise and viewpoints were felt through the United States Commission on Industrial Relations (CIR). Following the McNamara confession, President William H. Taft heeded the call for a federal investigation, after an intensive campaign led by such social workers as Jane Addams and Paul Kellogg, editor of *Survey* magazine, and supported by such academics as George E. Barnett, who had been a commentator on Adams' paper in 1906. In the U.S. Senate, the NAM lobby joined with the AFL and National Civic Federation lobbies in supporting the proposals for an investigation. The passing of the CIR bill on August 15, 1912, was a symptom of universal concern with the problem of industrial violence.[40]

Under the chairmanship of Frank Walsh, appointed by Taft's successor Woodrow Wilson, most of the money available to the CIR was expended on public hearings at the location of strikes. But in addition to its hearings, the commission supported a Research Division under the direction of Charles McCarthy, director of the Wisconsin Reference Library, who undertook his new task at the instigation of Commons.[41]

Whether by residence, profession, or academic training, most of those who produced reports on violence for the Research Division were associated with the University of Wisconsin, including W. Ballantine, Crystal E. Benedict, Luke Grant, Elizabeth A. Hyde, Blaine F. Moore, Daniel O'Regan, Margaret L. Stecker, F. P. Valiant, Inis Weed, and Edwin E. Witte.

Just as a broad spectrum of lobbyists had demanded an investigation on the basis of expected social upheaval, so the preoccupation with violence continued after the commission had been set up. Advocating workmen's compensation at preliminary hearings in 1913, McCarthy observed: "These things are coming up in a crowded country like America. . . . The problem of unrest is coming up, because men are not able to get out on the land, and get at the minerals, and get the things of nature." [42] The investigations of the intellectuals of the CIR were more cautious than those of Walsh, who sensationalized employers' violence in a series of widely publicized public hearings. But the Wisconsin team wished it to be known that they, too, had premonitions of social upheaval.

Americans living in the Progressive period built a composite picture of industrial violence. To discuss their views without heeding this and without grasping the contemporary definition of quantifiable violence would be unhistorical. We have already noted that contemporaries used a definition that included physical damage to property and injury and death to persons and assumed that acts of violence were illegal. Syndicalists regarded legality as irrelevant and capitalistic physical intimidation as "force," not "violence." [43] However, most attempts at quantification used figures for deaths, injuries, and arrests.

Yet there was little attempt to substantiate two out of the three common assertions about the prevalence of industrial violence in the United States. Numerous writers claimed that industrial violence in the United States was more extensive than in Great Britain.[44] They did not explain whether they meant contemporary Britain, or Britain in its phase of industrialization, whether they meant strike mortalities per head of population or some other yardstick of violence. Further, they neglected to inquire whether the incidence of strike deaths in Britain

THE ANATOMY OF A MYTH

was about average for industrial countries or in some way exceptional. Another assertion was that industrial violence was worse than other kinds of domestic violence. Few had the temerity to verify this point, although N. P. Gilman, in his opening comment on Adams' paper of 1906, stated: "I deprecate any attempt to minimize the amount of violence in labor disputes by comparing it with the amount of other crimes, for trade unionists belong to the intelligent and usually peaceful classes of the community and ought not to need such comparison to excuse them." [45]

A third major assertion about the incidence of industrial violence foreshadowed the propaganda of the "law-and-order" advocates of the 1960s. According to Federal Bureau of Investigation figures, the U.S. crime rate increased by 71 percent between 1960 and 1967.[46] In December 1904 S. S. McClure's account of the "increase of lawlessness" included statistics taken from the *Chicago Tribune* which showed that strike violence increased from 1895 to 1900, although compared with homicide it was insignificant.[47] This was consistent with the view expressed in *The Weekly Bulletin of the Clothing Trades,* which in August 1905 printed an apologetic article: "It is becoming evident, notwithstanding the influence and authority of labor leaders, that violence during strikes is on the increase." [48] There seemed to be a weight of evidence to support the view that industrial violence was increasing. The railroad journalist, historian, and biographer Slason Thompson tried to show in *Outlook* in 1904 that, taking into account figures for deaths, injuries, and arrests, there had been over the past two years "no abatement in the violence attending labor strikes." [49]

T. S. Adams accepted Thompson's figures and added some of his own concerning the incidence of violence in strikes before 1880 (although, as Barnett pointed out in his commentary, Adams' figures were not qualitatively differentiated: he did not "distinguish between large disturbances such as the railroad strikes of the seventies, and the smallest infractions of the law"). Adams thought that the United States in general was an exceptionally violent country. While the amount of violence per strike was decreasing, the level of lawlessness showed no sign of diminishing, because of the increasing number of strikes. Furthermore, Adams argued, violence was becoming doubly sinister because it was "too often cunning, systematic, and planful." [50] It may be concluded that the composite picture of industrial violence in the Progressive period had common elements, irrespective of sophistication of judgment or nature of bias. There was a widespread conviction that something would have to be done.

The Progressive concern with industrial violence appears in sharp relief when viewed against the background of declining interest in the problem after World War I. Fears of social upheaval became fixed, during the great Red Scare, on socialists or communists. In his 1920 book, *Is Violence the Way Out of Our Industrial Disputes?* John Haynes Holmes wrote, "The worst thing that we can say about a man socially is that he is an anarchist, or, in this day, perhaps, a Bolshevist; and this epithet has a forbidding sound to us all because it implies that the man to whom we are making reference believes in and practices violence." [51] Socialism being equated with violence and anti-democracy, but being for the most part inactive in the field of industrial relations, the union image became decontaminated. In the 1930s, when industrial conflict assumed grave proportions, unions escaped criticism with respect to genuine industrial disputes, even if racketeering and jurisdictional fights received more than a fair measure of attention. One reason for this was the exposure by the La Follette Senate investigations of employers' practices of keeping private arsenals. Again, private detective agencies had been effectively muckraked by Sidney Howard and Edward Levinson. These exposures not only made it difficult to inveigh against labor malpractices with consistent vehemence, but also made employers distrustful of what detectives told them about plots and intimidation among their workmen. [52]

The mood of the New Deal passed. Ironically if not untypically, the attention devoted to industrial violence increased as the annual strike mortality rate declined. Yet during World War II, even the most sensational case received sober coverage. In 1942, officials of the Brotherhood of Railroad Trainmen were arraigned in court accused of a widespread dynamite conspiracy and of plotting the assassination of George P. McNear, president of the Toledo, Peoria & Western Railroad. [53] In the first decade of the twentieth century, such a case would have been a national scandal. In 1942 it was relegated to an inside page of *The New York Times*. In the postwar years, respectable magazines complained of widespread strike rioting, and the Taft-Hartley Act of 1947 was symptomatic of the prevailing conservative mood. [54] But Taft-Hartley was not predominantly concerned with industrial violence as such: indeed, a note of objectivity had entered the discussion of that subject. When Malcolm Johnson wrote *Crime on the Labor*

Front in 1950, it received critical acclaim from many sources favorable to labor, for all its concentration on the racketeering then prevalent on the New York waterfront.[55]

Fears for the general condition of industrial democracy in America had not been entirely eliminated by the 1940s and 1950s. Newspapers in the Truman and Eisenhower years chronicled raids by "goon squads" on nonunion factories, directed by "communistic" organizations.[56] Employers' organizations still occasionally appealed to the survival instinct of the upper class. The concern of newspapers and businesses with industrial violence was, however, a minor rivulet compared with the flood of concern with communism in the McCarthy period.

The National Labor Relations Board, established in 1935, was effective in controlling exaggeration of labor violence. One of its press releases in 1960 recorded: "General Counsel Stuart Rothman of the National Labor Relations Board today reported that an injunction was granted in the first case under the new Taft-Hartley amendments as to whether picketline violence and misconduct may shorten the 30-day period for requesting an NLRB election after starting recognition and organization picketing." [57] Journalists clutching such a bulletin in one hand were not likely to snatch for the telephone with the other. They were as far removed from the Progressive excitement as were the New York cordwainers of 1809.

The Progressives' concern for industrial violence was distinctive in the international as well as the historical context. It was a normal tenet of the American attitude to industrial violence that while it potentially threatened the political fabric, it was rarely seen as an actual threat to national order. Foreign political scientists, such as Harold Laski, have remarked, along with American labor historians, such as Philip Taft, that the United States has suffered from a peculiarly high level of industrial violence.[58] But, outside the Progressive period, only polemicists have identified American industrial strife with European manifestations that threatened the stability of states and occasionally sprang from a homogeneous proletariat.

As a background to expectations concerning American industrial violence, it is worth referring to British expectations. Since the late eighteenth century the British have been concerned with dire threats to the body politic, rather than with mere blemishes upon it. Britain has been thought of as potentially revolutionary whereas America has been regarded as conservative but violent. Burke feared the overthrow of the English state in 1790; following the Merthyr rising of 1831, the premier Melbourne feared a nationally planned insurrection; in the 1830s and 1840s writers such as the historian Alison feared the extension of French revolutionary ideas to the British Isles.[59] In defining, in the 1840s, a problem of industrial violence without revolutionary implications, John Stuart Mill was exceptional.[60]

Earlier British anxieties about social revolution are important to bear in mind when assessing similar worries in the late nineteenth and early twentieth centuries. In the period just before the outbreak of World War I in 1914, the reactionary publicist A. C. Sutherland, the strikebreaker W. Collinson, the labor leader Ben Tillett, and the industrial relations expert Sir George Askwith were among those who predicted widespread and violent class conflict.[61] The significance of such evidence is debated by historians. Did it signify, as Phelps-Brown has suggested, the presence of a "sense of an impending clash, a civil war between capital and labor," or was it irrelevant to an age perceived by another historian, George Dangerfield, as one of soaring confidence? [62] Whichever view is preferred, it is sufficient to note for the purpose of our argument here that British premonitions of revolt formed part of a serious tradition, whereas American cataclysmic anxieties did not.

Compared to British responses, American attitudes toward the threat of actual revolution have been generally complacent. While such uprisings as Shays' Rebellion, the march of Coxey's Army, and the camping of the Bonus Expeditionary Force on the Anacostia Flats did cause consternation, they had relatively minor effect on general political tranquillity. America had had her Revolution to render further revolutions obsolete. The size of the United States, and the consequent absence of a strategically important metropolis, made it difficult to envisage a real threat to national security in isolated uprisings. It is precisely against this background, of distinctive confidence in her capacity to withstand social upheaval, that America's excitement in the Progressive period and 1960s stands out.

It remains to be shown that Progressive excitement about industrial violence was unjustified. In the first place, there can be no doubt that it was insignificant compared with other forms of crime. Often-cited *Chicago-Tribune* figures estimated the total number of murders and homicides between 1894 and 1900 as 62,812. Of these, only 365 were even alleged to have arisen as a result of strikes.[63] In mortal terms, the race problem, though in one of its quieter phases following the demise of Radical Reconstruction, was more serious than the "class" problem. More than a hundred blacks were lynched in each of the years 1891, 1892, 1894, 1895, 1897, 1898, 1900, and 1901; strike mortalities never matched these figures.[64] Industrial violence received disproportionate attention (just as racial violence did later) because it was regarded as an important social indicator. As such, it was further twisted and abused by the polemicists of the Progressive period.

Industrial violence was no more problematic in the United States than in other countries. Historians comparing social violence in various countries have generally matched trends rather than figures, arguing for example that European countries "peaked" in terms of social disorder as they went through the early stages of industrialization.[65] However, by using the definitions preferred by Progressives and their

Table I
Strike Mortalities in the U.S.A., 1890–1909

DATE	TOTAL NO. OF STRIKE MORTALITIES[a]	WORKERS INVOLVED IN STRIKES[b]	MORTALITY PER 100,000 STRIKERS	DISTRIBUTION OF MORTALITIES AMONG STRIKES[a]	NO. OF STRIKES LEADING TO MORTALITY[a]
1890	2	373,499	0.535	1,1	2
91	25	329,953	7.58	8,1,15,1	4
92	22	238,685	9.22	6,4,1,1,10	5
93	5	287,756	1.74	5	1
94	32	690,044	4.64	4,14,3,10,1	5
95	6	407,188	1.47	1,5	2
96	6	248,838	2.41	5,1	2
97	18	416,154	4.33	18	1
98	10	263,219	3.80	9,1	2
99	25	431,889	5.79	5,1,7,6,1,2,3	7
1900	20	567,719	3.52	3,11,5,1	4
01	17	563,843	3.02	3,3,2,1,5,2,1	7
02	8	691,507	1.16	5,1,1,1	4
03	17	787,834	2.16	3,3,3,1,1,1,1,4	8
04	41	573,815	7.15	30,1,3,1,4,1,1	7
05	20	302,434	6.61	1,2,14,3	4
06	17			3,9,1,1,1,2	7
07	7			6,1	2
08	0				0
1909	10			1,9	2
TOTALS	308				75

a. Extracted from the Appendix.
b. Florence Peterson, *Strikes in the United States, 1880–1936* (Washington, 1938), p. 34.

contemporaries, it is possible to impale the cataclysmic quantifiers on their own statistical barbs.

Early twentieth-century quantifiers placed firm emphasis on homicide figures, and these do lend themselves to definite comparisons because the figures themselves are, if properly examined and gathered, reliable. From Table I, it may be seen that in 1904, one of the peak years for strike mortalities, the number of strike deaths per million U.S. population (using the 1900 census figure of 75,994,575) was .54. This ratio does not begin to compare with the equivalent ratio for that bogey of social conservatives, the Paris Commune. When Thiers crushed the Communards, he executed at least 20,000 people (apart from those previously killed in the fighting and by his bombardment of Paris). This gives a ratio of 1,850 per million, given a French population of approximately 37 million. It may be argued that the Paris Commune was not a strike but an episode in Europe's history of twin revolutions—political as well as social—which was alien to the politically emancipated United States.[66] But in 1908, one of France's peaks for purely industrial violence, the ratio of strike deaths to people was .52 per million, which is not far removed from the American .54 for the proximate peak year 1904.[67] In 1911 Wales, by then a politically emancipated country, suffered a ratio of 2.5 per million—higher than anything the United States has ever experienced.[68] Future research may reveal that a case can be made for Welsh exceptionalism, illustrating a peculiar intensity of class strife in that country. Such an argument could be countered, however, by observing that Colorado has accounted for a great number of strike deaths in American history, and by asking, in the words of the title of a miners' leaflet published in 1904, *Is Colorado in America?* [69] The argument favored by Progressives and by many historians that the United States has had an exceptionally violent history is based on false or nonexistent premises and is groundless.

Both in the Progressive years and those of the "Great Society," protagonists in social debates held that disorder was increasing. The attorney and journalist Fred P. Graham has argued that the FBI presents crime figures in a misleading way, adopting unrepresentative base years for its ratio charts and achieving a "skyrocket effect" in its portrayal of increases in the crime rate.[70] Similarly, it is possible to challenge the view that industrial violence was increasing in the Progressive period. The ratio of strike deaths to population in selected peak years in the United States was 1.1 in 1877, .40 in 1891, .54 in 1904, .80 in 1913, and less than .35 in 1934. The two highest peaks occurred during the railroad riots of 1877 and the Ludlow, Colorado, troubles of 1913 (American concern over class conflict was actually *subsiding* in the latter year, when 74 men, women, and children lost their lives in industrial conflict in Colorado).[71]

When Progressives and their contemporaries held that industrial violence was increasing in their time, they usually took a shorter-term view than that offered above. And it may indeed be seen from Table I that 157 men lost their lives from 1900 to 1909, an increase of seven, or 4.6 percent, over the decade 1890 to 1899. However, on the basis

Table II
List of Strikes and Arrests for Four Occupations in Chicago, 1902–1904[a]

OCCUPATION (POLICE CLASSIFICATION IN PARENTHESES)	1902			1903			1904		
	DAYS LOST IN STRIKES[b]	TOTAL NO. STRIKERS	NO. OF ARRESTS[c]	DAYS LOST IN STRIKES[b]	TOTAL NO. STRIKERS	NO. OF ARRESTS[c]	DAYS LOST IN STRIKES[b]	TOTAL NO. STRIKERS	NO. OF ARRESTS[c]
Building trades (carpenters and plasterers)	8,948	6,909	1,268	9,475	7,338	956	9,051	9,356	733
Foundry and machine shop workers (molders and machinists)	2,110	3,947	1,348	3,944	4,863	1,250	2,352	2,088	259
Freight handling and teaming (teamsters)	1,049	6,852	3,248	829	1,719	3,898	322	1,389	3,208
Slaughtering and meat packing (butchers)	146	1,707	440	589	1,996	541	1,742	38,718	506

a. The figures in this table are extracted from: U.S. Department of Commerce and Labor, Bureau of Labor, *Twenty-first Annual Report of the Commissioners of Labor, 1906* (1907), pp. 172–181; *Report of the General Superintendent of Police of the City of Chicago to the City Council for the fiscal year ending December 31, 1902* (1903), pp. 44–45; *ibid., 1903*, p. 53; and *ibid., 1904*, p. 53. The following qualifications may be made: (i) The figures for arrests concern Chicago alone; those for strikes the state of Illinois. However, the four industries were concentrated in Chicago. (ii) The police classification "butcher" may not coincide with slaughterers and meat packers. On the other hand, the terms were interchangeable in strike parlance, and there is no other classification in the police statistics into which slaughterers and meat packers could fall.

b. Total number of days lost in all strikes. For example, there were 46 strikes in the building trades in 1902, with an aggregate of 8,948 lost days.

c. That is, the number of arrests of men in the particular occupations, throughout the stated year and whether on strike or not.

of the figures given in the table, there is no trend in the number of people killed per annum. Neither is there a simple relationship between the number of men killed in strikes and the number of men on strike.[72] The conclusion to be drawn from this is that industrial violence, physically defined, was not exceptionally rife in the 1900s.

When Thomas S. Adams tried to show in 1906 that there was no abatement in strike lawlessness because there was an increasing number of strikes, he implied two things: that there was a correlation between strikes and the crime rate among groups of workers affected; and that unions which called strikes inevitably caused lawlessness. An approximate indication of the relationship between strikes and arrests may be found in municipal police statistics. Chicago is a convenient example. Illinois, according to Slason Thompson, was third after Colorado and Pennsylvania in the table of strike mortalities for the years from 1902 to 1904. Frederick W. Job, secretary of the Chicago Employers' Association, complained that more than a hundred men had been injured in strikes in the city in 1903.[73] And yet Table II shows that, even in union gangster Martin B. "Skinny" Madden's building trades, there was no positive correlation between the number of men on strike in a trade and the number of the same occupation arrested.[74]

There can be no doubt that industrial violence, in several forms and with varying characteristics, persisted for several decades on each side of 1900. With the legitimization of trade-union activities, industrial violence received prominence in public discussion, with exceptional emphasis on this form of disorder in the Progressive period. But the latter emphasis, while it took different shapes and fluctuated in accuracy, was on the whole unjustifiable. Its different facets constituted a composite myth of industrial violence.

Chapter 3

The Making of U.S. Revolutionary Theory

THE EXAGGERATION OF VIOLENCE HAS HAD DELETERIOUS EFFECTS ON reform at least twice in American history. There is therefore a good case for explaining in detail why the exaggeration occurred.

In providing such an explanation, it is well to start in a negative vein, dismissing certain factors and characterizing others as long term, rather than immediate. For example, it is not helpful to say that quantifiers in the Progressive period exaggerated because they did not fully understand the science of statistics—for they exaggerated, as we saw in the last chapter, in terms of their own figures and definitions. Next, one ought to note that while there exist certain psychosocial reasons for exaggeration, they do not, in themselves, explain the advent of a sudden great fear (or hopeful expectation) of class revolt. For example, memories of bloody revolutions in the past form a constant rather than intermittent undercurrent. Again, fear of the unseen and nonexistent, the terror of a *supposed* conspiracy to subvert, rebel, or destroy is a constant that needs the goad of a specific precipitant to be converted into full hysteria. Nativism, yet another wellspring of distorted perceptions, embraces a constant if varied demonology—its evil genii include witches, Jacobins, Irishmen, blacks, Catholics, Jews, strikers, communists, and capitalists, but every evil genie must be rubbed into life anew by shorter-term factors.

31

Similarly, the motivation of rational men who deceive others in order to advance their own ends is something that does not vary in itself but only in the opportunities presented. Employers, labor leaders, and social reformers may all brand each other as fomentors of violent discontent so that they can present class warfare as the inescapable alternative to their own chosen avenues of social progress; journalists may exaggerate social disorder to please wealthy advertisers or to boost the circulation of their newspapers. But opportunism is impossible without opportunity. To explain the Progressive period's preoccupation with class conflict it is necessary to define medium- and short-term factors and to understand how immediate precipitants gave renewed life to long-term tendencies.

Journalists undoubtedly encountered new opportunities in the late nineteenth century. For example, the development of the Linotype, high-speed electric presses, and photographic reproduction in the 1880s encouraged the rise of the cheap "yellow press" in the 1890s, and the accompanying circulation wars stimulated irresponsible reporting. Lincoln Steffens claimed to have invented a "crime wave" in the late 1890s when the news was flat. Other journalists may have distorted industrial violence, though one should be on guard against assuming that they kept the public in a constant state of alarm. So frequent were stories of violence during the Kentucky mining troubles of 1901 that John Ireland, Roman Catholic archbishop of St. Paul, complained that "readers of newspapers learn of frightful outrages committed daily," but took little notice, indicating that "public opinion seems to be deadened or debauched." The effect of sensational reporting probably declined as people got used to it; nevertheless, for a short while around the turn of the century journalistic sensationalism in daily newspapers and "muckraking" magazines quickened the pulse of the literate public.[1]

Professional soldiers were another group with a vested interest in exaggerating domestic violence. Reacting against militarism following the Civil War, Congress had in 1869 limited the number of enlisted men in the U.S. Army to 25,000, a number that remained static until the Spanish-American War of 1898. Army expansionists found it difficult to persuade the nation that more soldiers were needed, because the geographic isolation of the United States lulled Americans into the belief that they would never be attacked. Exploiting the successful use of federal troops to restore order during the railroad riots of

1877, the military theorist Emory Upton and Secretary of War George W. McCrary called for an increase in manpower to meet domestic emergencies. The time was not propitious in view of contemporary attitudes toward the military generated by military rule in the Reconstruction South, and Army leaders dropped the tactic. In the 1890s, however, federal troops again saw service during the railroad strike of 1894 and the Coeur d'Alene mining troubles of 1892 and 1899. It once more became useful for Army men to talk about riot control. Their tactic was opportunistic: They were probably more concerned about a reformed career structure for officers and burgeoning U.S. imperialism than genuinely worried about the revolutionary potential of labor disorders, but whatever their reason, Commanding General John M. Schofield and others did contribute (though in a discreet and professional manner) to a mounting anxiety about class conflict.[2]

What gave the military arguments force on the eve of Progressivism was the renewed growth of the labor movement following the depression of the mid-1890s. The AFL and its affiliates showed that, unlike earlier organizations such as the National Labor Union and Knights of Labor, they were capable of surviving economic vicissitude. In spite of its inherently conservative nature, the revival of union expansion was widely interpreted as a sinister, subversive development. Yet—and this was a factor that worried anti-union employers—public opinion was beginning to show a pro-labor tendency. It was to prevent a major change in public sympathies that the capitalists, already reeling under antitrust and populist attacks, launched an attack on organized labor. As we saw in Chapter 2, open-shop businessmen were already in a good position to act in unison against unions, because so many of them belonged to organizations set up to act collectively in pursuit of high tariffs and foreign markets. It will also be recalled that, the principle of labor unionism having been established, employers found it necessary to attack labor's tactics, and so depicted labor violence in lurid terms.

Two developments in the Progressive period itself gave the rise of labor power an ominous appearance. First, there appears to have been an enormous increase in the homicide rate in the first decade of the twentieth century. Fabian Franklin, a former professor of mathematics at Johns Hopkins and associate editor of the *New York Evening Post,* pointedly remarked, in 1913, that violence was traditional and criminal, and not the symptom of a new belligerent labor power. His less well-

trained contemporaries in the preceding decade, however, understandably looked for a scapegoat for soaring crime, one of the issues of the
Progressive movement. The growth of the AFL all too conveniently
coincided with the rise in the general homicide rate.[3]

Another contemporary development leading to the disturbance of
social equanimity was the abortive attempt at revolution in Russia in
1905. This was followed by an increased flow of radical Russian Jewish
immigrants to the United States and proved to be but the prelude to
the Bolshevik take-over in Petrograd in 1917. Upheaval in Russia
reinforced concern occasioned by the development of radicalism in
the West following the U.S. Army's suppression of the Coeur d'Alene
miners' strike of 1899, the formation of the IWW in 1905, and the
spread of Wobbly militancy to the East after 1909.

The increase in aggregate membership in AFL affiliates after 1897
was crucial in provoking fears of industrial violence and class revolt.
The rise of labor provoked a myth of industrial violence for five
major reasons, all of them associated with labor's advance. First,
contemporaries were influenced by the development of theories of
revolutionary violence. Second, American labor leaders used violence
in pursuit of their ends. Third, the Western Federation of Miners and
the Bridgemen's Union embarked on what seemed to be a conspiratorial, masked war on society in the first decade of the twentieth century. Fourth, private detective agencies exaggerated labor violence because they made money out of it; the growth of the labor movement
stimulated an expansion in labor work for detectives, in detective
businesses, and in detectives' prevarications. Finally, the Progressive
movement, which was, it is true, partly a *response* to the threat of class
violence, also produced men and women who publicized and *exploited*
labor violence in the hope that this tactic would gain support for their
proposed reforms.

These five stimuli of the myth of industrial violence are examined in
this and succeeding chapters. Our first proposition, then, is that theories
of revolutionary violence developed in the late nineteenth century in
such a way as to increase expectations of social disorder. The writings
of Karl Marx and other socialists had, of course, created a revolutionary ideology in Europe by the middle of the nineteenth century.
But until 1886 the United States lacked an ideological stimulus of
sufficient force to create a preliminary audience for gifted social theo-
rists. The Haymarket Bomb Affair of that year supplied America with

her second Boston Tea Party and stirred the pens if not the hopes of some native writers.

On the evening of May 4, 1886, workers assembled in Haymarket Square, on Randolph Street in Chicago, to protest against the mortal shooting of a striker by policemen the day before. The anarchist August Spies, among others, addressed the meeting. Suddenly, a column of 180 policemen advanced on his audience, whereupon someone threw a dynamite bomb, killing one officer. Eight anarchists were convicted in connection with the crime.

The Haymarket Affair introduced a note of acute social concern into U.S. political rhetoric and convinced European socialists that America was no longer a backwater of radicalism. The English socialists Edward and Eleanor Marx Aveling, who toured the United States in 1886 and 1888, remarked in the aftermath of the execution of four of the alleged bomb conspirators that petitions on behalf of the Chicago anarchists had been signed by "thousands and thousands." Even in England (where George Bernard Shaw flourished a petition and obtained the signature of Oscar Wilde), "hundreds" had signed. Russian anarchist Peter Kropotkin remarked in December 1888 that the "commemoration of the Chicago martyrs has almost acquired the same importance as the commemoration of the Paris Commune." [4]

The Haymarket "martyrs" succeeded in persuading their contemporaries of America's revolutionary potential partly because they were presumed innocent and partly because they were presumed guilty. Presuming innocence, libertarians protested that the anarchists' trial had been unfair; the Avelings claimed that the men had been "condemned on no real evidence"; socialists stated that judicial bias in Chicago proved that the United States was as much affected by class divisions as other countries.[5]

On the premise that the "martyrs" were innocent, socialists could excoriate the American class system in a most satisfying manner. Just as exciting, however, was the prospect of their possible guilt. After all, the Christian martyrs had been charismatic not because they were framed but because they were "guilty" of faith within a secular Roman society. There is more than a little evidence pointing to the guilt of the indicted Chicago anarchists, a circumstance that helps to account for their impact. For example, on June 5, 1886, America's leading pacifistic anarchist, Benjamin R. Tucker, warned his disciple Joseph Labadie not to believe stories that the police had "planted" the bomb-making equipment found in the desk of the indicted (and later executed) August Spies: He knew the contrary to be true.[6]

Socialists, as well as the general public (who were subjected to a flood of newspaper abuse against Chicago's anarchists), were prepared to consider the possibility of the guilt of the "martyrs" and its implications. The American parliamentary socialist Robert Hunter traced the origins of the Haymarket explosion to the violent philosophy preached by Bakunin's disciple, the European anarchist Johann Most, who had arrived in the United States in 1882. He was in no doubt about the effects of Most's philosophy: "The advocates of direct action continued headlong toward the bitter climax at the Haymarket in Chicago in 1886." [7] In his book *Violence and the Labor Movement* (1914), Hunter described a trend within the international socialist movement against parliamentary democracy and in favor of revolutionary violence: Haymarket signified that the United States had been affected by this trend, which was to gather momentum in the succeeding years.

Hunter's views on violence merit close attention because they were those of an erudite socialist, conversant with American conditions, who both reflected and influenced contemporary fears of social disorder. Hunter was knowledgeable about European socialism and socialists: he crossed the Atlantic three times between 1899 and 1907, meeting Keir Hardie, Kropotkin, Lenin, and Leo Tolstoy. But his distinctive perceptiveness was due to his American background. Born in 1874, the son of a manufacturer of Scottish descent, he became interested in social reform after witnessing the effects of the Crash of 1893 on workers in his hometown of Terre Haute, Indiana. He worked at Jane Addams' famous social settlement in Chicago, Hull-House, and in 1904 published a classic study of social deprivation in which he claimed that ten million Americans lived "in poverty." He joined the Socialist Party of America in 1905.[8]

Hunter was particularly critical of syndicalism. He observed that this form of revolutionary activity had emerged in 1895 when the General Confederation of Labor was formed in France and Émile Pouget urged anarchists to infiltrate the labor unions. The French syndicalist philosophy abhorred by Hunter is best described in Georges Sorel's *Reflections on Violence* (1908). Sorel expressed disgust at the corruption of society in general and of parliamentary socialists in particular. He alleged that parliamentary socialists, such as Jean Jaurès, who had championed the cause of Alfred Dreyfus in the 1890s and condemned the conservatives' use of espionage and cover-up tactics, condoned, when it suited them, "a regular system of secret accusations." To eliminate informers, state spies, and social degeneracy, Sorel advocated a rejection of the state, the general strike, and violent revolution. Violence was, in any case, according to Sorel, natural to the workers. As a parliamentary socialist and a democrat (he was the socialist gubernatorial candidate for Connecticut in 1910), Hunter disagreed with this philosophy.[9]

Hunter believed that workingmen were by nature peaceful. Violence was in any case a poor working-class tactic because it alienated public opinion. Attacking syndicalism, he seized on the fact that violence so often played into the hands of reactionaries, who, for precisely that reason, frequently started it. Seizing on a distinctive feature of American industrial life, the detective agency, the parliamentary socialist showed that the U.S. labor movement, if it turned to violence, would be particularly prey to agents provocateurs supplied on a private-enterprise basis. In emphasizing this factor, Hunter was almost entirely alone and original among serious political scientists.[10]

Hunter's interpretation made an impact on his contemporaries for several reasons. First, it was supported by Morris Hillquit, founder member, leading theoretician, and executive board member of the SPA. Hillquit, too, attacked the anarchists, agreeing with Marx and Engels that their violence would "furnish freely to the reactionaries a well-trained gang of police spies" (Hillquit failed to grasp the point that private detectives were more important than government agents in the United States). Secondly, Hunter's views seemed to be supported by the McNamara confessions of 1911. Though the McNamara brothers were philosophically conservative, Hunter and Hillquit portrayed them as anarchists. Finally, Hunter's attack on anarcho-syndicalism was timed to help destroy the Industrial Workers of the World; IWW incursions in the East after 1909 threatened the AFL, whose alliance Hunter and other moderate socialists were seeking. The socialists' equation of the Wobblies with anarcho-syndicalism and violence smacks of opportunism, but it confirmed the worst fears of many citizens.[11]

After Haymarket, a theory of revolution was in the making with regard to the United States, but it never materialized. Nevertheless, Robert Hunter contributed a theory *about* the theory of revolution. This helped to create illusions of proletarian violence, giving the bourgeoning AFL, of which the McNamaras seemed such typical progeny, a sinister profile.

Theories *about* revolution once again triumphed over theories *advocating* revolution in the 1960s. This is not altogether surprising, for both the configuration and the causes of the violence-distorting tendency of the 1960s resembled their counterparts in the Progressive period.

One similarity in the configuration of violence in both our periods was that crime was on the increase in the 1960s as it had been sixty years earlier. Blacks were held to be responsible for a disproportionate amount of it, just as labor unionists had been previously; blacks and students were considered in relation to race and campus riots in the 1960s just as labor sympathizers had been regarded in relation to riots at the beginning of the twentieth century. Yet the violence of the 1960s, like its antecedent labor violence, may be placed in a less alarming perspective. Crime escalated in the 1950s and 1960s in London, Stockholm, and Sydney, not in the United States alone. It also continued to increase in the United States through the 1970s without provoking the extravagant responses of the 1960s. Furthermore, criminologists were able to show in the 1970s that the riots of the 1960s were less homicidal, inclusive of both whites and blacks killed, than the lynchings of the 1890s, which involved blacks almost exclusively and produced no "law and order" scare.[12]

Motives for distorting threats to the social order in the 1960s resembled those of our earlier generation. Like Army officers in the 1890s and private detectives a little later, FBI spokesmen were expansionists. To begin with, the FBI was on the defensive in the early 1960s. Indeed, it had been expected that the newly elected President, John F. Kennedy, would dismiss the agency's empire-building director, J. Edgar Hoover, in 1961. To reassure conservatives, Kennedy kept Hoover on, and FBI statisticians did their best to show that soaring crime justified the young President's trust in their appropriation-hungry institution. Trends published by these FBI statisticians did not seem improbable in a decade when television reporting had come into its own, bringing violence into instantaneous prominence in the American home in a way reminiscent of, but more effective than, the yellow press.[13]

The rise of the black civil-rights movement in the 1950s provoked responses with affinities to reactions in the late nineteenth century. After U.S. Supreme Court decisions in 1954 and 1955 had outlawed certain key forms of segregation in the South, the legitimacy of black protest could no longer be called into question, and (as in the case of labor unionism in the earlier period) its tactics were attacked instead. Radical leaders, such as Bobby Seale of the Black Panthers, were accused in much-publicized trials of "conspiracies" to foment riot. Moderate black leaders and white liberals bewailed, publicized, and exploited the activities of the "Black Muslims" just as socialists and Progressive politicians had utilized the Wobblies. Violent anticolonial revolutions in the nonwhite "Third World" reinforced domestic fears in a manner that is comparable to the effects of the Russian upheavals of 1905 and 1917.

Yet, in spite of attempts in the 1960s to formulate a revolutionary theory for the United States (radical students convened at Princeton University for this purpose in February 1967), no such theory emerged. The New Left's leading theorist, Herbert Marcuse, was repetitious in his analysis (for example, in warning students against agents provocateurs and violence) and pessimistic about the prospects for a revolutionary ideology. That such an ideology did not emerge from the troubles of the 1960s may be due to the general triumph of pragmatism over dogmatism in modern America or to the decline of books in the face of competition from the audio-visual media. It must also be a reflection of the fact that in the 1960s, no less than in the Progressive period, there was little call for revolution in a country where social change could be achieved democratically. Haymarket, the McNamara confessions, and race riots all failed to create a revolutionary ideology; rather, they encouraged talk about it.[14]

Chapter **4**

℘Workers and Violence, ——— 1886–1912

DID WORKERS NATURALLY RESORT TO VIOLENCE WHEN ON STRIKE? TO this question, which so fundamentally divided Sorel and Hunter, there is more than one approach. As we saw in Chapter 2, quantitative analysis suggests a negative conclusion for the Progressive period in the United States. But another approach is to examine the statements of articulate workers and labor leaders. From these statements, it may be seen that Sorel (who did not limit the applicability of his generalizations to France) was nevertheless correct in his observation that workers were collectively involved with violence, even though he did not analyze the role of labor leaders and drew the wrong conclusions about the character of workers' militancy. Sorel failed to see that the responses of labor leaders to violence were not indications of a revolutionary consciousness so much as a case study in minority tactics. Yet these responses were susceptible to misinterpretation by many Americans, as well as by Sorel, and contributed to fears of class conflict.

American union spokesmen of the post-Haymarket generation commented on violence in a way that alarmed many of their fellow countrymen to whom the Chicago explosion had been a frightening premonition of class conflict. Their comments indicate a willingness by various labor leaders on differing occasions to (1) advocate but not practice, (2) advocate and practice, (3) not advocate but practice,

(4) condemn but practice, (5) condemn but condone, and (6) condemn and punish violence. Critics of labor unionism tended to concentrate their attack on union leaders who condemned but condoned violence by their members. There were several reasons for this, not the least among them being that there were many ways of arguing the case but very few of refuting it. Another reason was that there was little proof available to show that labor leaders advocated or practiced violence—after all, no union leader wanted to provide evidence that would land him in jail. Nevertheless, it can, in retrospect, be shown that in some situations even the most respectable of union officials supported violence.

Two men who advocated violence in conflicts where neither they nor their organizations were directly concerned were Treasurer Hotchkin of the New York City Central Labor Union and Terence Powderly, Grand Master Workman of the declining but respectable Knights of Labor. Hotchkin spoke in the aftermath of the New York Central Railroad strike of 1890, and Powderly following the bloody gunfight of 1892 in the Homestead, Pennsylvania, steel mills owned by Andrew Carnegie. In each case, the Pinkerton Detective Agency had supplied armed guards in an effort to end workers' resistance. Both Hotchkin and Powderly advocated that Pinkerton men should be shot.[1] But since they were not personally involved in the practice of violence and since they advocated its use only when faced with dire provocation, their statements were not widely publicized.

Labor leaders explicitly advocated violence only when, in their opinion, the context justified it—for only then would the press let them off lightly. Rank-and-file union members recognized the need for caution. In the immediate presence of employers' coercion, Hotchkin's New York CLU audience had warmed to his theme; in 1896 the same audience, unpressed by any local emergency, grew restless listening to Isaac Cohen, a delegate from the strikebound Cleveland CLU, call for the formation of a union soldiery to combat the state militias.[2] Big Bill Haywood of the IWW had a set speech in which he asked "Do you blame me when I say I despise the law; that I am not a law-abiding citizen?"[3] He was indignant when the daily press printed the quotation out of context, a speech concerned with class repression and employers' corruption.[4] Haywood's reaction suggests that some violent utterings were made with a view to attracting attention to speeches concerned with social injustices, not to foment disorder.

Only by quoting out of context could anti-union propagandists indict the more judicious verbal insurrectionists without publicizing the enemy cause.

Labor leaders of stature who both preached and practiced violence were extremely rare, while the authenticity of their statements and the fairness of their court trials were sometimes questionable. In 1894, in defiance of the craft-orientated brotherhoods, which contained only a skilled minority of railroad employees, the majority of railroad workers rebelled against the magnates in a strike under the auspices of the recently formed American Railway Union. The strike leader, Eugene V. Debs, allegedly instructed a supporter in South Butte, Montana: "Save your money and buy a gun," but he later attributed the dispatch of the message to an irresponsible office boy.[5] Three days later *The New York Times* quoted the railwaymen's leader on the Chicago situation: "The first shot fired by the regular soldiers at the mobs here will be the signal for a civil war," but carefully attributed the report to a United Press journalist.[6] An injunction was granted against Debs and his fellow ARU officers on the ground, in part, that they employed "force and violence," and they were convicted on charges that accused them of "conspiracy to injure, oppress, threaten or intimidate" in the course of the strike.[7] But many thought of the ARU leader's conviction as an injustice; Debs shared this view and became a socialist in prison; he was the Socialist Party of America's Presidential candidate in the new century.

Ed Boyce was another labor leader accused of both advocating and practicing violence. Irish-born Boyce was among those who went to jail after the Coeur d'Alene, Idaho, miners' strike of 1892. After his release in 1893, he attended the founding convention of a labor organization covering the Rocky Mountain States, becoming the president of the Western Federation of Miners between 1896 and 1902. He was rearrested in the course of the WFM's Leadville, Colorado, strike of 1896. In May 1897 he encouraged local unions in Idaho and Colorado to organize rifle corps so that "we can hear the inspiring music of the martial tread of 25,000 armed men in the ranks of labor." [8] A few years later, the Boise *Idaho Daily Statesman* seized on what it retrospectively termed the "Boyce policy" of armament as an indication of union policy.[9] The opportunities for such attacks were, however, comparatively rare.

Some union leaders in the city building trades did not advocate, yet practiced violence. Like Boyce and the majority of union leaders in the United States, many of them were of Irish extraction. Here, however, the similarity ended, for, unlike the WFM leader, they were far from idealistic and largely inarticulate. The convictions of Sam Parks of New York in 1903, Tom Slattery of the same city in 1908, "Skinny" Madden of Chicago in 1909, and Olaf Tveitmoe of Los Angeles in 1912 on various charges of intimidation and extortion involved men of action, not words. According to Harold Seidman, a historian of American racketeering, Parks was semiliterate.[10]

Lack of verbal capacity went hand in hand with antidemocratic trends in the building trades. From the early 1890s the Board of Walking Delegates of the New York Housesmiths' Union met internal criticism with coercive tactics.[11] In Chicago, when an election of City Federation of Labor officials was being held in the Bricklayers' Hall on July 16, 1905, there occurred an instance of workers' violence that was a far cry from Georges Sorel's antidecadent, revolutionary ideal, and a vindication of Robert Hunter's view that social democrats should guard against violence. Six men armed with revolvers rushed in, smashed the ballot boxes, and badly beat up Michael Donnelly, socialist president of the butchers' union.[12] The *Chicago Tribune* had singled out Donnelly, in 1904, for his long-standing opposition to violence and his restraint during the meat packers' strike of that year.[13] Yet the Chicago union hierarchy failed to press for the prosecution of those who had committed what was probably an unprovoked attack on the butchers' leader. The *Typographical Journal* (official organ of the International Typographical Union) deplored the use of "magazine guns, billies and brass knuckles," which it identified as "the policy of the element who monopolize the limelight of labor matters in the Chicago Federation." [14]

Verbal incapacity was not the only factor that kept the likes of Parks from advocating their policies in public. It was not in the interest of corrupt union leaders to allow democratic debate and process, which might expose their activities or undermine their position. This was brought home in the Chicago City Federation of Labor election of 1905 when, in spite of the intimidatory and wrecking tactics epitomized in the Donnelly assault, the honest John Fitzpatrick acceded to the federation's presidency, seriously weakening the influence that Madden had hitherto exerted through his Board of Business Agents and the Building Trades Council.[15]

Whether involuntary or calculated, the inarticulacy of the corrupt deprived anti-union propagandists in the building trades of a source of ammunition. Even the relatively infrequent court convictions of such as Parks and Madden had to be handled with care. For union business agents sometimes entered into "sweetheart contracts" with certain employers, whose corrupt payments bought immunity from strikes for themselves and constant labor troubles for their competitors. Since court appearances by such agents sometimes had the disconcerting effect of exposing employers' corruption and connivance in the methods of union "plug-uglies," businessmen were not always eager to press charges.

The union leader's standard response to labor violence was to condemn it and demand the punishment of its perpetrators. Yet very few assumed the role of executioner themselves by expelling violent members from union membership. After all, if such expulsion took place prior to conviction for a criminal act, it might prove to be prejudicial to the jury's verdict; if expulsion followed conviction, the union member was being punished twice for the same offense. In any case, expulsion from membership was bad politics as every elected officer knew, for many rank-and-file members admired a man who risked prison on behalf of his fellow workers.

For these reasons, unionists wishing to see labor violence punished as well as condemned confined themselves to offering rewards for information leading to convictions. For example, the Sailors' Union offered such a reward after an explosion in San Francisco on September 24, 1893, which destroyed with fatal consequences Curtin's boardinghouse, a "crimp" establishment that advanced credit to sailors, thus keeping them in permanent bondage to the shipowners. So did the WFM after the explosion at Independence, Colorado, in 1904, when thirteen men died. Such union rewards should not, however, be taken at face value. The motives behind reward offers were sometimes indicative of partisanship rather than a desire to see justice done, in that union leaders refused to believe that their own men were the criminals. At other times, the motives were plainly ulterior, being coupled with professions of faith in union innocence, accusations about agents provocateurs, and actual guilt. The reward offer by the bridgeworkers' union following the *Los Angeles Times* explosion of 1910 fell into this category.[16]

Labor leaders were particularly vulnerable to the charge that they condoned violence by their followers even as they hypocritically condemned it. The plausibility of the charge rested partly on its conjectural nature. Against a background of social turbulence in the 1960s, criminologists Thorsten Sellin and Martin E. Wolfgang focused attention on the difficulty of assessing hidden criminality. They mentioned the following classes of crime: (1) direct harm to persons, (2) conspiratorial or consentual crime, and (3) crimes against the public order. They stated that there was general agreement that police statistics were not good enough to enable anyone to measure the incidence of crimes of the second and third categories.[17] What was true for the 1960s applied also to the period from 1886 to 1912. It was difficult to prove or disprove the existence of conspiracy, or tacit consent concerning violence, on the part of labor leaders. In such an area of uncertainty, circumstantial evidence received credence. Critics of the labor movement focused attention on the generally equivocal attitude of union leaders toward violence, their objections to the militia, their creation of a cult of martyrdom, their use of calculated or incendiary predictions, and their failure to discipline violent members.

Critics of unionism noted several forms of equivocation over violence on the part of labor spokesmen. For example, violent labor troubles in the West Coast shipping industry in 1892 and 1893 furnished an instance of indirect incitement to violence. An editorial in the *Coast Seamen's Journal* instructed union members that no oppressed people had ever won redress until they broke the law and "remedies by lawlessness are not always worse than the disease. As a rule that depends upon the extent of the lawlessness and the final result, defeat or victory. But we are not in favor of lawlessness."[18] The response of the Ship-owners' Association to such prevarication was as follows: "The Association does not charge the Union's officers with directly inciting or inducing the members to such awful deeds of bloodshed and destruction, but does charge them with stirring up by speech and action in a manner calculated to make individual members take just such steps of war."[19]

In the context of the Philadelphia streetcar strike of 1910, an anonymous contributor to *Collier's National Weekly* suggested that labor leaders feared not violence as such but the consequences of being caught: "The striking union car-men did not disapprove of the vandalism. On the contrary, they were glad it took place. But they had been carefully coached by their leaders to keep clear of violence themselves." [20] Other writers, too, thought that equivocation reflected a calculating attitude. H. R. Mussey, an economist and authority on trusts, argued that labor leaders bargained against a "backcloth of potential violence." [21] Labor sympathizers did not go quite so far, but some of them did admit that union leaders condoned violence. Henry White, a former president of the Garment Workers' Union, remarked in 1913 that union leaders could easily stop so-called irresponsible union violence if they wanted to, but rarely did so—yet they loudly disclaimed sympathy with violence in public. The editor and writer Fabian Franklin expanded on this view in an article for the social reform journal *Survey*. Franklin observed that social workers and labor sympathizers, like union leaders, failed to condemn labor violence unequivocably because they knew it was understandable.[22]

Union leaders who condemned violence lost credibility in several cases by objecting to the introduction of extra police or troops to areas that had become tense because of an industrial dispute. The Grand Master Workman of the Knights of Labor condemned the drafting of extra police to the Brooklyn streetcar strike of 1899, eliciting from *The New York Times* the editorial question "Why? If the Knights of Labor are not disturbers of the peace they will not come in conflict with the police." [23] The labor unionists' answer to this question was that policemen and soldiers actually disrupted hitherto peaceful situations by intimidating strikers. But this answer sounded like rationalization of an unsound position: in July 1903 *Independent* magazine claimed editorially that by attacking the character of the militia, union leaders ". . . virtually confess by their action that they expect to gain their ends by violence." [24]

After the Haymarket Affair, there developed a cult of martyrdom that reinforced the view that militant labor leaders condoned violence, however much they preached against it. AFL President Samuel Gompers immediately perceived the opportunity that the Chicago executions themselves would create for militant leaders in the future. In his plea for clemency after the Haymarket convictions he argued that martyrdom for the anarchists could spur on their followers.[25] Debs called the Chicago anarchists ". . . the first martyrs to a cause which, fertilized by their blood, has grown in strength and sweep and influence from the day they yielded up their lives and liberty in its defense." [26] Grover S. Cleveland, U.S. President at the time of the ARU strike, remarked that Debs himself chose prison, not bail on July 17,

1894, because he was aware of the charisma of martyrdom.[27] Similar arguments were advanced about WFM leaders Big Bill Haywood, Charles Moyer, and George Pettibone (all charged but acquitted of the murder of a former governor of Idaho in 1905), the Wobbly Joe Hill (executed for murder in 1915), and even about Sam Parks.[28] There can be no doubt that the publicity attracted by "martyred" labor leaders served as a warning to employers of a do-or-die spirit of militancy.

Union publicists drove the point home by treating labor's strike casualties like war heroes. In the West Coast seamen's strike of 1906, Andrew Kelner, a union picket, was shot dead when trying to board the nonunion schooner *National City* in San Francisco harbor. The union journal greeted the news with a comment that exalted death in battle: "Another name has been added to the list of our comrades who have given their lives for the Sailors' Union." [29] The union afforded Kelner a funeral with full honors. It was common for union journals to glorify "massacred" heroes of the labor cause, and mass funerals solidified the ranks of labor in support of strikers killed in action. Reportedly, seventeen thousand attended the Morewood, Pennsylvania, funeral of eight miners shot dead by deputies in 1891, and in Cleveland, only the late President James A. Garfield's funeral had exceeded that of William Rettger, a striking ironworker who met his death at the hand of a strikebreaker in 1896.[30]

In the funeral services for the Morewood victims and Rettger, Catholic priests made strong pleas for peace and urged union men not to use violence. Clearly, the implication was either that the unions had caused violence in the first place and were glorifying men who embodied their guilt, or that in the wake of highly publicized martyrdom the unions were likely to use violence in future: implicit in the cult of martyrdom, therefore, was a threat of violence.

Predictions of violence similarly verged on threatening behavior. President William Weihe of the Amalgamated Association of Iron and Steel Workers of America was reported by the *Pittsburgh Press* to have predicted during the Homestead strike of 1892 that the railway platform inside the steelworks would be torn down if an attempt was made to induct strikebreakers.[31] Because of its specific nature, this "prediction" can only be regarded as a threat, even if the idea did not originate with Weihe. Nor was Weihe's calculated prediction an isolated example. According to John Fitch, a sympathetic expert on steelworkers' working conditions, the Homestead strikers' Advisory Committee warned the Carnegie Company that it could not be responsible for the conduct of union members if smoke did not cease to issue from the factory chimneys.[32]

In an attempt to make their predictions of violence more frightening, some union publicists argued that Americans had always resisted oppression with physical force. In 1892 the *Coast Seamen's Journal* advanced the view that lawlessness was the necessary antidote to oppression.[33] In August 1901 an editorial with the apparently condemnatory title "Violence Deprecated" in the *Locomotive Engineers' Monthly Journal* made a similar point in the context of a discussion of pro-employer bias in the lawcourts: "Reform in this matter will come, and if not from peaceful means, from some other. The public will not stand still and have their natural liberties, even to free speech, placed in jeopardy without an effort to effect a cure, and violence may attend it, however much we may deprecate violence." [34] This statement published in the official journal of a conservative railroad Brotherhood epitomized the vulnerability of any union defense before the hostile accusation that labor organizations, however much they "deprecated" violence, condoned it. Where was the dividing line between a prediction and a threat of violence?

During the Pennsylvania anthracite coal strike of 1902 there occurred a concerted and highly publicized effort to show that John Mitchell, president of the United Mine Workers of America (UMWA), who had been notable for his condemnation of violence in industrial relations, in fact condoned its use by failing to discipline guilty members of his union. The debate over UMWA tactics during the long stoppage of 1902 engaged the attention of a wide audience because the threatened shortage of domestic heating fuel introduced millions of consumers to the prospect of acute suffering during the winter of 1902–1903. President Theodore Roosevelt, recognizing the emerging importance of the consumer as a force in politics, arranged for an Anthracite Coal Commission to arbitrate the dispute between coal operators and the UMWA. The commission held hearings, which afforded both Mitchell and his detractors an opportunity to publicize their views on violence.

John Mitchell had been born in Braidwood, Illinois, and, after being orphaned, went to work in the mines at the age of twelve. Though toughened by this experience, he was sensitive to the aspirations of an ethnically and religiously diverse work force, being the son of a Scotch-Irishman, yet a Catholic. He was well fitted to unite, to fight for —and, possibly, to pacify—miners from points as diverse as Silesia and Lanarkshire. Mitchell had always emphasized what he maintained was the peaceful character of the mineworker on strike. Sometimes his statements seemed to defy the evidence. Following a collision between law officers and strikers at the Coxe Brothers' Oneida Colliery in Hazleton, Pennsylvania, in 1900, which resulted in one death on each side and the conviction of fourteen strikers, Mitchell told a UMWA convention that the anthracite stoppage of 1900 was "remarkable . . . because of the entire absence of lawlessness on the part of those who engaged in the strike." [35] On the eve of Roosevelt's intervention in the great strike of 1902, *The New York Times* noted Mitchell's exhortation to five thousand miners at Dickson City: "If this strike cannot be won by honorable means, I say a thousand times it is better to lose it." [36] But Roosevelt confided to Winthrop M. Crane, governor of Massachusetts, that he had received "flatly contradictory" reports concerning Mitchell's responsibility for violence that had occurred after the introduction of a peacekeeping force of state troops to the anthracite region.[37]

Following Roosevelt's intervention, the Presidential Anthracite Coal Commission held hearings at various locations between October 27, 1902, and February 13, 1903. As early as October 24, the day when Roosevelt presented members of the commission with a letter of instructions, an editorial in *The New York Times* warned that proof of acts of violence was "likely to react powerfully to the disadvantage of the union and to prejudice the Commission of Arbitration against it, to the extent of impressing it with the impossibility of recommending its recognition in any form." [38] Realizing the importance of the issue of union violence, Mitchell had come to the hearings well prepared. Clarence Darrow, a champion of labor who was destined to become America's most famous criminal lawyer, acted as chief counsel to the mineworkers. Mitchell arrived at the first session of the commission, held in Washington, D.C., flanked by John Fahy, an organizer with firsthand experience of violence in the anthracite field, and Walter Weyl, soon to become one of the Progressive movement's leading intellectuals.[39]

Lawyers acting on behalf of the coal operators exploited the issue of violence in the course of the commission's hearings, introducing several nonunion men to testify to union brutality. Following a week of such testimony, Mitchell complained that the "non-union man . . . was brought here, for the same purpose he was put in the mines. He was put in the mines for the purpose of destroying the efforts of the men who went out on strike." [40]

Lawyers representing the coal operators accused the UMWA of pursuing the closed shop. They argued it was impossible to achieve the closed shop without violence and quoted extracts from union resolutions to show that coercion was being used. For example, David Willcox, vice-president of the Delaware and Hudson Railway Company, read from the proceedings of a convention held in 1901 in Edwardsville, Luzerne County: "Regularly moved and seconded that it becomes compulsory on the men of any mine employed in and around the mines to become a member of the United Mine Workers of America. Carried." [41] Wayne McVeagh, a former U.S. Attorney General representing the Pennsylvania Coal Company and the Hillside Coal and Iron Company, claimed that on September 6, 1902, locals of the UMWA had passed resolutions calling on all members to assemble in order to prevent men from going to work. The militia, he observed, had been unable to control violent incidents. McVeagh offered in evidence a list of fourteen strike fatalities.[42]

Counsel for the operators insisted that the union was productive of violence because that was the only deterrent that kept nonunion men from working. Union leaders did not personally instigate it but were guilty of creating an inflammable situation and then failing to discipline their men.[43] Public denouncements of violence did not impress such men as McVeagh, who remarked to Mitchell: "Of course orders [to avoid lawlessness] are given, and you give yours in sincerity. Sometimes they are not given in sincerity." [44]

McVeagh's allegations were given official credence when the commission published its *Report*. The editor of the report was U.S. Commissioner of Labor Caroll D. Wright, a pioneer in labor statistics for Massachusetts and the nation who might have been expected to take a prolabor position: indeed, the commission recommended a compromise on union demands, which, in the climate of the day, was a victory for Mitchell. But Wright had long been convinced that a tightening in union discipline was desirable and that the responsibility for control rested with labor leaders. The second recommendation of his report on the ARU strike of 1894 had been that a federal law should require union rules to expel violent members.[45] The Anthracite Commission *Report* of May 1903 differentiated between planned union violence and violence by individuals but castigated union officials for failing in their disciplinary responsibilities. The *Report* noted that violence had occurred in areas where operators were trying to work their mines: The failure of union leaders to prevent it was therefore a factor in deterring nonunion men from working, as McVeagh had averred.[46]

Mitchell proved resourceful in replying to criticisms levied against him, the UMWA, and, by implication, against strikers and protesters generally. In answer to the accusation that the union wanted a closed shop, he advanced a utilitarian philosophy, arguing that it was normal for a man to surrender some of his rights in the interest of society and that it was immoral for a man to sell his labor at a price that would undermine the wage rates of other workers. But he dissociated his union from violence in pursuit of the closed shop. He acknowledged that there had been violence in the anthracite region at the time of the strike but attributed it to the Coal and Iron Police, to fights among undisciplined nonunion men, and to small boys affected by the excitement.[47]

The UMWA president advanced peaceful, rather than pacifist, arguments. Replying to questions asked by George Gray, chairman of the Anthracite Commission, he claimed—in what was to become a standard union argument—that violence, far from winning a strike, was likely to alienate public opinion and injure the union cause.[48] It was no deterrent to potential strikebreakers in the coal stoppage because the troops provided adequate protection; the union's most potent weapon was moral, not physical—it was social ostracism.[49] Mitchell denied that union propaganda had engendered a violent hatred of strikebreakers. His critics had complained that the Hazleton, Pennsylvania, *Trade Unionist* had published an incendiary attack on former "scabs" who were to testify before the Anthracite Commission—"disgusting as the shoat of the swill pen and corruptive of moral virtue as the degenerates of prostituted society"—but the Hazelton publication was not, said Mitchell, an authentic union organ.[50] In contrast with the conduct of the private individual who published the Hazleton paper, local unions of the UMWA held special meetings to denounce violence, to prevent it, and to protect property.[51]

This was as far as Mitchell was prepared to go. Discipline, he maintained, was the province of the law: "We take the position that the courts are the proper persons to determine the innocence or guilt of a person arrested, and that until the courts have determined that, we have no right to proceed against them." [52] Not every union official would have agreed with Mitchell. The Brotherhood of Locomotive Engineers "strictly prohibited every violation of written or moral law," while *The Weekly Bulletin of the Clothing Trades* and *The Typographical Journal* advocated the expulsion of violent members from their respective unions.[53] However, public opinion was not powerful enough to induce Mitchell to assume extralegal authority for the UMWA, and his policy of nondiscipline endured in other unions as well as in his own.[54]

Mitchell not only refused to discipline violent UMWA members but provided union funds to pay for counsel to defend members accused of assault and murder.[55] He took his stand as one who defended his men, innocent or not, against criticism. At the same time, he tried to prove that the UMWA was a peaceful union. To a challenge by McVeagh, he replied: "I deny that there was this reign of terror. My information is that there was not. The reign of terror was very largely in the newspapers." [56] Mitchell attacked McVeagh's list of fourteen fatalities. The operators' counsel had used the *New York Sun* as his source, and Mitchell said the *Sun* reporter was "bitterly hostile" to the union and strikers.[57] The reporter's compilations of statistics of murders, assaults, and other forms of violence were based on his own unreliable reports and had been accepted by other newspapers and by McVeagh. By referring to police records, Mitchell showed that in only four cases of murder was suspicion directed against members of the union. The union president said that when the strike had been in progress for four months, he asked city officials and policemen whether the crime rate was high. The records showed that the number of convictions was below average. If Mitchell's estimates were accurate, he had not only welded a heterogeneous mass of immigrant workers into a fighting unit, but had also induced them, by persuasion rather than active discipline, to remain peaceful on strike. Though he refused in theory as well as in practice to accept the principle that lawless union men should be punished by the UMWA, he was able to claim that, on the whole, his union was a civilizing influence.[58]

Mitchell's assertion was neither new nor limited to claims on behalf of the miners. For example, the *Buffalo Morning Express* reported

that union men had been comparatively orderly during the Tona-
wanda, New York, longshoremen's strike of 1893: "The non-union
men, who are less intelligent and more inflammable than the original
strikers, have been won over [to the strike], and it has become necessary to send a portion of the National Guard to the Tonawandas."
The *Express* was not favorably disposed toward strikers, indeed had
failed to mention the longshoremen's dispute until newsworthy violence broke out. Union spokesmen naturally went further than the
press and highlighted evidence that, they maintained, showed unionism
was a healing social balm. In 1896 the *Motorman and Conductor*
claimed that strong union organization accounted for the peacefulness
of the Milwaukee streetcar strike of that year. James Regan of the
Chicago Lathers' Union argued in the context of the 1900 Chicago
building-trades strike: "Disorganization is the thing that produces
crime." The *Locomotive Engineers' Monthly Journal* in its August 1901
editorial depicted trade unionists as middle-class citizens who formed
the backbone of many respectable American communities: It took great
provocation to drive them to violence.[59]

Mitchell's argument and method of proof attracted publicity and
started a debate in which reformers, criminologists, socialists, and, in
later years, student and black militants were to join. Yet, like his
argument, his method of proof—his use of statistics and his attack
on the *New York Sun*—lacked novelty. As recently as 1901, the Catholic priest Father Peter C. Yorke had effectively used the records of the
San Francisco Central Receiving Hospital during the waterfront strike,
which was taking place that year under the leadership of Andrew
Furuseth, head of the Seamen's Union. According to Yorke and the
Coast Seamen's Journal, Chief of Police Sullivan and the newspapers
cooperated in issuing fabricated stories of riots in order to create a
climate of opinion that would tolerate rough strikebreaking tactics.
Like Mitchell, Yorke was prepared to excuse violence: In view of
police corruption, he said, "I am beginning to cast in my mind if there
be not worse things than violence." In yellow press magnate W. R.
Hearst's *Examiner,* the only pro-union and most popular newspaper in
San Francisco, the priest attacked swollen strike casualty figures published in the *San Francisco Call:* He protested that "the number of
cases treated in the hospitals is less than the number treated during the
corresponding period of last year." [60]

Mitchell's argument and proof were not novel; that they received attention was due to the economic importance of the anthracite strike, the personal stature of the miners' leader, and his eye for publicity. Mitchell made an impression on journalists and the public by dining and mixing with the nation's elite (he had social charm) and by hastening into print. In 1903 Mitchell and Weyl published *Organized Labor* under Mitchell's name. Parts of this book were devoted to a discussion of the civilizing influence of unionism, for example, a chapter entitled "The Moral Uplifting of the Workman," which they wrote to refute the contentions of employers that unions tyrannized, bred discontent, and injured the morale of workers. In another part of the work they related Mitchell's evidence before the Anthracite Commission and admitted on the one hand that there had been violence during the strike, "but the claim that the majority of the men were prevented from working in the mines by the force and intimidation of a minority was utterly misleading, utterly false, and, as was subsequently shown, easily and completely disproved." [61]

There can be no doubt that Mitchell made his mark on friend and foe alike. The Mitchellian point of view was reiterated and discussed in diverse sources.[62] Even in 1908 when Mitchell's mental and physical breakdown, coinciding with dissention within the UMWA, culminated in his resignation from the union presidency, the miners' leader was upheld by *The Teamster* as an example to union men. Officials of the International Brotherhood of Teamsters had recently been through a period of violent confrontation with employers and were already being charged with some of the malpractices for which Jimmy Hoffa became rightly or wrongly notorious in the 1950s. Recalling that only the UMWA leader's threat of resignation prevented an outbreak of disorder in the anthracite strike, *The Teamster* repeated Mitchell's view that "in almost every strike the heads of the labor organizations insist that no crime be committed, and were it not for this it is hard to tell where our persecuted people would stop." [63]

Many critics of union malpractices remained unappeased by Mitchell's pleas. The prominent journalist Ray Stannard Baker, who had been in the coalfields during the 1902 strike, lent a muckraking voice to the employers' cause in his articles for *McClure's Magazine*. Baker attacked intimidation and, using a phrase that was later attached to open-shop legislation on the state and national levels, supported the "right to work" of the 17,000 nonstrikers. Another magazine that became critical of miners' violence and Mitchell's position on it was *Outlook,* edited by Lyman Abbott. This magazine afforded steady support to Roosevelt, who was a contributing editor, and in July 1902 Abbott had allowed Weyl to argue in it the case for recognition of the UMWA. But in January 1903 an editorial in *Outlook* noted that Chairman Gray of the Anthracite Commission had criticized the mineworkers' union for not applying discipline before members were convicted in court. It took cognizance of Mitchell's protest that a union had no right to expel men until they were proven guilty, yet held "that the greatest enemy that the trades-unions have to face to-day is not the criminal aggression of Capital, but the criminal acts of their own members." Two years later, after the Colorado miners' and Chicago meatpackers' strikes had heightened apprehensions concerning labor militancy, Abbott published the Slason Thompson article that purported to put on a statistical basis the hitherto inferential argument on labor's violence: Thus, Mitchell's method of argument elicited a response in kind.[64]

Judging from the American experience at the time, Georges Sorel was correct in observing in the early twentieth century that labor unionists showed a proclivity for violence. Union leaders themselves realized they were vulnerable to this charge. Regardless of their social philosophy, such men were inextricably linked with violence. This was true not only of the corrupt and predatory, such as Parks, Madden, Slattery, and Tveitmoe, but also of honest leaders such as Hotchkin, Moyer, McNamara, Mitchell, Weihe, and Gompers, of such revolutionaries as Debs, Boyce, and Haywood, and even of idealists such as Powderly.[65]

Yet, if contemporary opinion is to be taken seriously, Sorel was wrong in regarding labor violence as primarily spontaneous, as the expression of a grass-roots yearning for freedom from oppression and corruption. Like Robert Hunter, many labor leaders professed faith in the intrinsic peacefulness of the worker, especially the unionized worker. Their statements may have sprung less from a tendency to idealize the working class than from a shrewd suspicion that labor leaders could never be cleared of the charge of exploiting such violence as did exist. Thus Mitchell was probably wise to emphasize rank-and-file peacefulness instead of union officials' verbal disclaimers of violence.

In spite of the efforts of Mitchell and other quantifiers, the problem of the extent of labor violence remained intractable in the Progressive period. Labor violence often fell into the Sellin-and-Wolfgang categories of conspiratorial or consentual crime and crimes against the public order because of the prevarications of union leaders. These prevarications were not new, but they had a greater effect in the post-Haymarket decades. The AFL, established in 1886, increased its aggregate affiliated membership from 447,000 in 1897 to 2,072,700 in 1904. Unlike the declining Knights of Labor, which had eschewed secrecy under pressure from the Catholic Church and which was in principle against strikes, the AFL's affiliates resorted to frequent and militant strikes planned, for obvious tactical reasons, in secret. As if this was not enough, Americans witnessed, in the opening decade of the new century, what appeared to be two major, subversive, and violent union conspiracies.

Chapter 5

Of Inner Circles ——————
and Masked War

LABOR LEADERS OF THE EARLY TWENTIETH CENTURY WERE, BY NATURE of their profession, conspiratorial and secretive. Tactical moves, especially during strikes, could be plotted by only discreet minorities. Secrecy was essential. But to the suspicious, secrecy meant that trade unionists on strike had something unsavory to hide.

What unionism's critics needed, and apparently obtained in the most dramatic form in the Progressive period, was proof of labor violence. The strikes of the Western Federation of Miners in Colorado (1903–1904) and of the International Association of Bridge, Structural, and Ironworkers generally (1905–1911) seemed at the time to be two particularly vivid examples of violent behavior by union leaders. In the opening years of the twentieth century WFM leadership appeared to be a secret, united "Inner Circle" with the object of terrorizing the Rocky Mountain states. But when WFM leaders appeared on trial, juries delivered frustrating acquittals. Believers in labor violence felt themselves vindicated, therefore, by revelations concerning the admitted use of dynamite by the IABSI in its so-called Masked War against steel contractors. These two complex examples of industrial violence reinforced each other in the Progressive period and, however exceptional, were widely perceived as typical.

Doubts about burgeoning American unionism were reinforced for many by the arrest of Joseph Valentine, president of the molders' union, on charges of dynamiting in 1904. W. G. Meritt, legal counsel to the open-shop National Erectors' Association, had already been frustrated in one attempt to land Gompers in prison because of his role in the Bucks Stove and Range Company secondary boycott (1907). But outstanding among these unsuccessful prosecutions of labor leaders was the outcome of the Steunenberg murder trial.

On December 30, 1905, Frank Steunenberg, who as governor of Idaho had suppressed a bitter strike in 1899, was blown to pieces by a bomb attached to the front gate of his house in Caldwell. Harry Orchard, later proved to be a prolific murderer, confessed to the deed. His evidence led to the arrests of Charles Moyer, William D. Haywood, and George Pettibone—president, secretary-treasurer, and former member of the Western Federation of Miners respectively—in connection with the same murder. All three were, however, acquitted.

To understand the expectations that the Steunenberg trial aroused and then temporarily disappointed, it is necessary to examine the reputation of the WFM. For in retrospect, it is by no means clear that the specific charges preferred against the WFM leaders following Steunenberg's murder were not entirely fabricated. The case against them would have appeared flimsy to contemporaries had expectations of guilt not been aroused by the recent history of the WFM.

Perhaps the most explicit use of violence by WFM leaders in Colorado occurred during the Telluride strike of 1901. On May Day 1901 two hundred and fifty workers in the Smuggler-Union mines struck. The management imported Mexican strikebreakers and armed them. In the gray hours of the morning of the third of July, the miners of the Tom Boy and Liberty Bell workings, having decided to help their Smuggler-Union comrades, marched in a body to the latter mine. The morning shift, which was about to go underground, was advised to cooperate with the strikers by not working. The "scabs" fired a volley at the pickets, and a gunfight ensued, which lasted six hours. Three men died, including a Mexican strikebreaker and an Italian picket. Superior odds forced the strikebreakers to surrender, and they were run out of the district after being beaten up.

The union achieved an advantageous truce: "It is hereby agreed between the miners' union by V. St. John, president, and the Smuggler-Union mining company by Edgar A. Collins that all work shall cease on said mine for the space of three days, ending Friday evening. Also that the said miners' union will refrain from violence either to persons or property in the same period." [1] This seemed to be a tacit admission of union responsibility for violence by Vincent St. John (later secretary-treasurer of the Industrial Workers of the World). Also present were James T. Sullivan of the WFM executive board and Oscar M. Carpenter, secretary of the local union. Further evidence of WFM approval of the violence was adduced from the fact that the union financed a funeral for the Italian victim and erected an expensive monument to his memory. Union approval and exploitation of violence did not of necessity amount to complicity, but actions of union officials in Telluride did little to give the WFM a good name.

The Telluride strike gave merely a foretaste of the Cripple Creek strike of 1903–1904. The miners at Cripple Creek came out on August 10, 1903, in support of strikers at the Denver mills of the American Smelter and Refining Company. It was Haywood, the radical secretary-treasurer of the WFM, who induced the Cripple Creek miners to walk out. In swaying the Cripple Creek miners, Haywood was aided by a circumstance that played into the hands of a strong-willed minority. Shortly before the strike began, poorly attended referendum meetings voted the power of calling strikes into the hands of a thirteen-man District Council. The council was unbalanced in that some of the small radical unions had equal representation with the rest.[2]

There was, then, a conspiratorial clique, or an "Inner Circle," as it came to be known, in charge of the Cripple Creek strike. But it should be noted that unions on strike, like democratic countries at war, as a matter of course invest their leaders with powers that would not be theirs in times of peace. In view of the fact that the WFM was infested with Pinkerton spies, it made good sense to limit discussion of strategy to a small band of trusted men. There is no concrete evidence to suggest that Haywood organized a conspiracy to dynamite, as opposed to a conspiracy to win. Ultimately, it was this distinction that most newspapers failed to make.

In no case was violence firmly pinned on the WFM, while in several instances the hand of the agent provocateur may be discerned no less clearly than that of a union militant. For example, on November 16 there was an attempted derailment of a Florence and Cripple Creek Railroad train carrying nonunion workers. H. H. McKinney, a former member of the WFM, was charged with the crime, which was supposedly the idea of Sherman Parker, president of District Union No.

1, WFM. This was disproved, as two independent detectives were involved in the incident. They were alleged to have been paid by the Mine Owners' Association (MOA) to discredit the WFM and so bring federal troops into the area. Eventually, an MOA attorney bailed McKinney out.[3]

Other incidents demonstrate the ambiguities of violence in a well-directed strike. Superintendent Charles McCormack and shift boss Melvin Beck were descending the mine shaft of the Vindicator mine on November 21 when an explosion killed them both. The WFM, and in particular Steve Adams, Harry Orchard's associate, were accused of complicity. But it seemed unlikely that the union alone could have been culpable, for the mine was guarded at the time of the explosion by state troops, which had been imported at the behest of the operators on September 4. The unionists claimed that the two men were accidentally killed while trying to fabricate the appearance of a new plot in order to ensure the continued presence of the militia.[4] Sergeant Claude C. Baldwin, the orderly of Colorado's adjutant general, Sherman Bell, later claimed that operators had planned the explosion but neglected to forewarn their two unfortunate employees.[5] Without doubt, the account of the Vindicator incident on the front page of *The New York Times* did the union an injustice: ". . . one of the most diabolical crimes that ever darkened the annals of Colorado, and . . . another step in the trail of blood which has been made by the Western Federation of Miners in this State." [6]

Cripple Creek was further troubled on January 28, 1904, when a cage bringing night-shift workers up the shaft of Stratton's Independence mine, Victor, failed to stop, touched the sheave wheel, and fell. A coroner's jury blamed the deaths of the fifteen men on the company's neglect of safety regulations, while the managers of the nonunion mine claimed that the machinery had been tampered with and WFM propaganda described the accident as a planned attempt to blacken the name of the union.[7] Even this incident, however, was to be overshadowed in notoriety by the Independence explosion, which brought the phrase "Inner Circle" to the attention of the nation.

At two o'clock in the morning, June 6, 1904, nonunion workers from the Findley mine, in the town of Independence, were waiting for a train at the Golden Circle Depot when a large quantity of dynamite exploded under the platform, killing thirteen of them. On June 10 the coroner's jury found, apparently without the assistance of evidence, that the Independence explosion was ". . . the result of a conspiracy entered into by certain members of the Western Federation of Miners." [8] During the Steunenberg trial and in his autobiography of 1907, Harry Orchard stated that he and Steve Adams had perpetrated the deed at the suggestion of Pettibone and Parker and with the approval of Haywood. The union disclaimed responsibility for the murders, and the WFM convention, then in session, voted to appropriate a reward for the capture of the dynamiter.[9]

The explosion did seem to occur at an inopportune moment for the union. Charles Moyer, imprisoned in connection with renewed trouble at Telluride, hourly expected a decision to be handed down on his *habeas corpus* application. At the national Democratic convention under way at St. Louis, Charles S. Thomas, a former governor of Colorado, was about to attack the "state of military despotism" existing in the Cripple Creek mining region and especially the conduct of Bell, one of Roosevelt's Rough Riders in the Spanish-American War of 1898, whose appointment as adjutant general of Colorado had been made at the request of the Republican President. The explosion occurred on the eve of his speech, and he failed to make headway against the effective counterpropaganda of the employers' associations organized under D. M. Parry.[10]

The most credible explanation of the Cripple Creek murders is that Orchard, Adams, and their like played both sides, making themselves useful by perpetrating the atrocities to which they confessed. But in the excitement of the 1900s Americans either swallowed Orchard's conspiracy theory or agreed with Clarence Darrow, union counsel in the Steunenberg case, that Orchard was "the most monumental liar that ever lived on earth." [11]

Orchard, who was prosecuting attorney William Borah's chief witness during the Steunenberg trial, based his story on the assumption that there was a rift between the followers of Moyer and those of Haywood during the 1903–1904 strike. Orchard pleaded that Haywood was responsible for WFM violence whereas Moyer, a conservative in tactics, was cautious in his use of force.[12] In the spring of 1904 both the renewed Telluride strike and the Cripple Creek strike were going very badly, and Haywood feared that as a consequence, power might slip away from minority radical control. He therefore resorted to tough measures both within and outside the WFM. He had already ordered the assassination of Lyte Gregory, who was known to have been a spy who betrayed union secrets. Now the secretary-treasurer threatened Third Vice-President James P. Murphy of Butte, Montana, with the fate of Gregory, in order to ensure Murphy's support for radical policies. The Independence explosion, although it took the lives of nonunion men, was similarly a reflection of internal union stresses. Haywood, whose presence at the WFM convention in Denver gave him a safe alibi, knew that Murphy was in Cripple Creek at the time of the explosion. Optimally, according to the Orchard story, Murphy would be arrested for the crime, thus removing a direct threat to Haywood's leadership, while Moyer would be forced by the crisis to stand by the radicals in order to ensure unity among the ranks of the WFM.[13]

After the Cripple Creek strike was over, Haywood became a prominent leader of the IWW and spent his last years exiled in Bolshevik Russia. But to assume that he was more radical than Moyer in 1904 would be to read history backwards. Moyer was himself a socialist. On May 28 he sent from his bull pen (the western colloquialism for concentration camp) a report to the WFM convention in which he referred to strikebreakers: "To these traitors can be charged the long-drawn-out struggle in the Cripple Creek district and they will surely receive their reward." [14] Had he known that the Independence explosion would occur a few days later, Moyer would not have sent such a message. If a WFM Inner Circle planned violence, Moyer was not a member of it. This was consistent with Orchard's story; on the other hand, the militancy of the statement could scarcely have been matched.

Just as the secrecy that shrouded the deliberations of the WFM Inner Circle encouraged tales of conspiracy, so the deliberations of detectives, capitalists, and Colorado politicians gave rise to speculation. For many who knew that James McParlan was head of the western division of the Pinkerton Detective Agency, credulity knew no bounds. McParlan, who secured the arrest of Haywood and his codefendants in 1905, already had a reputation for his part in bringing the "Molly Maguires" to trial in 1876. "Mollies" identified by McParlan had been convicted of assassinating Pennsylvania coal mine operators to further the cause of Irish-American mine laborers in the 1860s and 1870s, and had been duly hung. At the time of the Steunenberg trial, pro-WFM sources were not neglectful of the opportunity to revive the complaint that McParlan had been an agent provocateur to some of the Pennsylvania assassins. Since he had eight labor spies working for him in Colorado in 1903–1904, and since he coached Orchard to give evidence at the Steunenberg trial, union men drew their own conclusions.[15]

The Telluride strike of 1903–1904 illustrates the grounds of their suspicions. This strike, partly in pursuit of the eight-hour day and partly in sympathy with Cripple Creek miners, was inspired by Oscar Carpenter, secretary-treasurer of the Telluride Miners' Union and a personal friend of Haywood's. It was an "Inner Circle" strike—so much so that Moyer sent his own emissary to the scene. This man, John C. Williams, a WFM vice-president from Grass Valley, California, fell out with Carpenter, whom he accused of undermining strike morale through his foolish radicalism.[16]

When Governor Peabody declared "qualified martial law" on January 4, 1904, Williams and forty others were deported. On March 26 in Ouray, Colorado, Charles Moyer was arrested. He was then taken to nearby Telluride and charged with desecration of the American flag. The stars and stripes had been used as a background for the notorious leaflet *Is Colorado in America?* which enumerated injustices suffered by the WFM (this gave rise to the previously mentioned Moyer *habeas corpus* case, which the WFM leader lost on appeal to the Supreme Court in January 1909). One writer voiced the contemporary suspicion that the soldiers had arrested only conservative men, leaving the hot-blooded element free in the hope that they would incriminate themselves and the WFM.[17] If such a hope existed, it was frustrated, for no particularly bloody outrage occurred in Telluride. In this context, Moyer's radicalism was as strong as the next man's, and it seems likely that Haywood's Inner Circle was nothing more than a power faction within the WFM. What the Telluride arrests may very well reflect is the detectives' and operators' belief that there was an Inner Circle which, if given its head, would hang itself.

Each side in the Colorado war planned its strategy in secret; immediate and impartial investigation into various allegations was impossible because state politicians were pawns in the pockets of one side or another. In these circumstances, webs of mendacity shrouded every incident, so that individual interpretations were guided by existing loyalties rather than by cogitation. The divergence between different pieces of testimony was remarkable. Contrast, for example, Orchard's account of the Independence explosion with that of Bell's orderly, Sergeant Claude C. Baldwin. Baldwin claimed to have been present at a meeting of employers in Denver when the Independence plan had been discussed, and two men had been delegated to the task, although these two men had not been the actual murderers. According to this version, Clarence Hamlin of the MOA knew and approved of the commission of such atrocities.[18] There was no common ground whereon stories such as Orchard's and Baldwin's could be brought into perspective (the Steunenberg trial concerned only that particular murder). As a result, sensational stories remained untested, and bias accumulated for the next stage in the industrial struggle.

Before we leave the Cripple Creek struggle of 1903–1904 and the Steunenberg murder trial, it would be well to note that these events formed part of a thirty-year struggle in the mining regions of Colorado. They stood out from other incidents in the protracted confrontation for special reasons. Haywood, for example, became the IWW's most prominent leader: The IWW strikes, which spread to the East after 1908, therefore served as a reminder of bitter western battles. Rightly or wrongly, the western battles of 1903–1904 were presented by leading contemporary authorities on industrial relations as class conflicts, whereas western strikes in Colorado and Idaho in the 1890s had been dismissed as mere frontier disorders.[19] They were treated as a greater threat than the Ludlow strike of 1913–1914, which culminated in the machine-gunning of miners' wives and children by militiamen defending the interests of the Colorado Fuel and Iron Company. The bloodshed at Ludlow was considered less threatening to social order than the Cripple Creek strike and its aftermath because militiamen pulled the triggers, not workers, because the UMWA was involved rather than its more radical western counterpart, and because the news was quickly overshadowed by the outbreak of World War I. Also, the U.S. Commission on Industrial Relations held public hearings on the Ludlow incident in New York and Washington, a procedure that brought Colorado conflicts into the open and in so doing demonstrated their finite nature.

In contrast, the bridgemen's "Masked War," which we shall now consider, focused attention on the workers' potential for infinite clandestine violence. In the *American Federationist* of September 1901 a contributor had speculated that the convenient stick of dynamite (easily hidden on the person and cheap) would be the anarchists' answer to the Gatling gun, while employers, fearing the new undercover threat, would hire secret operators who, in turn, would exaggerate the dangers inherent in trade unionism.[20] This speculation was to prove a good fit for the bridgeworkers' strike, though its Marxist author shared Robert Hunter's inability to perceive that labor violence was not the sole prerogative of anarchists.

To understand the impact of revelations about the "National Dynamite Conspiracy" (1905–1911), it should be borne in mind that the Steunenberg trial had become ingrained in political memory. The effect of acquittal was to create expectations of innocence. The WFM arrests had involved kidnapping and illegal extradition, and the same was true of the arrest of John J. McNamara. Expecting a rerun of the Steunenberg trial, the labor movement was caught unaware by the McNamara confessions. Also lulled into a sense of reluctant security were those social reformers who sympathized with the labor movement. The WFM had seemed palpably guilty of a reign of terror. If social crusading was safe in the hands of a radical like Haywood (as the Steunenberg verdict indicated), it was safe in the hands of any labor leader. It took the violence of a conservative such as John J. McNamara to restore the liberals' faith in class disharmony.

The International Association of Bridge, Structural and Ornamental Ironworkers was an affiliate of the American Federation of Labor diversely known as the Bridgemen's Union, the Ironworkers' Union, and, in New York City, as the Housesmiths' Union. Its members erected steel girders for bridges and skyscrapers. In 1905 the tough IABSI members went on strike to achieve job control and better conditions; major contractors responded with a lockout. The ensuing struggle was protracted and irrefutably violent.

The IABSI strike was characterized by features that contemporaries found to be particularly suggestive. There was a conspiracy at the head of the association to intimidate nonunion workers through systematic beatings. In mid-strike, there was a cold-blooded policy decision to favor dynamite rather than personal violence, a shift designed to ensure deeper secrecy. Of similar interest to people who considered the strike in retrospect was the apparent complicity of Samuel Gompers, president of the AFL, in its violence.

The bridgeworkers' dynamite campaign is usually associated with the *Los Angeles Times* explosion of October 1, 1910. The proprietor of the *Times,* Harrison Gray Otis, was a declared and effective opponent of organized labor. A bomb was set off in an alley adjoining the Times Building.

The explosion took place on October 1, 1910, in the dead of night—

a precaution against loss of life. But the alley contained barrels of highly combustible ink, and twenty *Times* employees lost their lives in a lightning-fast, devastating fire.

Through the columns of his quickly restored newspaper, Otis lost no time in linking the explosion to labor and to socialist elements generally. Job Harriman, a hitherto strong socialist candidate for mayor of Los Angeles, was crushingly defeated.

As the history of events unfolded in 1911, it became evident to objective observers that the IABSI had had no part in the *Los Angeles Times* explosion. The *Times* affair, nevertheless, led to the exposure of violent tactics resorted to on other occasions by the International Association.

One of those who had plotted the *Times* explosion was James B. McNamara. A former member of the IABSI, and one of its paid dynamiters, he had helped damage Otis's building on his own initiative, not as part of union policy. But his brother, John J. McNamara, was secretary-treasurer of the IABSI, so when the brothers were arrested on charges arising out of the *Times* murders, the International Association was unavoidably implicated. Sympathizers with organized labor at first regarded the McNamara arrests as just another capitalist frame-up. The brothers were members of a Catholic labor organization, The Militia of Christ, and by definition nonsocialist. It came as a shock, therefore, when James (confronted privately with evidence that the prosecution would use against him) confessed on December 1, 1911, to complicity in the *Times* explosion. His confession paved the way for the portrayal of the socially supine AFL as a red menace.

On the day of his brother's admission, John J. McNamara also confessed, but not to the same crime. John admitted to conspiracy to dynamite the Llewellyn Iron Works in Los Angeles (this as part of union policy). John J. McNamara's confession marked the point of no return for the officers of his union, who became involved in an ever-widening morass of complicity and accusations.

The National Dynamite Conspiracy so unveiled was discovered to have implicated all who had served on the union executive board since 1906. The evidence of a turncoat eventually led to the conviction, on December 28, 1912, of the president of the union, Frank Ryan, and thirty-seven others on the charge of conspiring "to commit a crime against the United States, and of transporting, aiding and abetting the transportation of dynamite and nitroglycerin in interstate commerce in passenger trains and cars between the United States." [21] This one retrospective revelation gave rise to endless speculation about further unexposed conspiracies.

Ironically, leading IABSI officials resorted to dynamite in pursuit of a fight started by powerful New York delegates of whom they disapproved. This was an aspect of the Dynamite Conspiracy that seemed particularly ominous—it was the work of honest, nationally prominent men, not of the New York element, which was already known for its corruption and violence.

In New York, violence was endemic in the building trades unions. Until court prosecutions brought about his downfall in 1902–1903, the notorious Sam Parks had dominated the aggressive New York Housesmiths' Union. A County Down Irishman, Parks acquired physical toughness during his fourteen years as a Canadian North Woods lumberman and was reported to prefer fighting to eating.[22] He was by no means an intransigent enemy of the managerial class, but an exponent of the "sweetheart contract," which involved payoffs from unprincipled employers willing to disburse strike insurance. By the same token, however, Parks was the natural enemy of honest employers. Eventually, the employers of principle made a stand in the name of ideology and campaigned for the open shop.

In 1903 President Frank Buchanan of the IABSI ignored Parks' opposition in reaching an agreement with the American Bridge Company, a subsidiary of United States Steel and a major New York steel erection firm that had no interest in paying protection money. But the Housesmiths defied Buchanan and struck the company and its allies. An indication of the subculture of roughness and resistance that existed locally is given in the minutes taken during the September 9, 1903 meeting of the New York Building Trades Employers' Association: "One of the business agents, John Dolan, stated to one of the firms of the Iron League that he did not recognize the National Agreement and that he himself was the agreement and that the Employers had to do as he said, and the only use for the agreement was that it could [be] used for toilet paper." [23]

In the face of such attitudes held by local minorities, the harmony that Buchanan sought to establish broke down. In August 1905 militant elements within the IABSI forced the declaration of a strike against American Bridge and its subcontractors. In September, Frank Ryan, a known radical opponent of American Bridge, was elected president.

Partly because of the intransigence of the union, partly in defense of the liberties of nonunion men, and very largely because it cost "approximately $5.00 per ton less to erect industrial buildings with Open Shop men," [24] the employers inaugurated an anti-union offensive. Already in the steel and metal trades, unionism had been considerably weakened; it was now planned to attack the citadel of urban unionism, the building industry, using the financial resources of the metal trades that were available through the steel erection industry. On May 1, 1905, the National Erectors' Association (NEA, founded in 1903) declared for the open-shop principle. The Michigan attorney Walter Drew was made commissioner for the NEA and was entrusted with the task of union smashing.

In the protracted struggle between the IABSI and the NEA, each side used ruthless tactics. On January 6, 1906, a *New York Tribune* reporter pointed to the parallel between recent assaults and the tactics of "the late Sam Parks." Two months later the erector management in New York City, represented in the Allied Iron Association, gave union violence as their reason for not dealing with the Housesmiths' Union.[25] Assaults on nonunion men and retaliations occurred in Pittsburgh and New York City, sometimes with fatal consequences. In March 1907 an anonymous letter arrived at the open shop of Post and McCord: "These 1,500 or more men who are not anxious to be forced into the union . . . have become disgusted with the union because of its slugging and bulldozing methods, and the well known rottenness and grafting of its Officers and its paid Plug Uglies." [26]

Tom Slattery was the presiding genius of the paid plug-uglies. After his dismissal from the Brooklyn police force for assaulting a fellow policeman, Slattery had become Sam Parks' lieutenant and a walking delegate for Local 35 of the IABSI of Brooklyn. The former policeman was the ironworkers' most active agent in New York and in the years preceding 1913 was arrested several times for assault and indicted for bribery in the court cases arising. Slattery's usefulness and success after 1905 arose from his police and political connections (in this respect he was a true disciple of the deceased Parks, who had been noted for his Tammany pull). He was, indeed, a popular and semimythologized figure. The cause of his death in 1929 was reported to be a hemorrhage in an old bullet wound, brought on by a temporary abstinence from alcohol. The *Nassau Daily Review* paid him a front-page tribute on that occasion: "There were many in Brooklyn and Long Island who feared and hated 'Big Tom,' but there were a far greater number who looked upon him as 'regular,' as a friend and a champion of the weak against the strong." [27] It was this man who waved his fist in the face of open-shop steel erectors in the early years of the bridgeworkers' strike.

Tom Slattery's pugilism was, for all its popularity, an anachronism. Within two years of the beginning of the strike of 1905–1911 the leaders of the International Association decided to place their faith in dynamite in preference to fisticuffs. As a militant and controlling clique, they were able to effect this change in emphasis. Their goal was still the same—to secure the employment of union men and to achieve higher wages. But, whereas previously the method had been to curtail the supply of nonunion labor through violence, the new method was to destroy the property of uncooperative businessmen.

It was because they sought a secret weapon that the national executive of the IABSI decided to change to dynamite. The use of plug-uglies had required a certain amount of interchange in violence. Thugs would beat up men in a precinct other than their own, sometimes even in other cities. Now, a small elite of dynamiters would operate in any state in the Union, under central guidance from the union headquarters in Indianapolis. Such was the nature of the new method that it was possible to aver that the AFL unions retained a corps of dynamiters ready to participate in any anarchic scheme.

Plug-uglies were dispensable anyhow by the summer of 1907, because they were highly vulnerable to detection. Walter Drew tried to impoverish the Bridgemen's Union by dragging its members into court at every opportunity. David Marks, of the Housesmiths' "entertainment committee" (the prevailing euphemism for union plug-uglies), was sentenced to four years' imprisonment on February 1, 1906. On the twenty-sixth of the same month the *Tribune* predicted that arrests of union men for assault "may have a tendency to break the strike or do away with the dangers incurred by men who wish to work." Walter Drew's lawyers began to outwit Tom Slattery's political friends. On the first of May 1907, the firm of Eidlitz and Hulse, counsel for the NEA and the Allied Iron Association of New York City, sent Commissioner Drew a memorandum on assaults. It showed that in only one case since the beginning of the strike had their prosecution of union men been unsuccessful.[28]

Eidlitz and Hulse's one failure was even more damaging to the union than their many successful prosecutions. It concerned the several trials of John O'Brian, a New York gunman used to settle union affairs in several midwestern cities. O'Brian was initially convicted of assaulting a foreman in Ashtabula, Ohio, and made several appeals. Since the IABSI was paying for the defense, these court cases milked it of funds.

The association's difficulties were compounded in 1908 when Tom Slattery shot O'Brian for political reasons.[29] Slattery was usually able to get away with such acts because of his Tammany associations. On this occasion, with Drew and a whole battery of lawyers and detectives breathing down his neck, he had to flee to Canada.

This played into the hands of IABSI leaders with cooler heads than Slattery's. When the intemperate plug-ugly returned from Canada, he found that President Ryan no longer extended the palm of gold. In May 1909 executive board member Frank C. Webb wrote to John J. McNamara saying that Ryan had refused to sanction their plan to help Slattery financially and that he had to inform Slattery accordingly.[30] This was confirmed in 1910 when Slattery called a strike against a McClintic-Marshall pier job in Brooklyn. Slattery assaulted a rival walking delegate, William Dalton, and incurred the wrath of the Drew legal machine. To the union rank and file, Slattery remained a hero—they collected $2,000 locally toward the eventual out-of-court settlement—but Ryan refused to provide national treasury funds.[31]

The court expenses of union plug-uglies were bothersome but not necessarily prohibitive. In spite of its struggle with employers, the IABSI was an increasingly affluent union. There was, however, an underlying economic factor that made 1907 a propitious year for change. A recession set in following the "Bankers' Panic" of March 1907. By August, NEA Commissioner Drew was turning away from his employment bureau even highly skilled open-shop workers. Building had fallen off, and Ryan realized that personal intimidation alone would not triumph when there were hundreds of qualified men walking the streets of New York.[32]

The attraction of dynamite, above all, lay in its clandestine possibilities—it could be secretly deployed, thus avoiding not only the irksome attentions of unmanageable policemen but also the strident strictures of the open-shop press. It is ironic that dynamite, the instrument of secrecy, eventually occasioned maximum exposure for union violence.

Dynamite had been used for several years by strikers and agents provocateurs. Indeed, two members of the New York local of the IABSI had already been convicted of dynamiting, in November 1905, a derrick on a Post and McCord project.[33] Late in 1907 the National Dynamite Campaign was inaugurated. Targets for destruction included railroad bridges, steamship piers, and structural building materials in storage. These were difficult to guard, so that dynamiters could escape fairly easily. It was hardly worth insuring a plant, because dynamite caused only light damage to open structures. On the other hand, dynamiters had a high nuisance value in that they so often attacked completed property, forcing the clients of open-shop construction companies to hire union men to effect repairs. Technological advances made dynamiting more efficient. Union dynamiters used an "infernal machine," which consisted of "soup," or nitroglycerin, plus a clock, batteries, caps, and connections. This time bomb replaced the old-fashioned device of short-fused dynamite.[34]

It was Herbert S. Hockin of Local 25, Detroit, the eventual betrayer of the Dynamite Conspiracy, who hired Ortie McManigal in 1907 to dynamite property for the union. The prolifically destructive McManigal thereafter cooperated in his work with James B. McNamara, while the latter's elder brother, John J., kept the accounts and directed operations from Indianapolis. More than eighty explosions occurred during the National Dynamite Campaign. Open-shop advocates felt their very existence to be threatened. In Indianapolis in 1909 the use of several time bombs, transported in an automobile, enabled James B. McNamara to blow up four buildings simultaneously, confusing the police. The four buildings belonged to Albert Vansprecklesen, an open-shop contractor; one of the buildings was his home. So difficult was it to establish the identity of the dynamite conspirators that the Citizens' Association publication *Square Deal* vaguely attributed the Indianapolis explosions to "men supposed to be members of labor unions." [35] So did David M. Parry, president of the National Association of Manufacturers, which supported the open-shop drive of United States Steel and the NEA. Parry, who lived in Indianapolis, felt constrained to carry a revolver in each pocket and sent his family to Germany.[36]

Walter Drew sought an answer to union tactics in the employment of armed guards, labor spies, and criminal investigators. Early in the bridgeworkers' strike, Drew engaged the Thiel Detective Agency and the Corporations' Auxiliary Company to place armed men at disputed jobs. Meeting further requests from open-shop contractors, the NEA commissioner resorted to the services of men supplied from the agency of James Farley. But the guards proved to be a luxury few employers could afford, so Drew changed his main emphasis from the overt guarding of property to the hidden penetration of union ranks.[37]

In March 1907 Drew prevailed upon the Executive Committee of the NEA to endorse his plan of putting private detectives to work, with the object of finding out about union affairs and obtaining incriminating evidence. He was referred to the "Pinkerton Agency at Chicago as being most likely to have men suited to the purpose." [38] But by 1910 Drew and his colleagues had become disillusioned with the efforts of several detective agencies. F. W. Cohen, erection engineer for the Pennsylvania Steel Company, agreed with Drew:

> . . . that no detective agency is to be relied upon; their expenses run up enormously and they only give you enough to lead you on, and while once in a while they will give you information, they will not uncover the man who gave the information, and it is therefore of no legal value as far as convictions are concerned. . . . The men who give secret information as to the doings of the executive boards in the union play both sides and simply strain you.[39]

Drew had never relied entirely on independent detective agencies. He examined new approaches through subcommittees of the NEA— the Committee on Dynamiting in 1908, the Committee on Secret Service Department in 1909. Pursuant to a recommendation by the latter, the NEA set up its own fact-finding bureau, which improved the efficiency of a microscopic blacklist. This experiment, which the NEA financed through a special assessment on its members, was opposed by powerful members of the National Executive of the NEA. It declined in popularity as the months passed and union dynamiters stayed at large.[40]

Still seeking some proof of union perfidy, Drew was finally aided by the famous detective William J. Burns. Burns came to the erectors with a recommendation from the chief of the United States Secret Service. Professedly Progressive in politics, he protested convincingly that he was as much concerned for the welfare of labor as of capital. For some time, the wish had been expressed by the NEA and Drew to get "the men higher up" in union circles, who planned the ongoing national conspiracy. When Burns claimed that John McNamara had supplied the men who dynamited the Los Angeles Times Building, he was hired. So attractive was the prospect of landing national trade-union leaders on criminal charges that Kirby of the NAM and Chicago steel and railroad interests were induced to promise financial aid. It was thus that a well-primed legal juggernaut was launched successfully against the officers of the IABSI.[41]

In order to appreciate the national impact of the McNamara affair, it is necessary to take note of the nature of employers' and detectives' propaganda following the arrests. Burns believed, or at least pretended in public to believe, that the president of the American Federation of Labor was from the outset aware of the McNamaras' guilt. Following the arrest of John J. McNamara in Indianapolis on April 22, 1911, Burns hinted at Samuel Gompers' complicity through the columns of the *New York World*.[42] In 1913 Burns published his account of the Dynamite Conspiracy, with the immodest title, indicative of his theme, *The Masked War: The Story of a Peril that Threatened the United States by the Man who Uncovered the Dynamite Conspirators and Sent Them to Jail.* Drew was more moderate, and perhaps more persuasive, in his propaganda. He refused to talk in terms of a national peril or of war between capital and labor. But in a pamphlet defending labor injunctions entitled *Labor Unions and the Law,* he identified the policies of the IABSI leaders with those of the AFL, urging that nothing be done in Congress to increase their "ability to use their power for oppression, selfish ambition, civil war or plunder of the public." Drew was mainly concerned with dealing a blow to the trade-union movement, and to that end he argued that Gompers was the mouthpiece of the Bridgemen's Union.[43]

Was Gompers involved in the National Dynamite Conspiracy? The historian is not at his best in playing the retrospective detective, but it is quite legitimate to show that there was an appearance of AFL complicity in the Dynamite Campaign, which biased contemporaries would find difficult to ignore.

In the first place, Gompers appeared to be devious because he had stressed a partial and misleading version of the truth; he had repeatedly denied that the McNamaras were guilty of the *Los Angeles Times* explosion. The executive council of the AFL thought they had good reason to suppose that the *Los Angeles Times* charges were trumped up:

. . . long experience with the brutal side of many in the business world and their alliance with corrupt politics and unscrupulous detectives and *agents provocateurs;* the hostile employers association; the circumstantial evidence connected with the destruction of the *Times* Building; the fact that Harrison Gray Otis, owner of the Building and the *Los Angeles Times,* had for twenty years conducted a bitter, inexorable war upon organized labor—all this evidence, accompanied by the repeated disclaimers of guilt by the men, persuaded us into the full faith and belief that the men were victims of a vengeful plot to disrupt the labor movement of our country.[44]

American labor leaders understandably doubted the complicity of a union officer in the *Los Angeles Times* explosion, but their disclaimer smacked of hypocrisy when it was discovered they had done nothing to stop the National Dynamite Campaign.

Gompers certainly knew that the Bridgeworkers' Union had a history of violence. He was well versed in the problems of the building trades and knew several New York Irish labor leaders personally. Although John J. McNamara was not a close friend of his, he had met him on a few occasions. The AFL leader must have read in the newspapers of the confessions and convictions of Charles Moran and John Guthrie for dynamiting on behalf of the New York local in 1905. In 1909 Gompers wrote to Ryan, who was an AFL vice-president, insisting that the regular collection of union dues was essential to the outcome of any strike.[45] Yet the income of the IABSI had increased by 50 percent in the course of the year. Gompers may not have been aware of this, for the union's organ, *Bridgemen's Magazine,* had suspended its usual custom of printing financial reports. Yet it would be remarkable if the AFL president had not considered the question of expenditure as well as income and, in view of the criminal cases involved, pondered on the absence of published accounts. The foregoing considerations suggest at the very least that Gompers was not afflicted with a morbid curiosity.

The most suggestive evidence concerning Gompers' toleration of a Dynamite Campaign arose from his visit to Indianapolis. After the arrest of John J. McNamara at the IABSI headquarters in Indianapolis in April 1911, Drew went through the union papers, taking note of incriminating pieces of evidence. They included written directives from the national officers of the union concerning the Dynamite Campaign. There was also a copy of Slattery's derisive resolution sub-

mitted to the fourteenth annual convention of the IABSI in 1910:
"That no more bombs or explosives of any kind be exploded while
this convention is in session." [46] In June 1911 Gompers and members
of the AFL executive were shown the incriminating evidence in
Indianapolis, yet they continued to profess belief in the innocence of
the McNamara brothers. It is possible that they saw incriminating
letters concerning the Dynamite Campaign but chose to ignore them,
since the public scandal centered on the *Los Angeles Times* explosion.
Or Burns and Drew may have concocted a plot, contriving to create
the appearance of AFL complicity. In a letter to members of his
union, Frank Ryan complained bitterly three days after John Mc-
Namara's arrest that Drew had been allowed to take away from the
IABSI headquarters documentary evidence that was the property of
the union. Drew was also permitted by the Indianapolis superintendent of police to keep the keys to the union office. By removing from
Gompers' scrutiny certain vital pieces of evidence, Drew could have
been ensnaring the labor movement to associate itself publicly with the
arrested men.[47] Whatever the correct explanation, the McNamara affair
created a suspicion in the public mind that labor was waging a
"Masked War" against capital.

The McNamara affair alone does not explain the outcry occasioned
by the brothers' confessions. The release of pent-up frustration with
the policies of trade unions is evidenced in contemporary allegations
that union criminality was universal and in comparisons between the
dynamite trials and the Steunenberg trials of 1906–1908.

The accusation that the whole of the labor movement was implicated in violence took several forms. Ortie McManigal averred that
not all the dynamite explosions that had occurred since 1907 were
the work of the IABSI. Labor leaders in other unions had engaged in
violent practices "whenever the opportunity presented itself." Burns
claimed that the AFL had been so far implicated in the McNamaras'
policies that it had been prepared to bribe his son, Raymond J. Burns,
to drop the prosecution of the brothers. John Kirby, Jr., president of
the NAM, wrote that AFL leaders were brutal, unlawful, and un-
reasonable and comprised "a cold, merciless and murderous labor
trust." The *San Francisco Chronicle,* whose front page was monopolized by sensational coverage of the dynamite affair from the arrest
of the McNamaras to the end of April, hinted hopefully that there
would be widespread arrests of California labor leaders.[48]

The Union, an Indianapolis periodical that, like many prolabor sources, insisted that the McNamaras were two very pleasant people merely trying to improve working conditions, complained that the whole object of Burns and his brood was to discredit Samuel Gompers and other national labor leaders. Whether or not open-shop forces were so unscrupulous, they must have been satisfied with the national response. For example, the German-born editor and writer Walter V. Woehlke informed the readers of *Outlook* that 90 percent of trade-union leaders were fully aware of criminal acts committed on behalf of their movement and lent their support to these activities, whether by willing or reluctant acquiescence. Similarly, the *Nation* published an editorial on the IABSI that stated: "The history of the organization since its foundation in 1895 is an epitome of the history of most labor troubles in the United States." [49]

It was against the background of this kind of propaganda that in 1912 the Socialist Party of America decided to expel IWW's from membership, confusing them in the process with advocates of violence (the connection between the IABSI and the IWW was actually almost nonexistent, though Burns tried to make something of it, and David Caplan and Matthew Schmidt, alleged to have been among the *Los Angeles Times* dynamiters, had anarchist associations—but none with the IABSI). [50] Reactions to the McNamara confessions also encouraged President William H. Taft to create the United States Commission on Industrial Relations, which produced America's first blueprint for federal social reform.

Such events were the responses of men who were already predisposed to worry about labor conspiracies because they remembered recent industrial history. The Colorado strikes were the most notable of the various struggles that prepared the way for popular and political reaction to the McNamara affair. The metalliferous mine and construction strikes may be profitably compared with each other and with other strikes. In the first place, it is notable that each strike was supposedly conducted by conspiratorial, lawless minorities. This was a common supposition. Indeed, one authority remarked that most labor injunctions were granted in response to petitions that listed threats of violence and alleged "conspiracy to unlawfully injure the defendants." [51] The particular application of conspiracy theories to strikes reflected a general tendency in America to believe in conspiracies. The Populists had their "Hebrew" bankers, Woodrow Wilson his incongruous suspicion of "secret diplomacy," with which credulous attitudes toward "Inner Circles" and "Masked Wars" were entirely consistent.

Union leaders by their tolerance seemed to condone violence. Gompers' acceptance of New York plug-uglies is a case in point. It was natural to suppose that such leaders manipulated violence to their own advantage. Union leaders could have yielded to pressures to expel violent members from their organizations; Gompers could have called for the expulsion of the IABSI from the AFL, but to do so would have been clearly inexpedient. To union rank-and-file members, indicted or imprisoned leaders were martyrs in their cause. Again, discipline could not be meted out on the ground of suspicion. Only if a member was convicted of a criminal act could he justifiably be punished by his union—and why punish him twice for the same offense? These were the arguments that union spokesmen could and did plausibly advance. Employers constantly listened to the union argument that if they dealt fairly with labor, there would be less strife in their industry. Advocates of the open shop regarded this argument as a threat.

Finally, both the WFM and IABSI strikes were characterized by the enigmatic language of dynamite, and by the presence of detectives. The mysteries of dynamite, closely guarded by the Rocky Mountain antagonists, were blown open by the bridgeworkers' convictions. But McParlan and Burns were too discreet to allow anything stronger than speculation to flourish concerning the real work of detective agencies. Their presence in each strike at the capitalist elbow, and resentment of them in union quarters, are sufficient reasons in themselves for an examination in the next two chapters of the history of the detective agencies.

Chapter 6

Armed Guards ————————

THERE WAS, BY 1910, NO REFUGE FOR THE UNION DYNAMITER. AS HE approached his target in the freezing night, as he fumbled, all thumbs, with his volatile explosive, as he planned his escape via automobile, whiskey, and the woman who would supply his alibi, he ran the constant risk of discovery. Sooner or later, the detectives would break his cover. It might be through a guard's bullet, a drunken indiscretion, or a woman's betrayal, but inevitably he would become a marked man. Or so, at any rate, ran the publicity story of the private detective agencies.

The private detective agency was an important business institution by 1905. With the growth of industry and trade unionism and in the absence of proper state law enforcement, it met an apparent need. The detective agency was required to police industry and protect strikebreakers. It was further needed, in an era when trusts were being muckraked, to supply the countervailing facts about union violence. Large or small, detective agencies offered one or both of two services: armed guards, to be discussed here, and labor spies, to be dealt with in the next chapter.

In association or individually, many employers were capable of organizing their own strikebreakers, guards, and spies. Yet detectives were successful in representing their services as professional and efficient. They were more proficient than employers at creating the appearance of union violence and intimidation, even where there was none. Their success in this respect is reflected in the hostility they aroused in the ranks of labor and socialists. Detective agencies were adept at infusing the dramatic into strike situations at the expense of the mundane.

By 1914, however, the market was saturated. Furthermore, the growth of such institutions as the Pennsylvania Constabulary and the Federal Bureau of Investigation provided new competition. Some exposés of private detectives' methods began to appear, while the whole question of violence was put into perspective by the Great War. Private detective agencies were no longer expanding their collective industrial business by the 1920s; their period of maximum plausibility was over.

"Pinkertonism" was the eponym applied to the policy of using armed guards. It derived from the name of Allan Pinkerton, a Glaswegian who founded Pinkerton's National Detective Agency. One of his most lucrative sources of revenue was the Protective Patrol, which he established in 1850 to guard employers' property. Between 1874 and 1892, embattled property owners in several states had recourse to Pinkerton men on at least seventy occasions. By 1892 the Pinkerton Agency had offices in eight major cities. It retained an estimated 600 to 800 agents, and its Chicago arsenal was reputed to hold 250 rifles and 400 pistols.[1]

The Pinkerton Agency ceased to provide armed guards in labor disputes as a result of the censure it incurred in 1892. In that year there occurred the notorious strike in Andrew Carnegie's Homestead steelworks, just down the Ohio River from Pittsburgh. H. C. Frick, Carnegie's lieutenant, arranged for a force of Pinkerton agents to take over the works. The sheriff of Allegheny County, who had already failed to raise a posse for the same purpose, refused to deputize the private army. Three hundred armed Pinkerton men floated down the river in barges and attempted to land. Strikers successfully resisted them and after a long battle, resulting in several deaths, the invaders were taken captive. The strikers lost in the end in the face of the state militia and Carnegie's economic strength, but the Pinkerton Agency never recovered from the ignominy of its defeat and the notoriety of its attempt to take the law into its own hands.

The Homestead battle provided a focus for resentment, which already ran high, being expressed in the contemporary refrain:

> God help them tonight in the hour of their affliction
> Pray for him who they'll ne'er meet again
> Hear the poor orphans tell their sad story
> Father was killed by the Pinkerton men.

The public outcry after the Homestead shootings of July 1892 was so effective that in August Pinkertons were conspicuously absent from a New York Central railroad strike (two years previously, Pinkerton guards had been sharpshooting indiscriminately in a strike on the same line).[2]

The public demanded the suppression of not only Pinkertons but also "Pinkertonism." Petitions flowed into Washington protesting against private police forces that were used exclusively against workers and were "made up of the lowest, most vicious class, thugs and ex-convicts." Already some states had legislated against the importation of armed guards, and in 1892 Tom Watson attempted, even before the Homestead furor, to secure congressional legislation prohibiting them nationally. Although Watson's legislative campaign failed, two congressional inquiries followed the Homestead strike, one of which noted the "irreconcilable hostility" between Pinkertons and workingmen. A House committee reported that the Pinkerton Agency was now mainly concerned with private, or nonlabor, detective work. But simultaneously, a Senate report revealed that there already existed in Chicago and New York a few other agencies that specialized in providing armed guards.[3]

Into the breach vacated by the Pinkertons stepped James Farley. Farley specialized in breaking streetcar strikes, which became endemic as suburban lines snaked out from city centers and became essential links in the booming economy of the early 1900s. The unskilled nature of streetcar driving and conducting fostered an ease of labor substitution, which made it extremely difficult for the union to win against peaceful strikebreaking tactics. Nevertheless, Farley created an image of himself as one who outbraved riotous prounion crowds intent on obstructing traffic. Journalists referred to him as "the best known strikebreaker in the United States" and "the best hated man in this country."[4]

As a former hotelkeeper, Farley knew how to keep in touch with disreputable habitués of low-class hostelries who were the potential recruits for his "standing army of strikebreakers," which at the lowest estimate numbered four hundred. The Research Division of the Commission on Industrial Relations launched an inquiry into New York City-based detective agencies. Investigating for the CIR in 1914, William Zumach visited Mills Hotel No. 1 on Bleecker Street, Mills Hotel No. 2 on Rivington Street, and the Salvation Army Hotel on the Bowery, ascertaining that they all provided a roof for strike "busters." Another way of collecting men was to prowl the parks with a police-man, giving the "bums" a choice: four dollars a day as a strikebreaker or expulsion from the park.[5]

Farley had "captains" in major American cities to assess local man-power needs, which were then met by recruitment in New York City. Farley's stated policy was to import hard-core men to the scene of a strike and to keep them there until the job was safe for nonprofessional strikebreakers. He was reported to have made a million dollars out of strike jobs between 1904 and 1914. Farley paid his assistants Curry and Wendell handsomely; all three found they could subsist on their strikebreaking activities alone.[6]

Farley's role in the Chicago teamsters' strike in 1905 illustrates well the contingencies that made for the introduction of professional strikebreakers to urban industrial conflicts. He benefited from the after-effects of Debs' ARU strike in 1894. In 1895 a United States Strike Commission report had deplored U.S. Attorney General Richard Ol-ney's action in sanctioning the creation of a "mushroom" force of 3,600 deputy U.S. marshals that was put at the disposal of the rail-road companies. This marked a significant change in public opinion. Ever since, city and state executives of nervous political disposition had avoided taking a firm line that might be interpreted as prejudicial to the interests of labor. In 1905, when disorder broke out in Chicago, Republican Governor Charles S. Deneen refused to mobilize troops until asked to do so by the mayor. But the mayor of Chicago was a Democrat, Edward F. Dunne. Refusing to admit his inability to keep order, Dunne would not request troops.[7]

More than five thousand special deputies were sworn in to reinforce the regular Cook County force of a meager hundred and fifty deputy sheriffs but, in the absence of reinforcements from outside the city, em-ployers still felt it necessary to recruit irregular forces of strong-arm men. At first, individual employers of teamsters recruited their own plug-uglies. For example, Fred Gardner, secretary of E. F. Daniels' Coal Co., made the first delivery to Montgomery Ward & Co. (a boy-cotted firm), preceded by his own "wrecking crew" of fifteen "pugilists." But the expertise of Farley was not long ignored, as teamsters' strikes, like streetcar strikes, presented the basic problem of moving traffic through dense and sometimes hostile crowds. To this end, Farley's assistant Frank Curry recruited strikebreakers for Chicago and persuaded Police Chief O'Neill to deputize and arm them. Curry selected four hundred black strikebreakers in St. Louis. When not initially issued with revolvers, a hundred of the imported blacks went on strike. Evidently, they either realized the danger of being unarmed or intended to provoke an incident. To an already disrupted society, Farley had introduced the further divisive force of race. Certainly, Farley's men did not restore order to the city. The Department of Police estimated that fourteen people had been killed by the end of the strike. According to Walter B. Bremer and Palmer Stewart, special agents for the commissioner of labor, another thirty-one persons were injured by shooting. Cook County and Chicago had suffered from shrieval powerlessness comparable to that of Allegheny County and had taken a similar dose of "Pinkertonism." [8]

Farley took every opportunity to present his service to employers in a favorable light. One such opportunity occurred in 1907 when Farley and Curry took a carload of New York men to break an "out of town" strike in San Francisco against the streetcar system of Patrick Calhoun, United Railways magnate. Industrial strife in the West seemed to promise a new lease on life to the old breed of rural gunman—the "Robin Hood" image of the Jesse James type of bandit would have been well adapted to the vigilante-style offensive being mounted against western labor organizations. Urban strikebreakers like Farley therefore found competition: on arriving in San Francisco, for example, Farley learned that J. B. Hubbard, a "bad man" from Wyoming, had shot dead a Seamen's Union picket. But Farley was equal to the challenge. He emphasized his links with properly constituted law as opposed to popular sovereignty. And he advertised the superior toughness of his men by spreading the story—whether true or skillfully fabricated—that en route to San Francisco his men had stopped off on the outskirts of Hole-in-the-Wall territory, northern Wyoming, where they "beat up" a "bad" cow town.[9]

The indications are that the professional armed guard enjoyed his widest popularity, among employers, during the Progressive years. The impact that detectives had on the image of industrial relations is better understood in the light of this popularity. It is appropriate, therefore, to trace the growth of detective agencies, to discuss their distribution in the Progressive period, and to show how circumstances were then propitious for their success.

A gradual professionalization of service took place among agencies following the 1890s, and in the 1900s such professional agencies appealed not only to employers experiencing labor troubles for the first time but also to employers who normally hired their own guards. After 1900 armed-guard agencies acquired, and apparently throve on, a reputation that bordered on notoriety.

Detectives were not uniformly successful at first, but their image improved rapidly. In 1902 the professional strikebreaker A. F. Clark arrived in New Orleans to start the streetcars running, was beaten up, and "ignominiously failed." A note of thoroughness was evident in the Richmond, Virginia, streetcar lockout a year later: the management had professional agents to survey the battlefield in advance. In New York August Belmont, the business tycoon controlling the Interborough elevated lines, resorted to detective-guards. Soon W. D. Mahon, president of the Amalgamated Association of Street and Electric Railways, was to blame the failure of his organization in Kansas City and St. Louis on ". . . the outrages committed by Pinkertons in the employ of street railway corporations." [10]

In 1905 the National Association of Manufacturers gave its official blessing to the Farley agency. Firms hitherto self-reliant turned to the professionals: in 1906 the Allis-Chalmers Company, which had allegedly employed its own plug-uglies in the Chicago strike of 1900, engaged the services of the Burr-Herr Agency to combat striking machinists; West Virginia coal operators who had in the past displayed baronial independence turned to the Baldwin-Felts agency of Roanoke, Virginia. There was a lull in the strikebreaking business with the depression of 1907, but in 1909, as Farley busied himself with the Philadelphia streetcar strike, there occurred two disturbances that again brought publicity to agencies providing armed guards. Sam Cohen unsuccessfully tried to break the IWW McKees Rocks strike near Pittsburgh in a conflict so brutal that it resulted in a federal inquiry. One of Cohen's men testified to the existence of peonage: Strikers had been forcibly detained within the Pressed Steel car-manufacturing plant. In the course of his testimony, Cohen's man revealed that he had attended fourteen other strikes.[11]

In the same year (1909) the *Amalgamated Journal* made allegations of peonage concerning the abortive steel strike, the last stand of craft unionism in the steel industry, during which M. Frank's Labor Exchange of New York City provided the American Sheet and Tin Plate Company of Youngstown, Ohio, with strikebreakers. In 1939 the La Follette Committee completed a report on *Strikebreaking Services,* which indicated that ". . . by 1914 it is apparent that the strikebreaker had no status as a bona fide employee, but was simply one of an industrial mercenary army." This was an exaggeration, but it is true that, on the eve of the Great War, detective agencies had taken over most of the armed-guard business and a considerable portion of the strikebreaker trade. A reliable estimate of the number of agencies was made in 1914, based on New York and a few other eastern and midwestern cities. At a time when it cost five dollars per man per day to hire guards, more than 270 agencies undertook labor work—and found customers.[12]

Detective agencies undertaking labor work were to be found in communities all over the United States. Such agencies were in a particularly advantageous position, however, if they kept an office and a hiring hall in some large city, where guards could be recruited at short notice. Since large cities owed their preeminence to surrounding industry, the urban agency was well placed to service neighboring employers. They also, however, answered calls in distant, isolated locations. It was in some circumstances easier to carry guards from Cincinnati to Wyoming than to persuade the people of Wyoming to turn against each other.

Three large, prestige agencies were in a position to supply, through their branches and agents, armed guards at any location in the United States. These were the Pinkerton Agency of Chicago (supplying the Middle and Far West in the main), Farley's Detective Agency of New York (happier to operate east of the Mississippi), and the William J. Burns National Detective Agency (with offices from Los Angeles to New York).

New York was a particularly attractive location for armed-guard agencies. Some of them, like the Smithburger Detective Agency and M. Frank's Labor Exchange, were prepared to travel. Others preferred local work: the Dougherty Detective Agency, Waddell-Mahon Agency, Val O'Farrell Agency, United Secret Service Agency, and Sweeney Detective Agency, to name a few.

Chicago, as a railroad center, could quickly supply guards to the Midwest, South, and West. A. F. Clark and the Pinkerton men would travel huge distances. Other agencies preferred special areas. For example, the Employers' Detective Agency of Chicago had offices in Duluth and St. Paul, Minnesota. In spite of the wide-ranging activities of a few of its agencies, Chicago was not the only midwestern city where detectives had set up headquarters. Dunn's National Detective Agency of Detroit and the Coach Agency of Cleveland served the Midwest generally.

It is important to establish that although detective agencies flourished simultaneously with the industrial revolution, they came into existence independently of it. For to show that there were special causes of the rise of private detectives in America is to show that they were in a position to influence industrial conflict in the Progressive period, not merely being called into existence by it. Such special causes may be illustrated by drawing a contrast with Europe. In the history of that continent, the organized state preceded industrialization. Police services, therefore, did not lag far behind the needs of businessmen. Police work, espionage, and detection on the modern bureaucratic level at first aroused hostility but gained in respectability with passing decades. In Britain there was public uproar when it was discovered that government spies had played a part in the Cato Street Conspiracy (1820) and in the Richmond trials, which, in the next decade, occasioned the emigration to the United States of allegedly framed weavers from Glasgow. But, by the late 1850s, Britain was a well-policed state, and in the last quarter of the nineteenth century, the Criminal Investigation Department at Scotland Yard came into its own. There was no need for private detective agencies in the British Isles, where state machinery predated capitalism, and could be used to reach any area. Sherlock Holmes remained a fiction.

In America the urban dweller preceded the policeman into the wilderness. William Allan Pinkerton, son of the founder of the Pinkerton Agency, remarked on the thorough inadequacy of the Chicago police in the period following the Civil War. He claimed to be the only criminal investigator in the city, and no doubt profited from the situation, as did other private detectives in similar circumstances. Pinkerton's sons said their agency was necessary because of the weakness of the posse system. In the East, Philadelphia had established a professional police force in 1833; Boston and New York City followed suit in 1838 and 1844, respectively. But the forces remained ill-trained compared with Sir Robert Peel's "bobbies" in England; it was not until the Progressive period, when August Vollmer, chief of police in Berkeley, California, started a national campaign, that Americans faced up to the problem of police reform. This problem was compounded by the fact that the police had been locally controlled throughout the nineteenth century (in contrast to Britain, where the Crown had control); policemen were therefore subject to local influence. Employers had often controlled local politics in the Gilded Age, but from the 1890s they often worried about the increasing public sympathy for labor, which (in their view) led to chronic political indecision when disorders occurred.[13]

Detective agencies seemed to offer a traditional solution. Informal law enforcement had been a common occurrence in American history, particularly in primitive frontier communities. Even when lawless, rural America began to give way to policed, urban communities, "neovigilantes" set out to punish scapegoats blamed for society's ills: blacks, carpetbaggers, unmarried mothers, and labor leaders. The vigilante habit died hard, but it was beginning to die by 1900. As industry and labor unions recovered from the depression of the 1890s, detectives stepped in to fill the breach. They were independent of the law, yet represented a half step to legitimacy, for they presented themselves as a group who operated within the law.

One factor aiding the growth of detective agencies was the fact that absentee management was an unavoidable accompaniment of large-scale production and engendered both geographic and social distances between business executives and precinct policemen. Capitalists had to fall back on detectives to restore the common touch. In New York several agencies gave employers grass-roots contact. For example, the Smithburger Detective Agency was useful in that the proprietor's father was a police inspector. And as one investigator remarked of the Dougherty Detective Agency: "Dougherty is a brother of an ex-police Commissioner and the Commissioner himself is now a member of the firm, so these gentlemen might be permitted by the regular police force to resort to unlawful methods which would not be tolerated from an agency that is not 'Right.' "[14] Other New York agencies were run by, or retained the services of, former union men. To managers divorced from men, such agencies seemed a good weapon with which to fight the union menace.

Another factor that played into the hands of the industrial detective agent was a certain relaxation in law enforcement. Between 1889 and

1892, six states legislated against the use of nonresident police officers; after Homestead, further state legislation was specifically directed at armed groups, detective agencies, and Pinkertons; by 1899 twenty-six states prohibited their importation across state lines. But from the start, it was apparent that armed guards would not entirely disappear. Only a year after the Pennsylvania state legislature unanimously approved a measure against the importation of armed guards, coal operators assembled in Philadelphia to decide on a policy of "a deputy for every miner" with regard to the strike then in progress. Armed men guarded the mines and on May 24, 1894, those employed by the Washington Coal and Coke Company, Connellsville, shot four strikers dead. A few days later, Local Assembly 5539, Knights of Labor, Krebs, Indian Territory, complained in a memorandum to Senator W. V. Allen of Nebraska that the Great Choctaw Coal and Railway Company had imported blacks and "hired" deputy sheriffs not "to guard as they say," but in fact to provoke riots and provide an excuse for the arrival of troops. Coal operators felt confident enough in Illinois in 1897 to break the law, by sending black strikebreakers to Virden, as the annual report of the State Bureau of Labor Statistics put it, ". . . under the protection of Winchesters in the possession of men disqualified to perform police duty under the Laws of this State." [15]

There was in a few states a legal avenue toward the hiring of professional detectives. Loopholes in the letter of the law—for example, in Kentucky, South Dakota, and Utah, guards could be armed after their arrival—brought into disrespect the spirit of the law after 1900. The letter of the law was simply ignored long before the La Follette investigation showed in the 1930s that no one took any notice of statutes restricting the use of guard-detectives. Attacking "class labor legislation in different states," Walter Drew of the National Erectors' Association wrote in 1914:

> many laws, of course, are designed to aid the union in its industrial battle by limiting the employer in different ways in the matter of guards and securing workmen, etc. While these are in many instances unfair and vicious, they do not compare as legislative crimes with a law such as the full-crew railroad measure in force in several states.

Drew's appraisal was based on the knowledge that his own detectives had operated unimpeded.[16]

What were the functions of detective agencies in providing guards?

According to the agencies themselves, their function was clear-cut. A Detroit agency informed an Indiana employer in 1920: "We will furnish guards on very short notice, and will break a strike in a way that will obviate the necessity of your being forced to use union or other employees not of your own choosing." [17] How a detective agency could achieve such an end more efficiently than the employer himself was never made quite clear.

Whatever detectives might have wished him to think, the American capitalist was capable of looking after his own affairs. The capabilities of the American businessman are indeed manifest. Strikebreaking was a time-honored occupation in the United States as elsewhere, and employers themselves were the leading exponents of the art. Individual employers were constantly accused of provoking violence in order to discredit organized labor. For instance, P. J. McGuire, founder member of the Socialist Labor Party and secretary of the Brotherhood of Carpenters and Joiners, recounted how, during an iron molders' strike in Troy, New York, in 1883, Sleicher, an employer, goaded his armed strikebreakers into killing two union men by telling them that their lives were in danger.[18]

In areas where public opinion remained hostile to trade unionism, employers resorted to direct intimidation. This was particularly the case in the South, where the vigilante tradition still flourished. Those who were, in Eugene Debs' words, "lynched, tarred and feathered, manhandled, deported and outraged in every conceivable manner" were usually union leaders or organizers rather than rank-and-file strikers. A devil theory of "agitation" throve in the South where, indeed, a few hunted individuals rather than spontaneous discontent often accounted for the appearance of unionism. *Free Lance,* a coal operators' organ published in Birmingham, Alabama, in 1908 attacked W. R. Fairley, a member of the United Mineworkers of America national executive board, with the exhortation: "Deport El Hassassin and His Henchmen. . . . No Bonds for Criminal Aliens, Negro or Native Desperadoes, Alabama must be white at any cost." [19]

Single corporations, while they could not depend upon the personal following of southern employers, sometimes managed to recruit their own force of armed guards without resorting to professional agencies. Henry Ford is notorious for having resisted unionism, partly through employing ex-convicts whom he claimed to be "rehabilitating" and who, on occasion, taught union pickets an unsavory lesson in pugilism. The La Follette investigation exposed in the 1930s the existence of private armories kept by large corporations.

With the crucial growth in trade-union membership in the late 1890s and early 1900s, employers' associations became very active. In 1893 the General Managers' Association of leading Chicago railroads formulated a contingency plan to assess members for $10,000 and scoured almost twenty cities for strikebreakers during a dispute with switchmen. In 1894 the GMA levied $36,000 and recruited 2,493 strikebreakers. Employers' associations made special resources available to relatively small firms; for example, in 1894 the GMA supplied its largest number of strikebreakers to the Atchison, Topeka, and Santa Fe. An expansion of this type of facility occurred in the opening years of the twentieth century. The socialist W. E. Walling claimed in 1904 that, since 1901, manufacturers' associations had established strikebreaking employment exchanges in seven major midwestern and western cities.[20]

The National Erectors' Association, though it retained only one full-time detective, ran a clearinghouse for nonunion men. Ever in the forefront of the open-shop movement, the National Metal Trades Association announced inside the back cover of its official organ that "it furnishes the men and money to break unjust strikes . . . it operates a National Employment Department for benefit of both employers and employees." Completing a formidable array of employers' associations in the metal trades was the National Founders' Association. Bitterly antagonistic to the molders' union, the NFA was reported by a government investigator to have organized its own secret service corps, in addition to having retained a Milwaukee supplier of armed guards. The association recruited strikebreakers on an annual contract, which stipulated that the signatories had to accept an agreed wage and had to be on call to work at any locality. These signatories were reported to have filled strikers' places, intimidated union molders, and furnished indications of lawlessness so that injunctions could be obtained.[21]

It is evident that American employers could look after themselves; it is also clear that they were well equipped to do so in the Progressive period. Why, then, was this the period of maximum prestige for detective agencies?

In spite of their proved ability to handle labor troubles, many employers seemed to lack the will to do so on their own. For some employers had never had to confront unions before 1900. How was a businessman, perhaps elderly, comfortable, and slightly infirm, to cope singly with a youthful, aggressive negotiating committee? If his men went on strike, he might have the resources to win, but did he know how to use them? Feeling isolated in his own business, such a man would seek security elsewhere.

Apparently, several employers resorted to guard agencies out of genuine fear. Of course, the employing class was not, as a whole, oppressed. H. D. Lloyd once ridiculed the employer's attitude as being "I would kill any sheep that bit me." But individual employers did feel that they were being singly victimized. This helps to explain why they sought collective security in employers' associations, and why they employed detectives. The trend of the timid is easily observable in open-shop literature. *American Industries* titled its article on Farley "New Methods of Self-Preservation," while *Open Shop* commended the National Metal Trades Association for its prevention of "... *individual manufacturers being singled out, trapped, bullied, or blackmailed by walking Delegates."* The NAM endorsed a further kind of security for the frightened employer. Its journal in 1906 carried the announcement of the Joy Detective Service of Cleveland: "WE BREAK STRIKES . . . We guard property during strikes, employ non-union men to fill places of strikers." Most important in understanding the popularity of these agencies is the fact that the obscurity of detectives' operations led to a misinterpretation of their function. Employers, trade unionists, and socialists shared one false assumption about armed-guard agencies. The assumption that such agencies helped employers against the workers completes the explanation of why professional guards were hired at all.[22]

It is inconceivable that employers would have hired armed guards through detective agencies if they had not believed that this would help them in their struggle against strikers. Open-shop employers could, of course, phrase their justifications in terms of altruism. Why, they asked, should union plug-uglies be allowed to infringe on the individual freedom and right to work of nonunion men? According to this logic, armed guards were obtained to protect nonunion workers and private property. It was useful to resort to professional agencies because private guards filled the vacuum left by inadequate police forces.

Opposed to these explanations was the union view that employers were out to make money and preserve the dominant position of their class. According to this view, private guards were hired to intimidate strikers and oppress workingmen. Boss strikebreakers were useful for their police and political contacts.

Early twentieth-century gangsters had strong ethnic and community identification: "Umbrella" Mike Boyle (so-called because he collected protection money in an upturned umbrella) in Chicago, Sam Menz (Russian-Jewish) in St. Louis, and Paul Kelly, Monk Eastman, and the Cherry Hill gang in New York. Consequently, they were useful to employers. A clothing-trades union official complained in New York: "The private detectives employed by these agencies are recruited from East side gangs, the same gangs that support the politicians," with the result that politicians persuaded the police to side with employers. In 1909 a Vassar graduate gave an eyewitness account of how a thug caused a disturbance among striking female shirtwaistmakers, whereupon policemen rushed up at the prearranged cue and arrested twenty-eight girls.[23]

The purpose of introducing guards was to provoke incidents that would blacken the name of the union and induce an anti-strike injunction and the introduction of troops. The purpose of such measures, employers and union men agreed, was to break the back of a strike.

Trade unionists and socialists assumed that detectives were loyal to employers. Their reasons for so assuming throw an interesting light on their respective interpretations of the labor movement. In each case, the assumption was based on dogma rather than on observation. The assumption that detectives helped employers was a blind one. Trade unionists failed to open their eyes; moreover, they contributed to the strength of the employer-detective alliance by denouncing the professional guard at every turn.

Union spokesmen followed the lead of Samuel Gompers in arguing that capitalists used force because labor organization was incomplete. This made strikebreaking feasible, violence probable, and the presence of armed guards inevitable. The corollary to this was that violence was less common in the skilled, well-organized trades. The whole explanation was really an exhortation to organize rather than a reasoned analysis of employers' attitudes.[24]

Trade unionists were mistaken in believing that well-organized trades were less prone to violence. Even if the skilled workers in an industry were well organized and disciplined, there was no guarantee that they could control the affairs of those workers in their industry, usually in the majority, who were less skilled. As the Christian Socialist W. D. P.

Bliss pointed out, professional agencies had hundreds of thousands of would-be strikebreakers at their disposal, over whom trade unions had no control.[25]

While union spokesmen did not approach an understanding of the employers' position, they exemplified the workers' emotional response to strikebreakers and their guards. Social investigator Luke Grant characterized professional strikebreakers as "industrial misfits" who could find no regular employment; "neighborhood morality" deterred local men from acts of disloyalty. As a generalization this was questionable —local men did break strikes—but government researchers more than once mentioned that strikers reserved a particular contempt for professional strikebreakers who did not pretend to be bona fide workingmen. In any dispute the appearance of outsiders was certain to produce a strong psychological reaction. The epithets bestowed by union men on strikebreakers—"scabs," "rats," "snakes," and "scalies"—and on armed guards—"goons," "ginks," and "finks"—demonstrate this.[26]

In assuming that the workers were innocent of violence, the socialists resembled the trade unionists. Robert Hunter theorized that since criminals were an idle class, it was a contradiction in terms to equate them with workers. He overlooked the fact that, in a serious strike, workers were idle for long periods. The same writer portrayed detectives as violent class oppressors and as simulators of workers' violence. With reference to only three main examples—the Homestead, American Railway Union, and Cripple Creek strikes—Hunter asserted that thugs hired by capitalists were never prosecuted. But, in fact, local police sometimes did arrest detectives, for example during the New York Central strike of 1890, in the aftermath of the Virden, Illinois, coal riot in 1899, and during the 1909 steel strike; in Colorado in 1894 state forces effectively opposed employers' gunmen, armed guards, and detectives. Indeed, employers argued that it was bias on the part of local authorities that necessitated the use of armed guards. The socialist theory of class oppression may be inverted to show its Achilles' heel. It was sometimes assumed by his opponents that an employer's resort to arms was an admission that he was hard-pressed; that guards were hired not out of deliberation but out of desperation. When the 1904 strike by the United Garment Workers of America in Chicago was a month old, the *Weekly Bulletin of the Clothing Trades* announced that "the manufacturers have become desperate and the tactics usually credited to labor organizations, that of slugging, have been adopted by employers." [27]

The real difference between the trade union and the socialist interpretations was that the former regarded detectives as employers' agents trying to prevent the spread of union consciousness within a trade, whereas the latter saw them as emissaries from the capitalist class aimed at stemming the tide of working-class consciousness. The trade unionist claimed that he was interested in organizing the unorganized to prevent them from falling prey to the provocative tactics of detectives; the socialist insisted that the size of the slum proletariat (*lumpenproletariat*) had to be reduced to prevent its exploitation by capitalist undercover operators. Some socialists, anxious to win over trade unionists, thought that the slum proletariat could be reduced by expanding trade unionism within each industry. Others, despairing of educating trade unionists, maintained that their attitude put them beyond the pale of socialism. Austin Lewis, a socialist in the left-wing democratic fold of the Kerr publishing company, in 1907 proclaimed that it was the cupidity of trade-union leaders that forced many good workingmen to join the slum proletariat. Similarly, the economist H. R. Mussey in 1912 wrote that union leaders, by advocating a "trade" policy, ". . . have been unconsciously encouraging violence." The argument here was that detectives exploited a labor movement weakened by false doctrines. The socialist argument, like that of trade unionists, was ideological propaganda rather than an attempt to understand why professional guards were hired.[28]

If the polemical nature of discussion of armed guards attests to anything, it is to the skill of detective agencies in suggesting that they were able to break strikes and counteract union violence. By their protests, trade unionists and socialists reinforced the suggestion. But, in fact, professional agencies profited from this very bluff.

Frequently, imported strikebreakers were fakes; labor injunctions and troops were secured, as often as not, in order to further the impression of imaginary violence on which they were based. There was little class loyalty among private detectives. Employers who realized this sometimes dispensed with agencies; others found it convenient to exploit the illusions that detectives furnished and throve upon.

Whatever trade unionists thought, strikes involving skilled men were as vulnerable as any to the strikebreaking tactic of bluff. The New York Central strike of 1890 occasioned a good example: In an attempt to give the impression of normal service, the railroad shuttled one or two trains in and out of the New York City terminal; similarly, during the Homestead strike of 1892, when the unskilled steelworkers came out in support of the minority of skilled men thought to be essential to the running of the mill, strikebreakers lit smoky fires under the smokestacks to give the impression of normal production.[29] Each strike involved skilled men; in each strike it was possible to use bluff to indicate that employers were winning. Employers evidently knew of the utility of bluff; no doubt they tolerated its use in their own interests. What they did not comprehend was that they too could be bluffed by detectives who created the appearance of violence and intimidation by union men and, in retaliation, by themselves.

The detective's reputation for loyal toughness would not have survived close scrutiny. But, as expert investigators, detectives were naturally adept at evading scrutiny. When the Taft and Wilson administrations set up a Commission on Industrial Relations, it was suggested that W. J. Burns be retained to look into some of the less reputable detective agencies. Burns had worked for the government as a Secret Service agent in 1898, but on this occasion he demanded an impossibly high fee. He agreed to advise two University of Wisconsin students on how to infiltrate some New York agencies with a view to discovering their method of operation. But it soon transpired that Burns would accede to no investigation that would throw real discredit on detective agencies. When labor economist J. R. Commons asked the student investigators to find out about strikebreaking, Burns demanded to know exactly what the "Professor" was up to. Burns' sensitivity may have risen from the fact that his own agency was supplying strikebreakers, labor spies, and armed guards to employers in Ohio. He may have feared the exposure of some detective agencies' practice of exploiting gullible employers. Whatever his motive, Burns' failure to cooperate with federal investigators typified an attitude that impeded the immediate unmasking of detectives' behavior in labor disputes.[30]

Typical of the difficulty frustrating researchers was the wall of silence confronting Daniel O'Regan, a member of the New Jersey bar and a federal investigator of conditions in New York in 1914. O'Regan reported that he had no reason to doubt the veracity of stories told by labor leaders about assaults on union men by hired thugs. However, his informants could supply him with no proof, as they themselves never seemed to witness atrocities. Ex-detective "converts" to unionism could not be traced, and lawyers suffered from selective amnesia whenever questioned about plug-uglies.[31] The gist of the evidence is that detectives enjoyed an inflated reputation. In the face of such evidence, there is no reason to discredit widespread reports that private detectives smashed employers' property, particularly late-running streetcars on the outskirts of suburbia, in order to create a simulated crisis and thereby stay in business at the employer's expense.

That detectives deceived their employers through simulated violence was confirmed by the observations of William Zumach, one of the Wisconsin students who in 1914 provided illuminating evidence on the strikebreaking trade for the Commission on Industrial Relations. Zumach found a loquacious if self-inflating informant in Mr. Baysdorf of the Schmittberger Agency. Baysdorf appears to have been a typical armed-guard operator. In a story independently corroborated by his mistress, he related how, in a strike at Marinetta, New York, a riot had been staged, and Winchesters fired in the air, to keep things lively. The underlying purpose was to prolong what was a very lucrative job. There was little hostility between the gunmen and the strikers. To keep on the good side of the "detectives from New York," strikers plied them with drinks and cigars.[32]

Detectives dissimulated about their purpose at the scene of a strike: they were also capable of serving the union side. In 1897 "Monk" Eastman supplied some thugs to unions. Haywood was rumored to have employed Hole-in-the-Wall gunmen. In the 1909 New York shirtwaistmakers' strike, the inability of girl pickets to fight back against employers' gangsters created after 1910 a readily supplied demand for gangsters in the textile unions. "Dopey Benny" Fein protected the International Ladies Garment Workers Union after 1913. Detachment is the hallmark of the professional. There was no reason why he should want to serve mainly employers, except that employers could pay him more.[33]

Another function of detective agencies, which labor and employers overrated, was the procurement of injunctions restraining unions from "further" violence, threats of violence, and so on. It is true that the appearance of armed guards, together with stockades and the other trappings of industrial warfare, impressed judges and secured injunctions. Labor leaders leaped to attack this practice, however, without thought of the real consequences, which were not so harmful as they seemed.

Union spokesmen advertised the injunction, as they did the private detective. They attacked the "injunction record" of judges up for re-election. An anti-injunction law was second only to the eight-hour-day demand on the list submitted to the Fifty-fifth Congress (1898) by the legislative committee of the AFL. The Trades Assembly of Victor, Colorado, sent a resolution to Senator Henry M. Teller informing him ". . . there is not before that Body [the Senate] any single measure of equal importance to the mass of the people of the United States." On the other side, employers organized a powerful lobby to obstruct the passage of the anti-injunction law. Their point of view on the proposed measure is represented in this extract from a protest letter: ". . . we are against the passage of the Anti-injunction bill because it is calculated to produce disorder and riot, to subject person and property to the perils of mob law, and is a slander upon the integrity of the courts of injustice [sic] and honourable judges presiding over them." Each side to the industrial dispute felt strongly about the issue of injunctions.[34]

The Progressive period was one in which Americans looked at legal questions in a fresh light, a light shed by social experience. Edwin E. Witte, a research student and government investigator, who later became a leading New Deal brain truster, distinguished between the legal aspect of the injunction controversy and the results of the use of injunctions in labor disputes. A literal reading of writs of injunction would suggest, Witte pointed out, that they were intended to prevent violence while obviating the necessity for armed guards or troops. Witte noted further the argument that injunctions were expedient from the employers' point of view because, unlike prosecutions for criminal conspiracy, they were quickly dealt with by judges, not slowly deliberated by juries. The actual intention of employers in seeking injunctions was to break strikes by tying up union funds and prohibiting picketing.

In practice, Witte argued, there was no reason to suppose that injunctions reduced the level of violence—on the contrary, they embittered strikers and therefore increased the likelihood of disorder. Two of his conclusions are of particular interest in relation to the functions of private detective agencies. First, that, as contempt proceedings in reality could prove just as cumbersome as conspiracy cases, and as there was little evidence that judges were in such cases biased in favor of employers, injunctions did not operate to the disadvantage of labor. Second, that injunctions did nothing to improve the efficiency of local police.[35] In other words, if detectives were skilled enough to secure injunctions, they did not thereby serve the employers' interest—instead, they fortified artificially an impression of violence and ensured themselves continued employment without hindrance from the proper police arm of the state.

As a consequence of the apparent disorder produced by armed guards, state troops were at times dispatched to the areas afflicted by labor troubles. In the seventy-five strikes giving rise to mortalities between 1890 and 1909, deputized law officers were introduced on forty-two occasions, state troops on twenty-eight, and the federal army on three. The purpose of the troops was to restore order or to prevent outbreaks thought to be pending. In spite of the impartiality of most military units, trade unionists opposed the introduction of soldiers to industrial disputes. They did so because the presence of troops made strikers appear to be lawless. Apart from any consideration of public support, the strikers were demoralized by the thought that their chances of success had, by implication, depended upon the use of force. They further regarded the introduction of troops as a sign of official disapproval, which engendered bitter frustration. Their desperate denunciation of the militia lost them public support, because they appeared to disapprove of the agents of law and order. Furthermore, in opposing the use of troops, trade unionists encouraged the use of detectives.

The introduction of troops and its consequences sometimes followed upon the hiring of armed guards—for example, in the Colorado strike of 1903–1904. But on the whole, troops arrived in spite of, rather than because of, detectives' intentions. For, once troops had arrived, the services of armed guards could be dispensed with. Perhaps the optimum situation for the professional agency was that of the Chicago teamsters' strike of 1905. The strikers' leader, Cornelius Shea, denounced the militia before their introduction was ever considered, thus creating an impression of lawlessness from which Farley profited, while deferring any military competition for the professional strikebreaker.[36]

In spite of the inevitable obscurity of the subject, the piecemeal evidence regarding the function of detective agencies in providing armed guards makes sense when put together. Here is the armed guard in a series of typical poses: assisting the employer in the bluff that a strike is broken; avoiding actual fights to the extent that determined investigators find little evidence of intimidation; simulating sabotage; firing shots in the air and fraternizing with strikebreakers; serving unions affluent enough to pay him; seeking cause for injunctions, themselves a form of bluff. The armed guard is not to be confused with the policeman or state militiaman. His advantage lay in procrastination, his salary ended with the settlement of a strike. Little wonder that contemporary investigators encountered deliberate obfuscation.

During the Progressive period, when they throve, detectives contrived to inflate the myth of industrial violence. Yet, by 1914, they were on the verge of decline. Both these points were verified by the federal investigator William Zumach. One day, Zumach was sitting in a restaurant with David Silverman, an official and executive board member of the Neck Wear Makers' Union. As they were chatting, in walked Max Schlansky, of the United Secret Service Agency, 1133 Broadway. Schlansky entered into conversation with Silverman about the strike in progress against the business of Oppenheimer, Franc and Langsdorf. The guard business arising out of the dispute was being handled for the notorious Val O'Farrell Agency by its chief agent, Schultz. The engagement was yielding $300 weekly for Schultz, but was now coming to an end. Schlansky averred that Schultz did not know his business, for he had let slip by many opportunities to prolong the strike. Perceiving an opportunity to extract some money from the situation, Schlansky proposed to Silverman that the union leader hire some of his plug-uglies to beat up Schultz's men. Schlansky pointed out that in this event, Oppenheimer and partners would probably fire Schultz and engage Schlansky. Then, presumably for a further fee, Schlansky would ensure that the union won the strike.[37] It is evident that too many agencies were competing for too few customers.

By 1914 public opinion was becoming receptive to exposés of detective agencies in their role of supplying armed guards. In 1909 the *Milwaukee Sentinel* exposed the tactics of agencies during the iron molders' strike in the city in 1906. In 1912 these tactics were sufficiently notorious to be ventilated in "Limiting Federal Injunctions" hearings before a Senate subcommittee. In 1911 hearings before the House Committee on Labor revealed the occurrence of thuggery in the 1909 McKees Rocks strike. At the request of Commissioner J. R. Commons, the Commission on Industrial Relations undertook several frustrating inquiries into armed guards. Government investigations of armed-guard agencies testified to politicians' concern with the problem. Public opinion became increasingly difficult to ignore. Since sheriffs were political creatures, they sometimes refused to deputize detectives when community opinion was adverse to strikebreakers. It was on such occasions inadvisable to send in nondeputized armed guards, for whose actions providing agencies were in certain circumstances liable. Although laws limiting the freedom of agencies were not often enforced, employers were increasingly wary of hiring guards whose depredations would perhaps alienate a state legislature potentially empowered to assist businessmen with favorable legislation.[38]

While public opinion was awakening to the tactics of professional guards, employers were doubting their efficacy. The World War not only brought full employment and good industrial relations, but put domestic struggles into perspective beside the European bloodbath. The improving efficiency of regular police forces became apparent at the same time, leading not so much to the displacement of private detectives, as to the loss of their prestige and credibility.

A mutation of function was already under way in the detective world. It is interesting that proscriptive legislation was usually directed at the guard function, not the spy function, of detectives. There were exceptions—Minnesota was one state that legislated against labor spies —but undercover operators were naturally difficult to detect. There had been a dawning appreciation that clandestine operations were viable in the face of hostile officialdom. Inis Weed, investigating for the Commission on Industrial Relations, found that in Colorado detectives running in fear of the law had on occasion worn masks as they applied dynamite to union men's houses. As Gompers uncharitably put it, progressive public opinion forced employers to become clandestine in their open-shop activities. Doubts concerning the desirability of armed guards strengthened the appeal of that arch fomenter of misconceptions, the labor spy.[39]

Chapter 7

Labor Spies

IN THE PERIOD OF THE RISE OF THE AFL, FROM THE LATE 1890s TO the early 1920s, detective agencies sought to supply employers with labor spies as well as armed guards. Labor spies operated differently from armed guards, secrecy being as essential to them as conspicuousness was to their more bellicose colleagues. But their objective was the same, to make money by exaggerating the threat of violence and class conflict.

The rise and decline of the labor-spy business occurred for reasons similar to those governing the history of armed-guard agencies. For example, the physical inadequacies of police forces, which produced private armies, were matched by a scarcity of public facilities for criminal investigation. Private detectives supplied the need and were well equipped to infiltrate factories and spy on workers.

There were, however, dissimilarities between the armed-guard and labor-spy causative factors. Labor spies claimed to be offering a more advanced service than armed guards in that they prevented strikes and removed the necessity for physical confrontations. On the eve of World War I, some labor spies expected to supersede what they represented as the antiquated legions of private thugs. Indeed, they owed their existence to a factor that was to become more evident in the future, the relative absence of working-class consciousness in America,

which meant that there was less of a taboo against renegades. Ironically, however, labor spies throve on the illusion of class conflict, and
that illusion owed a good deal, as we saw in the last chapter, to armed
guards.

Whatever their early expectations, labor spies declined in importance after World War I along with armed guards, but for different
reasons. Whereas armed guards supplied by detective agencies were
gradually forced out of business by police reform, employers' skepticism, directly recruited employers' armies, and public opinion, labor
spies in many instances quit industrial relations voluntarily, because
their skills received lucrative rewards elsewhere. The increasingly so-
phisticated scientific techniques of U.S. industry produced a demand
for "industrial espionage" directed at competitors' research and development plans, not at labor unions. The proliferation of laboratory
secrets and the sharp rise in the divorce rate in the Progressive period
created a demand for clandestine operators that only private agencies
could supply.[1]

Another difference between the armed guard and the labor spy was
that the latter submitted analytical reports and contributed to American ideology. To study labor espionage is to study the propaganda of
class conflict. As we saw in Chapter 3, socialists such as Robert
Hunter took up the challenge. In 1912 the Socialist Party of America
purged itself of advocates of revolutionary violence in order to eliminate the agent provocateur, or labor spy. Most Americans took this
to mean that there *were* revolutionaries in the socialist movement. Since
the Progressive period, there has been a widespread tendency to equate
capitalism with democracy, socialism with force. This was an idea that
labor spies carefully nourished. There are, then, good reasons for
examining the growth, characteristics, and relationship to socialism of
private detective agencies specializing in labor espionage.

The equation of violence with labor agitation and socialism was
consistently made by the Pinkerton National Detective Agency. This
agency, which provided armed guards until the Homestead debacle,
dealt also in labor espionage. Its founder, Allan Pinkerton, could speak
from personal experience of class conflict. Born in Glasgow in 1819
and a member of the Coopers' Trade Union, he was reputedly active
in the Chartist cause before emigrating to America in 1842. In the
land of his adoption, there was a crying need for criminal investigators. The population growth in frontier and immigrant cities out-

paced the foresight of civic leaders, who neglected to establish urban detective services. William Allan Pinkerton, son of the Scottish immigrant, spoke of the thorough inadequacy of the Chicago police in the Reconstruction period, when he claimed to have been the only criminal investigator in the city. The Pinkerton Agency became famous for tracking down criminals and created its own mantle of prestige.[2]

In 1869, in a letter to a Glasgow newspaper, Allan Pinkerton expressed strong sympathy with organized labor. Yet, as we saw in the last chapter, he had formed a "Protective Patrol" to guard employers' property in 1850 and began in 1874 to supply guards on a regular basis to capitalists whose workers were on strike. In the meantime, he had also entered the labor-spy business, for in October 1873 he hired out James McParlan to Pennsylvania coal operators. Using the name James McKenna, McParlan penetrated the Irish-American organization known as the Molly Maguires. The Mollies, sometimes with the full knowledge of McParlan, if not with his collaboration, continued their policy of assassinating English, Welsh, and Scottish operators whose management of the mines they regarded as being inimical to the interests of the Irish-Catholic workers. For his success in procuring evidence good enough to hang nineteen Mollies in 1876, McParlan was made superintendent of the western division of the Pinkerton Agency, which was now a celebrated institution.[3]

If Allan Pinkerton approved of labor unions in 1869, he had certainly changed his mind by the end of the Mollies trial. There may have been many reasons for his change of heart: hatred of the Irish, shock in the aftermath of the Paris Commune of 1871, old age, hypocrisy, commercial opportunism, or a belief that Scotland needed unions but America did not. Whatever the reason, he set the tone for future detective-agency rhetoric in his autobiographical *Strikers, Communists, Tramps, and Detectives* (1878). Propagating an ideology far removed from his youthful Chartism, he wrote:

> Every trades-union has for its vital principle, whatever is professed, the concentration of brute force to gain certain ends. Then the deadly spirit of Communism steals in and further embitters the working man against that from which his very livelihood is secured; and gradually makes him an enemy to all law, order and good society.[4]

From the 1870s, the Pinkerton Agency provided labor spies as well as armed guards. So much opprobrium attached to Pinkertonism as a result of the Homestead riot that, according to its own spokesman, the agency thenceforth "steadfastly refused to accept any security arrangements that might be construed as strike-breaking." [5] Yet, the Homestead debacle did not mean that, overnight, Americans placed their trust in the legal arm of the state. During the turbulent Brooklyn streetcar strike of 1898, A. J. F. Behrends (author of *Socialism and Christianity* and a critic, if a mild one, of out-and-out laissez-faire) recommended the use of state power to deal with rioters because, but only because, of the current prejudice against Pinkertons. While attempts to improve the military and police forces of America met with opposition from sections of every social class, the Pinkerton Agency itself returned to favor. In 1903 there were Pinkerton Agency offices in Montreal, Boston, New York, Philadelphia, Chicago, St. Louis, Kansas City, St. Paul, Denver, Portland (Oregon), Seattle, and San Francisco—an increase of four since 1892. Between 1903 and 1907, new offices opened in Buffalo, Pittsburgh, Cincinnati, Cleveland, Minneapolis, Omaha, Spokane, and Los Angeles.[6]

The growth of cities in the West explains in part the proliferation of Pinkerton branches beyond the Mississippi, while the unabated energies of McParlan in organizing labor espionage helped to ensure the agency's continued success. Morris Friedman, who early procured some Pinkerton Agency reports, and whose lengthy testimony at the Steunenberg murder trial helped to bring about Haywood's acquittal, thought that there were by 1907 three kinds of Pinkerton operatives: special (temporary), general, and, "the main source of revenue and profit at every branch of the Agency," secret, or labor, spy. Friedman showed that McParlan, from his Denver office, controlled a wide network of labor spies, whom he identified by name and number. According to Friedman, McParlan invented the conspiracy theory of an "Inner Circle" of WFM plotters in the metalliferous mining industry, with the fulfilled purpose of inducing employers in twelve industries to hire his agents.[7]

In support of his arguments, Friedman quoted the reports of some Pinkerton agents. He used, for example, a communication from operative No. 42, A. W. Gratias, president of local 93, WFM, Mill and Smeltermen's Union, Denver, to McParlan, dated September 29, 1903: "I reported at the office and received instructions to speak to members of the Smeltermen's Union in a careful way, and try to make them believe they are entitled to some money or some benefits from the WFM, to cause them to become dissatisfied." Clearly, this was an example of "preventive" labor espionage. The operative was claiming to undermine the morale of the local of which he himself was president. Charles A. Siringo, who had been at different times a cowboy, a labor spy, and James McParlan's bodyguard, added to Friedman's account in a similar, if less authoritative, vein. Writing in the wake of the McNamara affair, he criticized the activities of what he termed "the inner circle of Pinkerton's National Detective Agency." [8]

Nor did the Pinkerton Agency confine its activities to the West. It elsewhere lent its services to open-shop militants for the purposes of criminal detection. Walter Drew of the NEA in 1907 wrote to Asher Rossiter, superintendent for the agency in Chicago:

> Regarding No. 72, I wish you would put him to work at once. Boyd of the Pittsburgh Local of the Iron Workers' Union and Smith of the Cleveland Local, have a gang of thuds [thugs] who have been beating up our foremen and even killing in some instances. There are a number of assaults not yet cleared up and a number of men now under indictment. I wish, if possible, to get a conviction of Boyd and Smith for planning and directing these things.

Again in 1920, H. Scott, New York superintendent of the Pinkerton Agency, while too cautious to commit himself to paper on the question of industrial espionage, offered to send a personal representative to see food manufacturer Paul Furnas, as he had no literature available on labor spies. [9]

Reticence concerning labor-spy activities continued to be the official policy of the Pinkerton Agency in the 1930s. Beginning in 1936, the La Follette Civil Liberties Committee investigated employers' strong-arm practices and the role of labor spies in industrial relations. By this time, the Pinkerton Agency had offices in thirty-five cities. At least part of its expansion was based on labor espionage; the La Follette investigation turned up correspondence proving that the United States Rubber Reclaiming Company, Buffalo, hired Pinkerton men to spy on union meetings. The La Follette committee also found that there were fifty-two Pinkerton spies in the United Automobile Workers at various times between 1934 and mid-1937. In April 1937 the directors of the Pinkerton Agency decided to give up labor spying because of adverse publicity (a full forty-five years after the Homestead strike, which had led the agency to abandon armed-guard contracts). But Asher Rossiter, by now vice-president and general manager of the Pinkerton Agency, defended the ideological role of his detectives. He claimed that the Pinkerton men were trying to root out communism, not spy on unions. The equation of agitation with subversion had originally been made by Allan Pinkerton, and once again in 1953 a vice-president of the agency claimed to be working against communist infiltration into offices and plants.[10]

It is clear that by 1914 the United States was covered by a network of spy agencies in competition with the Pinkerton Agency. A number of agencies—the Joy Detective Service, Thiel Detective Agency, Murphy Secret Service, and Corporation's Auxiliary Company—would supply any midwestern town. The Manufacturers Information Bureau Company had offices from Seattle to Chattanooga. A few agencies—the CBK Detective Bureau and James J. Maloy of New York City—confined their services to one urban area. But the flexibility of the labor spy was better typified by Louis Wein of Washington, D.C., and W. J. Burns, who between them covered the English-speaking world from Australia to England.

The geographic mobility of labor spies resulted in part from the former experience of several private detectives in the United States Secret Service. John Elbert Wilkie was chief of the Secret Service from February 1898 until 1912. He trained counterspies during the Spanish-American War (Burns was one of his protégés) and these men learned to operate in cities all over the United States and Canada. Several of his men became private agents, although not all of them sympathized with employers. Among those offering their services to Samuel Gompers and the AFL were Doyle's Detective Service Company of Seattle and Boyle's Secret Service Agency of Monmouth, Illinois.[11]

The discontent expressed in trade-union journals is one pointer to the expansion of labor espionage. After 1900, increasingly after 1903 and the beginning of the open-shop campaign, and especially in 1907, because of the Steunenberg trial, union journals protested against industrial espionage. The Brotherhood of Locomotive Firemen's magazine summed up the affronted feelings of the most conservative unions in its headline of June 1906: "A Long Established Fundamental and Vital Principle [peaceful collective bargaining] Superceded by 'Secret Service' Methods."

After the arrests of the McNamara brothers, it was widely felt in trade-union circles that detective agencies had assumed the form of a menace. The feeling was not confined to journalists or labor leaders. For example, a motion from the floor during the 1911 convention of the Massachusetts State Branch of the AFL demanded the abolition of private detective agencies, which had exerted a malevolent influence in Pennsylvania, Idaho, and Indiana, threatened to Russianize American society, and had "assumed formidable proportions." [12]

Advertisement was another indication of the growth of private spy agencies. In the mid-1900s some agencies expanded their existing facilities to provide a comprehensive service. The Joy Detective Service purported to "handle labor troubles in all their phases" and to that end announced its armed-guard service in the May 1905 issue of the NAM's *American Industries*. But the agency prefaced its offer to provide armed guards with the statement, "We are prepared to place secret operatives who are skilled mechanics in any shop, mill or factory, to discover whether any organizing is being done." In July 1905 the eastern district manager of the Manufacturers Information Bureau Company of Cleveland explained to an employer how his agency would identify labor agitators. His letter was headed with a printed listing of the Bureau's branches at St. Louis and San Francisco. But the Bureau had so recently opened new branches at Denver, Seattle, and Chattanooga that their names had had to be typed alongside the printed letterhead. [13]

There was varying testimony to the degree of penetration, money-making powers, and extent of detective agencies. In 1907 Samuel Gompers claimed that national union officers were on agency payrolls. Employers seemed prepared to pay dearly for their inside information. The new manager of the Wabash Railroad demonstrated this in 1905 when he abolished "spotting" on his system because it was useless and cost from $75,000 to $100,000 per annum. A year later the economist T. S. Adams was of the opinion that employers spent vast amounts of money each year on strike defense. Writers aware of, or believing in, such expenditures made confident estimates of the size of the labor-spy industry. The federal investigator O'Regan estimated that there were 275 agencies engaging in industrial-relations work prior to the First World War. In a spate of awareness in the 1920s, the left-wing writer Jean Spielman claimed that 75 percent of Pinkerton, Thiel, and Burns detectives (or 135,000 operatives) were secret agents. At the same time, Sidney Howard thought that labor espionage was practiced by the majority of the "great employers" of the United States. As a result of such reports, spy agencies were losing their prestige by the 1930s. However, detective fiction began to flourish in the 1920s, reaching a wide audience through such periodicals as the *Black Mask*. The private eye came to represent poetic justice to American readers, and possibly a few employers disillusioned by reports of police corruption in the Prohibition decade. The La Follette investigation again pilloried private detectives in the 1930s, but one writer was moved to remark of it: "The widespread publicity which attends such investigations informs employers who otherwise would not have thought of this method." [14]

According to Leo Huberman, who popularized relevant sections of the La Follette inquiry in *The Labor Spy Racket* (1937), there was by the 1930s a spy in every union local. The mining industry, apparently impregnable to the professional spy a generation previously, now provided thirty-two customers for detective agencies—perhaps a symptom of softening group morale. Another feature of the decade, which Huberman brought out in a revised edition of his book, was the infiltration of burgeoning white-collar unionism. In 1939 Sears Roebuck & Company, a long-term opponent of unionism (Sears had opposed the Teamsters' Union in the strike of 1905), helped to promote and finance Nathan W. Shefferman's effort to establish his firm, Labor Relations Associates of Chicago. Originally established with the purpose of opposing unionism in the Chicago store, LRA had by 1955 offered its services to about four hundred clients. These included such large-scale employers of nonmanual workers as the Allstate Insurance Company, Blue Cross, and American Express.[15]

The long-established, conservative unions were by no means free of labor espionage during Franklin D. Roosevelt's Presidency. The Brotherhood of Railroad Trainmen had been organized in 1883 (being known until 1893 as the Brotherhood of Railroad Brakemen). In 1891 the union's magazine had complained of the detectives' practice of simulating sabotage in order to discredit the Brotherhood: "Every strike of any importance for the past ten years, particularly in railroads, has been characterized by resort to this foul and infamous method." [16] Judging from an account given in *The New York Times* in 1942 of the trial of three railroad workers on charges arising from a strike against the Toledo, Peoria, & Western Railroad, little had changed in the intervening half century:

> Attorneys for the railroad . . . told the jury that not only did strikers plan to blow up the Walnut Creek Bridge near Eureka, in Woodford County, but also offered 25,000 dollars for the slaying of George P. McNear, president of the road.
> The three men on trial are Paul Brocaw, publicity man for the Brotherhood of Locomotive Firemen and Enginemen; Delmar C. Newdigate, chairman of the T.P. & W. Lodge of the Brotherhood of Railroad Firemen, and H. J. Diley, a striking fireman. They are accused of plotting to violate an injunction, issued by Federal Judge J. Leroy Adair, against violence in the strike.
> The principal witness against them will be William Wheeler, a private investigator. Mr. Fitzgerald told the jury that Wheeler was an ex-convict and an Army deserter. Wheeler has admitted being hired to blow up the bridge by Brocaw, to whom he was introduced by Diley.

Defense attorney Arthur M. Fitzgerald alleged the private investigator had helped to arrange a frame-up involving members of the railroad brotherhoods. Whatever the truth, it is clear that the conservative railroad brotherhoods were still afflicted by "spotters." [17]

Professional labor espionage continued to thrive in diverse industries well into the 1930s and on into the 1940s and 1950s. Yet, it seemed to attract less publicity than in former days. The extent of labor espionage was not necessarily smaller. Indeed, there are no reliable estimates, and it may have become greater; expansion may have been disguised by greater secrecy. But the Peoria and Western Railroad affair, occurring as it did in World War II, was passed over much more lightly than it would have been in the Progressive period. What is suggested is that the private labor-espionage business was conducted in a lower key.

What were the characteristics of the professional labor spy? To begin with, extreme secrecy and discretion were goals that the spy could ill afford to ignore, whether he operated in the 1900s or 1930s. As in the case of armed guards, obscurity is a clue to the motives and plans of detective agencies surviving on industrial conflict. They claimed to disrupt unionism; they constantly warned of agitation; what they wanted to hide was the fact that their own interest lay in fostering the appearance of conflict, so that they could live at the employer's expense.

Although it was natural enough given the nature of the subject, the alleged failure of government inquiries to "expose" detectives stimulated disgruntled comment. Sidney Howard in the 1920s complained that the inquiry into espionage conducted by the Senate in 1893 was the only such exposure; furthermore, that inquiry mainly concerned armed guards, merely digressing from its main body of concern in order to condemn mendacious labor spies who demoralized laborers and mechanics.[18] Daniel O'Regan conducted a field survey of detective agencies for the Research Division of the Commission on Industrial Relations, but he was forced to admit overall failure in his quest for information. His superiors on the commission inferred that he was incompetent; O'Regan himself blamed trade-union officers for withholding information. "Sometimes," he wrote,

> it seems as if they don't want these agencies curbed at all or else they are afraid to give any information against them. It might be that the detective agencies can be used as an excuse by the strikers for any violence at the scene of a strike and that a regulation of these agencies might remove the excuse and consequently the justification of rough methods used by strikers in many cases.[19]

It is further possible that union leaders were unwilling to expose the activities of detectives because they were inextricably enmeshed with them, because they thought they could control them, or simply because the interests of detectives were, in spite of frequent disclaimers, complementary to those of union men who welcomed a fearful reputation for violence.

Like union leaders, detectives themselves were reluctant to indulge in effusions about espionage. O'Regan's colleague Inis Weed interpreted the lack of evidence concerning detectives' activities in certain strikes as a conspiracy of silence. Indeed, the success of many agencies depended upon ignorance of their real purposes. This was hinted at by W. J. Burns. Justifying the high cost of a proposed investigation by himself in 1915, Burns protested, ". . . I render daily reports, and on these reports place the amount of money expended each day, which no other detective agency does." [20]

Detectives were sometimes candid about their purposes. Robert J.

Foster of the Foster Service promised one employer in 1910 that his men would ". . . carry on an intrigue which would result in factions, disagreement, resignations of officers and general decrease in membership" of the union concerned.[21] Nevertheless, there were limits to candor even in correspondence. Detectives were reluctant to detail their nefarious or real aims in a letter, because their correspondent might turn out to be a dummy (there is some evidence that such a ruse was employed) and because the employer was the last person they wanted to take into their confidence.

Two further letters hint at detectives' real intentions. The first was a reply from E. H. Murphy of Murphy Secret Service, Detroit, to an inquiry made by an Indiana manufacturer:

> We have the reputation of being several jumps ahead of the old way of settling capital and labor difficulties, and we feel that anybody who allows his affairs to reach the labor-strike stage, especially if operating on the open shop theory, is very much behind the times. Our service aims to keep our clients informed through the medium of intelligence reports, as to the loyalty of the workers.

The inference here was that armed-guard agencies were passé, a theory to which a number of open-shop employers had already subscribed. The important thing to note is that the appeal of the new type of agency was to the commercial sense of the employer, on the basis of the now widely suspected commercial rapacity of the old type of agency (F. W. Cohen of Pennsylvania Steel had complained of detectives as early as 1910 that "their expenses run up enormously and they only give you enough to lead you on.") [22]

In a final example of correspondence dated 1920, Captain B. Keleher of CBK Detective Bureau, New York City, wrote to a food producer: "My concern does not handle strike work. I have been trying to build up a business to prevent strikes. Thuggery on either side is always bad, if the employer resorts to thuggery he ties around his neck a band of men who may do his bidding, but they will be around his neck for many a day." [23] The irony is, of course, that this attack on armed-guard agencies was motivated by Keleher's desire to be around his client's neck for many a day and more, providing permanent protection.

Labor-union attitudes provide a corroborative perspective. The spokesmen for labor organizations were publicly hostile to labor spies;

there were men who, in private, evinced more subtle approaches. A few found it expedient to exploit the spy. Another attitude was that the spy was best ignored, that labor attacks on the spy only invested him with sufficient prestige to "lead on" his employer.

It may have been a sound idea, in principle, to ignore the labor spy. But restraint was difficult when one had been hounded by detectives over a number of years. Big Bill Haywood had particular reason to hate private detectives as a result of his false imprisonment during the Steunenberg trial. He belittled them, yet at the same time gave them publicity, in a colorful diatribe printed on postcard pamphlets for dissemination: "That you may know how small a detective is, you can take a hair and punch the pith out of it and in the hollow hair you can put the hearts and souls of 40,000 detectives and they will still rattle. You can pour them out on the surface of your thumb and the skin of a gnat will make an umbrella of them." Like the WFM, railroad brotherhoods had also been afflicted by the attentions of labor spies. In 1909 John F. McNamee, editor of the *Brotherhood of Locomotive and Enginemen's Magazine,* vindictively hinted that death was too good for the labor spy, writing that "in warfare the punishment of the spy is death," but that the labor spy was not even fired by patriotism.[24]

McNamee deplored the fact that, although the practice of espionage had become (in his view) a serious threat to unionism since the entry of the NAM into the open-shop fight in 1903, the spy was still underestimated. Even in his own industry, it was true, there were those who did not share his concern. An editorial in the *Railroad Trainmen's Journal* in 1906 ridiculed the spy system as serving no useful purpose: The spy, although a "downright rascal," was a "joke." It seems plausible that some labor leaders, far from respecting the sleuth, may have used spies to relay false information to employers. Frank Buchanan of the IABSI claimed that in 1903 he knew the identities of eight labor spies, whom he fed with false information.[25] Such claims may have been based on arrogance, but they confirm what some employers suspected.

Another revealing opinion was that detectives relied on an inflated reputation to which labor leaders themselves (for example, Haywood and McNamee) contributed. Hugh Frayne, a labor organizer acquainted with New York detective agencies, firmly voiced this opinion during the McNamara crisis. Before the McNamara arrests, Samuel Gompers had received warnings from various self-styled friends of labor, ranging from Populists to detective agencies, that certain agencies were out to discredit the AFL. After the arrests he was plagued with offers of help from several agencies, whose proprietors usually offered to dig out some information that would discredit Burns. Gompers took an interest in one such offer, from James J. Maloy of New York City. He asked the advice of Frank Morrison, secretary of the AFL and of the McNamara Ways and Means Committee, and of Hugh Frayne, the AFL general organizer who was then in New York. Frayne replied:

> I know from my personal experience here that this city is thoroughly honeycombed with concerns of this kind and any publicity or antagonism shown them by the labor movement would only tend to boom their business and give them recognition in the eye of certain employers that they would never hope to receive otherwise. . . . Mr. Morrison thinks as I do, that any publicity given these people would only tend to advertise them.

If Gompers was semicredulous, Frayne was entirely skeptical. Following the principle of self-abnegation, Frayne actually withheld from the federal investigator William Zumach (whom he distrusted, as Zumach was theoretically under the direction of Burns) any information that might have suggested to Zumach's colleague, O'Regan, a successful formula for legislating against detectives' malpractices.[26]

Derived as it is from several sources, the evidence about detectives' motives points to a firm conclusion. While several agencies, notably the higher echelons of the Pinkerton and Burns enterprises, were or claimed to be ideologically motivated, it was the purpose of all agencies to make money. As a business proposition, spy agencies tried to inflate their reputations as formidable oppressors of labor; out of discretion, they kept the actual nature of their operations secret. Their own correspondence obliquely confirms the commercialism of strike-prolonging detectives. Employers like Cohen and labor men like Frayne directly alleged that spies depended on bluff. Certainly the prestige of detectives was occasionally reinforced by an achievement, such as the McNamara convictions, but the gist of the evidence is that labor spies actively fomented misconceptions about themselves and industrial conflict.

As we saw in Chapter 3, the question of labor espionage occupied an important place in American socialist ideology in the period when

Robert Hunter and Morris Hillquit were at the height of their intellectual powers. It may be added that socialism occupied a significant
place in the propaganda of several detective agencies. The Pinkerton
Agency opposed anarchism, socialism, and communism in turn. A revealing light is thrown on the possible motivation for such an attitude
by Louis Wein, the previously mentioned private detective operating
from Washington, D.C. Republican Congressman G. W. Ray of New
York asked Wein for advice following the assassination of President
William McKinley in 1901 by the self-declared anarchist Leon Czolgosz. The private detective recommended the prohibition of anarchism,
anarchist meetings, newspapers, and immigration. A further recommendation of Wein's revealed his naked commercial ambition: Once
a mystery had been created through legislation forcing anarchists underground, Wein wanted the U.S. government to employ detectives to
track them down.[27] In 1903 Congress did pass the first of a series of
laws that made criminals of anarchists and other radicals and created
jobs for government-retained detectives.

The U.S. Secret Service already existed as a supplier and employer
of detectives who might be used against radicals. In July 1908 Attorney General Charles J. Bonaparte established the Bureau of Investigation (known as the FBI from the 1930s) as an agency of the
Justice Department. In the face of Congressional criticism, he conceded that the "class of men who do [detective] work as a profession is
one you have to employ with a good deal of caution." [28] It is possible
that Bonaparte conceded too much in making such a statement, for a
distinction may be drawn between government detectives who draw
a regular salary and have no day-to-day financial worries and private
detectives who sometimes have to invent conspiracies in order to make
a living. Important though such a distinction may be, however, it
should not be overdrawn. The government detective agencies have
sometimes borrowed the private sleuth's propensity to exaggerate; indeed, the Bureau of Investigation relied, in the World War I and Red
Scare emergencies, on the help of private detectives.

William J. Burns drew salaries on several occasions from government agencies. In addition to his service for the Secret Service in 1898,
he had by 1915 secured evidence that sent a dozen corrupt members
of the Ohio and West Virginia legislatures to prison. Between 1921
and 1924, Burns headed the Bureau of Investigation. It is clear that
Burns, like Wein, knew how to profit from the current popular mood.

In investigating legislative corruption, he was exploiting one of the main obsessions of Progressive reformers. Two circumstances suggest that he was not motivated by a personal aversion to corruption: First, he was not philanthropic enough to investigate Wisconsin politics at a reduced fee, when invited to do so in 1915; second, during the corrupt administration of Attorney General Harry Dougherty in the 1920s, Burns continued without a qualm as Bureau of Investigation chief. It was not by losing money over scruples that Burns had by 1915 built a private agency listing twenty offices in the United States, with one in London.[29]

It was his good business instinct that prompted Burns to attack socialism during the Progressive period and the 1920s. In 1913 he made a determined effort to link anarcho-syndicalism with what was probably his main source of revenue, the labor struggle. Of the AFL leaders, he remarked: "With the cause of labor in the hands of such men only wreck and ruin is ahead of it for the law prevails in this country and it is going to continue to prevail despite the efforts of men of the Gompers type who have made the unions gang-ridden and lawless." Employers in Ohio and elsewhere who used Burns' labor spies probably warmed to Burns' rhetoric without realizing that it was commercially motivated.[30]

Employers, socialists, and journalists exploited violence and fears of class conflict for their own reasons. Labor spies, as well as the armed guards also supplied by private detective agencies, played a special role in fueling and igniting these tendencies in the two decades after 1900. It remained for Progressive reformers and politicians to translate the bush fires of inflated violence into the holocaust of illusory revolution. Even as they did so, however, a great statesman of the Progressive era was reviewing the police role of the state in a way that was to lead to the curtailment of the private detective's scope for activity in industrial relations.

Chapter **8**

Truckling to the Labor Vote: Theodore Roosevelt's Presidential Departure

PRIVATE DETECTIVE AGENCIES PROSPERED AS DEFENDERS OF "LAW AND order" in inverse proportion to the efficiency of police forces. Yet on numerous occasions in American history, neither detectives nor policemen proved equal to the task of preserving order. Faced over a long period with Revolutionary riots, farmers' rebellions, slave insurrections, ethnic disturbances, and frontier disorders, politicians recognized a need not just for the reform of social conditions, but also for the firm and prudent use of military force.

The regular use of soldiers to restore order in the United States reinforced the American people's self-image as a disorderly nation. The Revolution had immortalized the image of disorderliness. Tories in the 1770s had predicted the consequences of what they perceived to be a unilateral repudiation of the Lockean social contract. In 1774 the New York clergyman Samuel Seabury averred that "if *one* has a right to disregard the laws of the society to which he belongs, *all* have the *same* right; and *then* government is at an end." [1] This Tory prediction became the constant fear of the legatees of the Revolutionary patriots: How could a nation of rebels be cajoled into behaving as law-abiding citizens?

The struggle between labor unions and employers revived the question of what government should do about disorder. Because the protagonists were articulate, they clarified the issues involved. For the nature of the problem had changed since James Madison and other lawyers had so intelligently discussed it during and in the aftermath of the Revolution. By the end of the nineteenth century, the threat of disorder emanated from the towns and cities, not from the backcountry of the Carolinas. The rise of a worldwide socialist movement had brought a new ideological dimension to riots, and the advent of labor unionism suggested sinister new possibilities of organized violence. In this context, President Theodore Roosevelt, through his handling of the anthracite coal strike of 1902, created a new style of response to serious conflicts and made a contribution to the understanding of the urban law and order problem.

By the end of the nineteenth century, strikes were providing regular and ample evidence of the apparent intractability of the law and order problem facing government officials. Strikes rarely posed a self-evident threat to law and order. Consequently, the initiative for governmental action often came not from public officials, but from partisans. No fair-minded politician accepted the word of a partisan without question, but many such found difficulty in acquiring accurate information. The susceptibility of the press to exaggeration, and the paramount need for speed, meant that the executive official concerned had to depend on quick investigations by local contacts or simply on the advice of friends. For example, J. Addison Porter, secretary to President William McKinley, received the following telegram prior to the dispatch of troops to the Coeur d'Alene in 1899: "An armed mob has destroyed valuable property in Wardner, Idaho, in which Jack Hammond, James Houghteling, and others of your friends are interested. The governor has asked for Federal troops. Please lend your interest to this appeal with the President." [2]

There was great indignation in Congress when it was discovered that this and similar communications, comprising an apparent abuse of friendship, had been received in the White House. Under pressure from Democrats, the Republican-dominated House Military Committee published a few of the Coeur d'Alene communications but not all of them. Representative John Lentz of Ohio alleged there had been a cover-up: "It is exceedingly hard to say, but it is an old and well-known maxim that 'the man with a pure heart and a clean record has nothing to conceal.' " Critics of the business-dominated McKinley Cabinet were not reassured by the fact that Houghteling was a Chicago banker and Hammond a colorful adventurer. (A mining engineer with western interests, John H. Hammond had worked for Cecil Rhodes in South Africa. He was sentenced to death following the Jameson Raid of 1895 but bought his way out of trouble by paying a fine of $125,000.) In the light of such evidence, Lentz may have been right in his contention that there had been a conspiracy to send troops to Idaho. But the incident also shows how the best intentioned of politicians would have found it difficult to arrive at the truth about local disorders when far removed from the area of contention and dependent on unreliable advice and telegraphic communications.[3]

But why did a President of the United States have to get involved in a distant local labor struggle? The history of vigilante movements and detective agents suggests an inherent weakness in local American law enforcement at least until the First World War. As we shall see below, the weakness was partly one of will: Politicians were too often afraid to use the force at their disposal. However, one of the instruments of law enforcement was chronically sick. This was the seventeenth-century English transplant and hero of western mythology, the sheriff.

Contemporary journals sometimes castigated local police officers undiscriminatingly. For example, *Collier's* referred to Philadelphia law officers on duty during the streetcar strike of 1910 as "a weak police force, fed by the company and friendly to the strikers, the tools of all factions, and the masters of no situation." On the other hand, the Commission on Industrial Relations concluded in 1915 that municipal police were less partisan than sheriff's deputies and even state militia, because they were always publicly financed. Investigator Luke Grant of the CIR's Research Division came to a similar conclusion, stating that city police were trained in methods of handling crowds. That there was some truth to this is evident from one of the examination questions asked of New York City police officers seeking promotion to the rank of police inspector on May 25, 1905: "Assume there is a strike, involving some thousands of men and accompanied by violence and threatened rioting. Assuming any other facts you please, write a report of your action as inspector in this case." Compared with the municipal police officer, the sheriff was by common consent the weak man of American law enforcement in an era of industrial strife. His weakness necessitated frequent municipal, state, and federal intervention in labor disputes.[4]

The task of the sheriff in a major industrial dispute was an unenviable one. He was an elected, not an appointed, law officer. He was more likely to owe his position to personal popularity and some deed of valor in his youth than to professional expertise or training. On the outbreak of a strike the sheriff might find himself advanced in age, encumbered with family responsibilities, and easily intimidated by the slightest show of force.

The sheriff's democratic support did not insulate him from factional demands or the exigencies of office. During the miners' strike at Cripple Creek, Colorado, in 1903, Sheriff H. M. Robertson was forced to enroll as deputies men chosen by the Mine Owners' Association in spite of the fact that his sympathies lay with the union. In 1904 the Citizens' Alliance forced him to resign under penalty of being lynched. Whatever the nature and extent of the support for a sheriff on election day, there was no guarantee that he would be helped in a crisis. For example, when in the course of the St. Louis streetcar strike of 1900 the sheriff of St. Louis County swore in a huge *posse comitatus, The New York Times* noted that many prominent citizens, including veterans of several wars, had refused to do duty. Such refusals stemmed from loyalty to one side or the other, from exaggerated fears of the dangers involved or skepticism concerning the same, or, as the *Nashville American* complained in the following year, from fear of prosecution for manslaughter after clashes with strikers.[5]

The ineptitude of the sheriff was therefore endemic and not necessarily an adverse reflection on the man in office. The sheriff of Allegheny County, Pennsylvania, is a case in point. Although Sheriff William H. McCleary earned the epithet "a very inefficient officer" from one federal report, he appears to have borne in mind the $4 million bill footed by the county for property damage in the 1877 railroad strike and to have done all in his power to preserve the peace during the Homestead steel strike of 1892. His attempt to take possession of the Homestead Steel Works (which was surrounded by union pickets) was unsuccessful, but his decision to avoid a violent confrontation at the factory gates was due in some measure to the fact that only fifty-two men joined his posse after he had sent writs to four hundred men to serve on it. In mitigation of McCleary's failure, it should be noted that seventeen years later, during the McKees Rocks strike of 1909, the sheriff of Allegheny County was again described as "inefficient" in a congressional document. In 1909 as in 1892, the sheriff had to receive support from a source external to the county:

Such evidence suggests that the sheriff's job in industrial society was beyond the capabilities of most men.[6]

It was no secret that the sheriff and his few deputies were ill equipped to handle a major strike. In many instances the introduction of the state militia to the scene of a strike was therefore automatic following an immediate request from a sheriff. In the large cities the sheriff very often existed merely to call upon other agencies of law enforcement. But he might organize, as an alternative to troops, a "mushroom" force of "specials" or temporary deputies. U.S. marshals and, more often, city police chiefs were given to similar practices. Thus municipal police forces, which were often undermanned, were not in many instances in a position to substitute professionalism for the amateurism of the sheriff's men. For the system of hiring "specials," whoever organized it, was open to abuse.

Father Peter C. Yorke, the priest who supported the union cause in San Francisco, delivered a typical attack on "specials" in 1901. He criticized the city's police chief, William P. Sullivan: "There is a secret body of wealthy men, unknown to the Constitution and above the law, who have full power over an armed force of about 1,289 men." Yorke claimed that these men were not, like soldiers, subject to immediate discipline.[7] In spite of this disadvantage, "specials" seemed, to citizens too frightened to volunteer themselves for posse duty, to constitute a solution. In fact, however, professional agencies increasingly supplied the "specials" in the 1900s, and the deputized mercenary specialized in aggravating the appearance of violence. Potential volunteers remained terrified, and politicians were confronted with artificial anarchy.

Often the weakness of local law enforcement, the agitation of the press, and the difficulties of factual corroboration, in addition to their own biases, induced politicians to mobilize armed forces in disproportionate numbers to the threat of violence and with unconvincing reasons. During the Colorado metal miners' strike of 1903 a *Denver Republican* reporter asked N. C. Miller, the state attorney general, why troops had been called out when Victor, the alleged trouble spot, was quiet. Miller earnestly replied that everyone in Victor had taken cover. This sort of logic may be amusing in retrospect, but it infuriated labor leaders, who often maintained that business and political bias were prime causes of violence. Gompers still adhered to this point of view in his autobiography (1925): "Situations that have been followed by acts of violence indicate that the major responsibility rests not upon wage-earners but upon those who have control over determination of industrial and social policies." This point of view had its support in Congress in the 1890s. In the context of a contemporary anthracite strike Representative C. H. Grosvenor of Ohio admonished the House on July 19, 1897: "Do not tell me that the miner has committed indiscretions. That may be so, and you may condemn it, but I say that the political power in this country that was hurled at him like an avenging Nemesis is to blame. . . ." [8]

But if some labor apologists regarded probusiness political bias as a provocation to disorder, it should be added that prolabor bias in officials entrusted with law enforcement was a problem of growing proportions. The labor vote was a factor of increasing political importance in the late nineteenth and early twentieth centuries. Indeed, it became part of standard newspaper invective to maintain that such-and-such a politician was, by pursuing a controversial law and order policy, "truckling to the labor vote." [9] Such allegations sometimes distracted attention from the need for local police reform, yet at the same time drew attention to the fact that in some cases policies, not policemen, were defective.

Labor had been able to count a number of victories in the 1890s. For example, D. H. Waite, who had been elected governor of Colorado on a Populist Labor ticket, in 1894 dispatched soldiers to Bull Hill in the Cripple Creek region, where a thousand armed deputies were about to attack a fortified encampment of striking miners. In a protest to Congress, the Mine Owners' Association complained that the state troops had protected lawless strikers and thereby forced employers to accede to union demands.[10]

Illinois was another state where the labor vote was important in gubernatorial elections. In that state John R. Tanner, of McKinley's party, vied for popularity with Democrat John Altgeld. Altgeld was regarded as a radical champion of labor because he had pardoned the surviving Haymarket anarchists, objected to the introduction of federal troops to Chicago during the Pullman railroad strike of 1894, and opposed the granting of political favors to corrupt businessmen. Governor Tanner had to do something for labor in order to help the Republicans to survive politically. In 1897 Tanner refused to send troops to Coffeen after Sheriff Henry N. Randall had predicted that strikers would raze the town and that there would be killings. Just before the midterm elections of 1898, when the rivalry of Altgeld seemed dangerous, Tanner refrained from sending troops to Pana. Then, when coal operators tried to introduce black strikebreakers to Virden, the state executive ordered the militia to meet the train and prevent their disembarkation. A partisan report by the Illinois Bureau of Labor Statistics described the latter incident as the first example in American history of protection of the rights of labor through the "military power of the law." Tanner was more frank: "Perhaps in placing the embargo upon imported labor I am a little in advance of statutory enactment." [11]

The St. Louis streetcar strike of 1900 illustrated dramatically the danger of "truckling to the labor vote" but at the same time drew attention to long-term problems posed by the nature of the American political system. On May 8 there began a general strike for the reinstatement of dismissed union men, affecting three streetcar companies in the state of Missouri: the St. Louis and Suburban Railway, St. Louis Transit, and, in Kansas City, the Metropolitan Street Railway. In St. Louis the Suburban Railway Company, which was to be prosecuted for political corruption in 1902 by future reform Governor J. W. Folk, induced Mayor "Uncle Henry" Ziegenheim and the Police Board to hold "law-and-order" meetings and to use the concentrated resources of the police force to open one Suburban line. The combination of massed police forces, strikebreakers imported from Mobile, New Orleans, Savannah, and Charleston, and large lunchtime crowds immediately produced riots. It became obvious that if the strike was to be broken in the name of "law and order," there was a need for better protection for nonunion labor.[12]

The Republican city administration of St. Louis was subject to three political pressures. The first two came from corporations and labor, interests that were impossible to please simultaneously. A third was imposed by the need to keep order at a time when a $5 million appropriation was being sought in Washington toward the cost of holding the World Fair centenary of the Louisiana Purchase in St. Louis. The city administration did not want to alienate labor, a potential source of support for the World Fair bid (the bid ultimately succeeded and the Louisiana Purchase Exposition opened to the public in 1904.) Yet the failure of the halfway measure, the stratagem of protecting just one line, was apparent. The Republican mayor now authorized the formation of a huge *posse comitatus* and the issuance of repeating shotguns, but the already bitter strike erupted into violence on June 10, when four people died in a riot, bringing the total number of strike deaths to ten.[13]

Lou V. Stevens, the governor of Missouri, was a Democrat. He immediately capitalized on the opportunity to castigate his opponents in the city machine. On the day following the major June riot he stated: "A similar strike upon the street railways was ordered in Kansas City about the same time the St. Louis strike was ordered, but proved a failure because the Mayor, the newspapers, and the Sheriff all cooperated with the Police Department." The governor assumed that the strike continued in St. Louis only because the forces of law and order would not combine to suppress violence (it seems equally plausible that the violence was a response to the hasty yet indecisive use of force). Yet the governor himself was empowered to use the state militia, a more effective force than the sheriff's posse and the outnumbered urban police. Stevens threatened to use troops but did not do so. The St. Louis strike was violent and continued to be violent because the politicians involved were indecisive, afraid of the electorate, and, because of the nature of the political system, disobliged to come to each other's aid.[14]

The changing attitude of Richard Olney shows that there was an increase in respect for the labor vote on the national as well as on the state or municipal level, and that the Pullman strike of 1894 was an educative influence on federal executive officers. Olney, a corporation lawyer from Massachusetts, was in turn U.S. Attorney General (1893–1895) and Secretary of State (1895–1897). In the Reconstruction period, he had respected states' rights insofar as the principle favored conservative white men: In 1875 he championed states' rights when President Ulysses S. Grant sent federal troops to Louisiana to uphold Reconstruction government.[15] But in 1894 he neglected to consult Governor Altgeld of Illinois when, as Attorney General, he interpreted the Pullman strike as a conspiracy leading to interference with U.S. Mails and to obstruction of interstate commerce, and advised Grover Cleveland to send federal troops to suppress alleged rioting in Chicago.

The federal government's intervention in the Pullman strike provided an illustration of a further potential for disunity and irresolution arising from the federal political system. Altgeld was joined by the governors of Missouri, Colorado, Oregon, and Kansas in protesting against Olney's tactics (federal intervention occurred in several states because the Pullman strike, though centered in Chicago, tied up railroads all over the United States). This furor shook the assumption that Washington rightly represented the people against striking workers.[16]

It is in the context of the Pullman outcry that an omission of Olney's in the following year becomes significant. In 1895 a U.S. attorney in New Orleans requested federal troops after a British ship's purser had been wounded in waterfront strike riots. Intervention was in this case possible under the terms of an act arising out of the 1891 lynching of Italians, also in New Orleans, whereby the federal government could mete out punishment for the violation of treaty rights afforded to foreigners. But in 1895 Olney refused to supply troops. He replied to the request: "Application to State authorities ought to be made and denied or proved unsuccessful before the United States interposes." The *New Orleans Times-Democrat* attributed the government's noncompliance to "severe criticism" arising out of the Pullman strike.[17]

The preceding examples show that an expanding labor vote and changing public opinion induced certain politicians to take a neutral or prolabor position during strikes. The examples are not, in fact, representative. They illustrate an emergent rather than a dominant trend. Nevertheless, it may be concluded that politicians were becoming increasingly sensitive to the labor issue in the 1890s and it is possible that labor leaders became commensurately less bitter.

Two years before the assassination of McKinley elevated Roosevelt to the Presidency, the issue of military intervention in labor disputes received a further airing. The dispatch of federal troops to Shoshone County, Idaho, in 1899 illustrates more than the difficulties of ascertaining truth at a distance and the resultant opportunities for misrepresentation. The Coeur d'Alene intervention was a point of departure in two ways. First, it set in train a course of events that exacerbated the industrial bitterness of the 1900s, culminating in the revolutionary thrust of the IWW. But, second, whatever McKinley's critics may have said, it demonstrated that the federal government was learning to be circumspect in its use of force in labor disputes.

Federal troops were sent to Idaho following an incident on April 29, 1899. On that day, between six hundred and a thousand men, many of them armed and some of them masked, congregated at Wardner, having traveled there on stolen railroad trains from their respective towns of Burke, Gem, Mullan, and Kellogg. While they were in Wardner, the quartz mill of the Bunker Hill and Sullivan Company, one of John D. Rockefeller's enterprises, was completely destroyed by giant powder stolen from the Helena-Frisco Mining Company. Two men were killed. The congregated men then dispersed and many fled the state for fear of being arrested. Immediately after the riot of April 29 the governor of Idaho, Frank Steunenberg, asked the Acting Secretary of War for federal troops. This was the only military force available because the state militia had volunteered for service against Spain in the Philippines. But Steunenberg was vulnerable nevertheless to a charge of high-handedness, because he ignored the constitutional provision that required the convening of the state legislature before a request for federal troops was sent. This constraint did not, of course, apply to the government in Washington, and, on the day following the riot (the day on which McKinley's secretary received telegrams from interested capitalists), Adjutant General H. C. Corbin directed Brigadier General Henry C. Merriam to send troops to the district and alerted troops throughout the West to stand by.[18]

With the rapid dispersal of the prime movers in the Bunker Hill explosion there was no continued threat to public order. To a few, the federal intervention in Idaho therefore seemed unjustifiable from the start. Many more came around to this view retrospectively because of the state authorities' abuse of their newly acquired military power. Steunenberg's appointee as state auditor, Bartlett Sinclair, used the military to enforce a blacklist against members of the Western Federation of Miners, and all able-bodied men hostile to the employers were incarcerated in "bull-pens" or makeshift concentration camps. Rumors to the effect that black troops were molesting bull-pen prisoners' wives gained currency in union quarters. To labor sympathizers it seemed unjustifiable that troops should have been sent to Idaho in the first place, that they were allowed to remain, and that state politicians and capitalists were able to manipulate a national force in their own interest.[19]

The partisan role permitted to the federal troops in Idaho contributed to the heritage of bitterness that characterized industrial relations in the western metalliferous mining industry. The assassination of Steunenberg in 1905 and the ensuing arrest of the leading officers of the WFM were a part of that heritage. But equally interesting about the intervention on a broader scale is the national response to the situation. Many city newspapers published what *The New York Times* feared were unduly embellished accounts of military atrocities in Idaho. Black soldiers were almost immediately withdrawn, and when Elihu Root succeeded R. A. Alger as Secretary of War in May 1899, he threatened the complete withdrawal of federal troops. But in Washington Representative Lentz and Senators Richard S. Pettigrew (South Dakota) and William V. Allen (Nebraska) continued the bitter attack on the Administration. Five Congressional reports on the Idaho affair, the last of them at a strategic interval before the 1900 Presidential election, served to emphasize that politicians were awakening to the labor question.[20]

Government officials entrusted with the preservation of order tried to present the appearance of being fair, yet firm. Changing public opinion was yet another factor, to be added to the difficulty of obtaining accurate information, the weakness of the shrieval system, and the endemic problems of federalism, which politicians were obliged to take into consideration. Theodore Roosevelt's exemplary handling of the law-and-order problem in the anthracite coal strike of 1902 owed much to his prior understanding of these factors, gained as governor of New York State at the time of labor disputes in 1899 and 1900.

Roosevelt's experience prior to becoming Vice-President helps to explain his successful blend of principle and political sensitivity. His principles were that legislative reform should improve the lot of labor without conflict, but that when violence threatened, authority should ruthlessly suppress it. Such principles if carried to an extreme might have proved impediments to Roosevelt's political aspirations. In pushing for reform, however, the governor was flexible enough to avoid a breach with the more conservative Republican Party boss, Senator Thomas C. Platt.[21]

In his attitude to strikes, Roosevelt had two useful attributes. He was known to be tough, yet he was politic. He was successful in handling strikes such as that in Buffalo in 1899. Late in April that year Roosevelt alerted state troops in connection with the strike of longshoremen, grain shovelers, and grain-elevator employees in Buffalo. Memories rankled in Buffalo of the conduct of Governor Roswell F. Flower in 1892 who, after signing a ten-hour-day state law, used troops to snuff out the railroad switchmen's attempt to enforce it. In 1899 some newspapers attempted to create an appearance of violence where there probably was none. *The New York Times* and the

Buffalo Morning Express both reported, under headlines on the Buffalo strike, the sandbagging of grain shoveler Michael McNamara and the shooting of W. H. Kennedy. Unmoved by such reports and in the absence of any proven connection between violence and the strike, Roosevelt did not deploy the troops he had alerted. After a display of preparedness, the future President avoided activating troops in a city that had, in the contest for gubernatorial nomination, provided him with political support.[22]

Roosevelt's subtle blend of principle and political expedience emerges against the background of the strike by Italian immigrants helping to construct Croton Dam, a public contract in Westchester County. When these unskilled laborers struck in April 1900 against low wages and the *padrone* system, Roosevelt met the request of Sheriff Molloy for troops, and the state militia broke the strike. Yet it was never proved that the Italians had offered any violence. A young sergeant in the militia was killed on April 16, but when troops from "Camp Roosevelt" searched the Italians' houses, they found no weapons. Roosevelt probably had the Croton Dam strike in mind when, on the day of the militia sergeant's assassination, he wrote to a political aide estimating his chances of gubernatorial renomination: "If, for instance, we had strikes which led to riots, I would of course be obliged to preserve order and stop the riots. Decent citizens would demand that I should do it, and in any event I should do it wholly without regard to their demands. But once it was done, they would forget all about it, while a great army of laboring men, honest but ignorant and prejudiced, would bear a grudge against me for doing it. This might put me out of the running as a candidate." Roosevelt clearly perceived what many of his contemporaries failed to see: that "public opinion" could not force the hand of a public executive in the immediate term, but that retribution at the hands of the voters was to be feared in the long term. It might be argued that the Croton Dam Italians received shorter shrift than the Buffalo grain shovelers because they were not enfranchised. On the other hand, the future President feared that labor would respond as a class to his stubborn stance. He adopted his tough approach, therefore, against the background of an intelligent appraisal of the political circumstances, not out of a false courage born of ignorance.[23]

Roosevelt believed in fair play. If he upheld the principle of order, he was also scrupulous in his reluctance to act hastily or unwisely when troops were demanded. He was aware of the bitterness that unjust or apparently unjust military intervention created, and feared that bitterness itself produced disorders. During the anthracite strike of 1902 he wrote of those who demanded federal troops: "The coal operators and their friends and allies of the type of the New York *Sun* have been attacking me. . . . Do they not realize that they are putting a very heavy burden on us who stand against socialism, against anarchic disorder?" In spite of the fact that capitalists put as much pressure on Roosevelt as on his predecessors in the White House, he resisted premature action and stressed the importance of acting only when in the possession of the fullest possible knowledge. He had initiated inquiries into the New York strikes of 1899 and 1900 through the State Board of Mediation and Arbitration. Armed with this memory, he fondly recalled in his *Autobiography* (1913) that he had suppressed the Buffalo and Croton Dam strikes with equal vigor and that his "chief opponents and critics were local politicians who were truckling to the labor vote." His response as President to the 1902 coal strike was, of course, to set up the Anthracite Commission, which gave each side in the dispute an opportunity to present its version of the violence that had taken place.[24]

The anthracite strike began on May 14, 1902. It provided the new and untested President with a challenging opportunity to show what he meant in practice by his "Square Deal," a slogan used by Roosevelt in speeches that shocked the Republican Old Guard by calling for the governmental regulation of big business as well as labor. On the other hand, the strike supplied the unelected, unmandated President with tempting reasons to favor one side or the other.

The New York Times noted that there was an enticing reason for Roosevelt to truckle to the labor vote: Congressional elections, the first judgment on his Presidency, were due in November. The pressure for military intervention on the side of the employers was as virulent, if more narrowly based. Roosevelt's stand on the labor question alienated some of the Republican Party's fund donors (though he may not have foreseen this consequence in 1902). The *New York Sun* attacked Roosevelt for what it portrayed as his military weakness. There was a danger that the public would demand drastic action and retaliate, in its absence, at the polls. Anthracite coal was a domestic heating fuel. Roosevelt was the first nationally prominent statesman to perceive that the consumer was a potent third force in politics, and he feared that a winter coal shortage would be "bad politically." In addition there was a general fear of "anarchism," a term loosely employed and associated anew with violence following the assassination of President McKinley by an avowed anarchist in 1901. In his address to Congress recommending the exclusion of foreign anarchists, Roosevelt had himself indicted "the deliberate demagogue, . . . the exploiter of sensationalism, and . . . the crude and foolish visionary who, for whatever reason, apologizes for crime, or excites aimless discontent." In the course of the anthracite dispute he had to discard the clamor of those who associated strikes with anarchism.[25]

The nature and history of the anthracite region exemplified some of the weaknesses in the law-and-order apparatus in America and invited the open inquiry supplied by Roosevelt. The region covered less than five hundred square miles in northeastern Pennsylvania. It contained mountain barriers and isolated mining patches and towns. Of the 630,000 inhabitants, 144,000 worked in coal mines. Of the remaining half million, many depended on mineworkers or on their employers for a living, whether as members of their families or as suppliers of their needs.[26]

This meant there were few local people with sufficient objectivity to mediate in industrial disputes. Employers complained that unions brought monolithic working-class pressure to bear on them: For example, during the Scranton streetcar strike of 1901 UMWA president John Mitchell asked miners to boycott the Scranton Railway Company. Even schoolchildren went on strike during the anthracite dispute, their action disrupting fourteen schools.[27]

A. M. Simons, who in 1902 ranked as a left-wing socialist, presented the other side of the picture. Writing under the temporary *nom de guerre* "A Black-Listed Machinist," he remarked of the anthracite combatants: "The capitalists are class-conscious. The big merchants cut off the credit of the small retailers, and force them to shut down on their customers (in this case, the striking miners), in order to starve the latter into submission to the exactions of the mine owners and operators, who are members of the capitalist class to which the big wholesalers belong." Given such pressures, tradesmen had to choose one side or the other in order to ensure their own survival, and sometimes they became actively involved in strikes. Thus after the major riot of the anthracite strike, that at Shenandoah, Schuylkill County, early in August, the coroner found that a butcher and saloonkeeper were responsible for its instigation. When Roosevelt set up a commission of arbitration to end the strike, he exercised a mediatory and restraining influence that no one in the anthracite region itself had been able to provide.[28]

Another factor making for bitterness in the anthracite region and inviting federal intervention was the tradition of ethnic animosity between workers and law officers. This had existed since the days of the Molly Maguires, when the chronically weak system of law enforcement had led to the introduction of the Pinkerton detective James McParlan. In 1902 it was still true that most of the workers were recent immigrants, while the mine officials and law officers frequently belonged to an established, English-speaking generation. The workers' resultant distrust of the forces of order extended beyond the local police to the state militia. This was evident when on October 6, 1902, Governor William A. Stone called out units of the National Guard of Pennsylvania in the anthracite regions, on the ground that in seven counties the civil authorities were no longer able to preserve order. In furious reaction came the *Mahoney City Daily American*'s characterization of the National Guard: "Gobin's drunken or crazy mob of mounted curs." [29]

Brigadier General John P. S. Gobin had earned the animus of the Schuylkill County paper for his participation some years earlier in an affair a few miles north of Mahoney City, in Hazleton, Luzerne County. On September 10, 1897, Polish, Italian, and Hungarian strikers from Hazleton set out on a march to Lattimer, where they hoped to persuade working miners to strike in sympathy. They were unarmed, marched behind two American flags, and, so the *American Federationist* later claimed, had received permission to picket from Chief of Police Evans Jones. James Martin, an English miner's son elected sheriff of Luzerne County in 1895 with the aid of the Republican machine, said later he had not been aware that the marchers were acting legally and thought they were heavily armed and drunk. He recruited a posse of about eighty-five men, many supplied by Thomas Hall, chief of coal and iron police for Lehigh Valley Coal Company. Though legitimized by a Pennsylvania statute of 1866, the coal and iron police were really a private army appointed by and loyal to various employers like the Lehigh company. Backed by this dubious reinforcement to his authority, Sheriff Martin obstructed the path of the Hazleton marchers. Following a verbal misunderstanding between

Martin and the immigrant miners, the posse fired two volleys into the uncomprehending crowd, killing nineteen and wounding forty.[30]

The labor press was indignant at the Hazleton massacre, which it portrayed as oppressive and unjustifiable. The *American Federationist* claimed that the posse had been forced on Martin by the mineowners. Some newspapers, such as the *Pittsburgh Press* and Joseph Pulitzer's *New York World,* joined in criticizing the sheriff, causing the lawyer David M. Means to complain that the press "gushed with sympathetic zeal" for the miners' cause. *The New York Times,* however, commended Martin's decisive action as a deterrent that would prevent a repetition of the Pittsburgh riots of 1877, when property had been destroyed. Two days after the shootings, the *Times* concluded in an editorial: "To talk of indicting Sheriff Martin for murder is an encouragement to crime and lawlessness." [31]

Martin was indicted, together with a number of his deputies. Crime reporters from the major city newspapers predicted that the sheriff and his deputies would be acquitted because of the money of the operators. The law officers were indeed acquitted on March 9, 1898, and labor spokesmen unrelentingly complained that the removal of the trial venue to Wilkes-Barre had been part of an attempt by mineowners and their helpers (including the trial judge) to influence the course of justice: Prosecution witnesses had to travel a long distance to testify at the risk of dismissal by their mineowning employers, while District Attorney Palmer (whose father, as Luzerne County sheriff in the 1840s, had criticized Irish immigrants) lost no opportunity to emphasize their foreign birth. D. Douglas Wilson, International Association of Machinists vice-president and editor of his union's magazine, reacted to the Wilkes-Barre verdict with the comment that "when crime is committed in the name of the law at the behest or suggestion of rich men, it is not likely to meet with punishment." [32]

Gobin, sent by Governor Daniel H. Hastings to command the National Guard at Hazleton just after the disorder, came to be associated then and thereafter in the eyes of labor sympathizers with what they saw as a miscarriage of justice. The brigadier general refused for several days to allow civil authorities to arrest Martin, on the ground that the military were subordinate to the sheriff. The *Philadelphia Public Ledger,* as well as Eugene Debs' old publication, the *Locomotive Firemen's Magazine,* imparted to Gobin the decision to hold the trial in Wilkes-Barre, where a procapitalist bias enabled a charge of manslaughter, not murder, to be lodged.[33]

The unionized anthracite miners never forgave Gobin. Aware of the hostility felt toward him, the general complained to the chairman of the Anthracite Commission: "I would sit on the streetcar or ride along the street, and I would hear somebody say: 'Just wait until the sons-of-bitches of soldiers leave, and then we'll do them strikebreakers up.' I have heard that frequently, sir, thrust at me—talked at me; not *to* me, but *at* me." According to Stewart Culin, who served during the anthracite strike as a private in the Pennsylvania National Guard at Shenandoah, near Mahoney City, the local people still hated Gobin because of his attitude toward the Martin case in 1897–1898. Gobin's actions in 1902 provoked renewed resentment, for his opinions had not changed. He refused to allow the arrest of a militiaman for shooting dead a deaf man who did not heed a verbal challenge and remained convinced that only the presence of troops safeguarded the persons of nonstrikers.[34]

Gobin's attitude was matched by a reverse sentiment in the ranks of the state militia. Many of the locally recruited National Guardsmen sympathized with the union cause. Culin recalled that his fellow militiamen had given odd jobs around their encampments to strikers' boys, distributed food to the boys' parents, and played baseball with the miners. With the anthracite strike in mind, Mitchell remarked: "If the militia were coming out I would rather that the militia were composed of members of my union." The idea of a thoroughly neutral police force had yet to take root in the inhospitable coal patches of eastern Pennsylvania.[35]

President Roosevelt was faced, in the anthracite coal strike of 1902, with a heritage of industrial bitterness, polarized local politics with little hope of any impartial industrial mediation, and an endemically inadequate system of local and state law enforcement. His reaction was, first of all, to ascertain the truth about violence and industrial conditions. He complained to Winthrop Crane, the Republican governor of Massachusetts, of having received "flatly contradictory" reports about violence that had recurred after the introduction of state troops to the anthracite region. But in the end he decided to believe Mitchell about the peaceful nature of the strike. Even Gobin later confirmed the wisdom of the President's decision not to send in the U.S. Army, testifying that although he had insufficient men under his command to be able to guarantee order, his modest force had succeeded in giving sufficient protection to the public.[36]

Having decided there was no case for U.S. military intervention,

Roosevelt set up his commission on October 14, 1902, to investigate industrial conditions and, incidentally, to give a full airing to the vexatious question of labor violence. A week later, the strike was over. Though technically impartial, Roosevelt's decisions were a victory for American workers, who had never before been given a Presidential "square deal" in this way. Knowing this to be the case, Roosevelt took pains to ensure that his policies were acceptable to public opinion. Newspapers across the nation accepted Roosevelt's view, expressed after meeting Mitchell and the employers on October 3, that the operators were of "a most insolent frame of mind." Public opinion was ready to accept the President's point that "turbulence and violence . . . is just as apt to come from an attitude of arrogance on the part of the owners of property and of unwillingness to recognize their duty to the public [a reference to the operators' refusal to go to arbitration] as from any improper encouragement of violence." In choosing restraint and impartiality and in taking pains to popularize his decision, Roosevelt steered America away from class violence just at the moment when so many of his countrymen were becoming so acutely worried about it.[37]

Roosevelt's judicious handling of the anthracite strike forced the Republican Party managers to adopt him as their Presidential candidate in 1904, when he was for the first time elected to the White House in his own right. In his second term, he continued to wield his "Big Stick," verbally reproving workers and capitalists alternatively and reinforcing the principles of the "Square Deal." That his attitude, and even his slogan, lived on in various adopted forms, is indicated in the histories of Franklin D. Roosevelt's "New Deal" and Harry Truman's "Fair Deal."

The spirit of 1902 reappeared in Theodore Roosevelt's second term during the Chicago teamsters' strike of 1905. It will be recalled (see Chapter 6) that on this occasion the Republican governor of Illinois and the Democratic mayor of Chicago were at odds about the use of state troops, and that private armed guards were used. At one point the introduction of federal troops to the Chicago strike was seriously under consideration. The attitude of Cornelius P. Shea, president of the International Brotherhood of Teamsters, illustrates the fears that trade-union leaders still entertained that governmental authorities would act in a suppressive manner on the basis of an illusion. On April 30, Shea wrote to Governor Deneen because he had heard that Levy

Mayer, the Employers' Association attorney, was calling for the introduction of state and federal troops for the purpose of "intimidating
and coercing our members to return to work under military protection." Armed guards and strikebreakers, Shea insisted, had been guilty
of such violence as had been committed. His letter continued: "We
respectfully protest against the [apparently intended] ordering out of
troops. . . . We respectfully request that before any such action is
taken you investigate the conditions as they exist, and upon whom rests
the responsibility for the disorder now existing in Chicago." [38]

On May 10 President Roosevelt visited Chicago to be presented with
another union petition appealing to his sense of fair play but unwisely
implying that federal intervention might not be impartial. The petition
claimed that employers refused to go to arbitration because "they
openly boast that they can spurn it, and that the troops under your
command will shoot down him who dares to openly protest against
their action." Roosevelt pounced on the implied questioning of the impartiality of federal troops, regretting that Shea "should have spoken
in the letter at all of the use of the federal army as you have spoken.
In upholding law and order, in doing what he is able to do to suppress mob violence in any shape or way, the mayor of Chicago, Mayor
Dunne, has my hearty support." The *Typographical Journal* later recalled with regret that the strike had not spread in a successful manner because of Roosevelt's interdiction, "Back of the city stands the
state, and back of the state stands the nation." But, confronted
with disorders far worse than those of the Pullman strike of 1894,
Roosevelt had in fact behaved with remarkable restraint.[39]

It should not be concluded from all this that 1902 was a once-and-
for-all turning point in the U.S. government's approach to order.
Roosevelt himself departed from his oft-stated principles when dealing
with the West and with revolutionary socialists. His reaction to the
Steunenberg murder trial became notorious. On February 17, 1906,
W. D. Haywood, Charles Moyer, and George Pettibone were appre-
hended in Denver, Colorado, and spirited away by special train to
Idaho, where they were charged with Frank Steunenberg's murder.
Certainly, the death of the former governor was not deeply regretted
by western miners. John M. O'Neil, editor of the WFM's *Miner's
Magazine* regretted the death of Steunenberg because, as he wrote
vindictively in the *Western Clarion*, when the fatal bomb exploded outside his home "the gate was completely wrecked." But this attitude,

however widespread, was not enough to convict Haywood, Moyer, and Pettibone. Their defending counsel, Clarence Darrow, hinted that the Pinkerton Detective Agency was trying to frame them.[40]

At this juncture, Roosevelt delivered one of his periodic chastisements of bad capitalists and, in the interest of the square deal, bad workers. He has since become famous for his remark that the ruthless railway magnate Edward H. Harriman was "at least as undesirable a citizen as Debs, or Moyer, or Haywood." [41] In making this judgment before Haywood went on trial in 1907, the President failed to adhere to his principle of fair investigation before condemnation. By January 4, 1908, Haywood, Moyer, and Pettibone were all, in fact, to be acquitted.

Roosevelt's judgment about the West was clouded by his long and fondly remembered associations with the region and its people. He portrayed the cowboys of his Chimney Butte Ranch in the Dakotas as individuals who looked down on labor unions and strikers, particularly at the time of the Haymarket Bomb Affair. Like the novelist Jack London, he perhaps thought of the Rocky Mountains in undifferentiated terms as the stalking ground of the pioneer and of the cities as the cockpits of threatening class conflict. He was, for whatever reason, intolerant of WFM activities.[42]

Ignoring his own guidelines and WFM objections, Roosevelt sent troops to Morenzi, Arizona, in June 1903 without preliminary investigation. In December 1903 the WFM, harassed by the tactics of the Citizens' Alliance and the Colorado state militia during the Cripple Creek strike, itself attempted to obtain federal intervention. Senator Thomas M. Patterson, proprietor of the *Rocky Mountain News* and *Denver Times,* joined his fellow Democrat and Colorado senator, Henry M. Teller, in petitioning Roosevelt to intervene. The President, whose western friend F. J. Bonfils ran the *Denver Post* in opposition to Patterson's pro-union papers, replied that he had "neither the power nor the right" even to investigate.[43]

So entrenched was Roosevelt in his support for the Colorado operators that he refused to recommend the subsequent Congressional inquiries into the strike.[44] His action in Morenzi and failure to act in Cripple Creek contrasted strangely with the nature of his intervention in the anthracite strike and with his nonintervention in Chicago in 1905 or, for that matter, in a streetcar strike in Houston, Texas, where troops had been requested but proved unnecessary in June 1904.

The WFM blamed Roosevelt for allowing democracy to be undermined in Colorado, and when the first IWW convention met in Chicago on June 27, 1905, the western miners were heavily represented. In one notable area Roosevelt had reaped the kind of retribution he had warned his fellow Americans to avoid. The history of Colorado was not, however, to exceed in influence the history of Pennsylvania and other industrial states. Roosevelt's principles were to live on.[45]

Chapter 9

Government and Order ——

THEODORE ROOSEVELT RELINQUISHED THE PRESIDENCY IN 1909, BUT IN 1910 once more focused public attention on his opinions concerning industrial violence. Unhappy with the state of politics under the Presidency of his chosen successor, William Howard Taft, Roosevelt made a speaking tour of the nation between August 23 and September 11, 1910. His speeches were published before the end of the year as *The New Nationalism,* a book of essays that helped to launch him as a third-party Presidential candidate in 1912. In the essay on "Labor and Capital" the irrepressible Roosevelt inveighed against "violence, lawlessness, and mob rule." In another essay based on a speech at Columbus, Ohio, he struck the familiar note of fairness: "I find that my speech was put down as being a speech upon law and order. I have asked that it be changed—that it be put down as a speech upon law, order, and justice." [1]

But was Roosevelt's emphasis on fairness typical of a more general change in heart during the Progressive period? Did this general attitude, if it existed, survive his Presidency? Did it affect future responses to nonlabor disturbances, such as race riots? And if, indeed, Roosevelt's attitude was symptomatic or causative of a more enlightened public opinion, did it do anything to counteract the hitherto endemic weaknesses of the American law enforcement system?

Roosevelt's idea of impartiality did not immediately appeal to those professionally entrusted with law enforcement. For example, U.S. Army reform was seldom regarded as something intended to redress the social balance; rightly or wrongly, both sides in the industrial conflict thought such reform would help the anti-union employers. It was generally supposed that Army reform was related to labor troubles as well as to imperialism and national defense, in spite of a disclaimer in the *Army and Navy Journal* in 1904.[2] During the 1890s, Lieutenant-General John M. Schofield, Commander of the Army of the United States from 1888 to 1895, emphasized the need for a strong federal force for the preservation of domestic peace. On the eve of his retirement in September 1895, Schofield visualized an internal danger to stability as exemplified in the Pullman strike of the previous year. He himself had not neglected his duty. In the course of the Pullman strike *The New York Times* had reassured its readers editorially: "The new tactics of the army and navy contain a very complete street-riot drill." The very concept of a standing Army had long been distrusted in America, and it was only after a struggle with Congress in 1902 and 1903 during which stress was laid on foreign commitments in the aftermath of the war with Spain that Roosevelt's Secretary of War, Elihu Root, was able to effect a further reorganization. Even then, he was forced to abandon a plan for the incorporation of the state militia into the regular Army.[3]

Root's reorganization was opposed by self-interested state militia officers, by traditional libertarians, and by labor, but supported by many employers. For although the U.S. Army rarely became involved in strikes, there was some psychological weight in Roosevelt's warning, "back of the state stands the nation." This was especially true where employers suspected the state militia of being sympathetic to the workers. For example, the *Nashville American* complained in 1901 that Kentucky's soldiers "were little better than a bodyguard for the union agitators" in that state. In the same state three years later the Newport Iron and Brass Foundry Company complained of inadequate protection against "mob violence" under state laws, moved its officers to Washington, and incorporated under the laws of the District of Columbia (administered by Congress). Its lawyers apparently believed that this move would bring federal military protection on a pro-employer basis. The *Louisville Courier-Journal* reported: "The plant will be operated as an open shop and managed by an executive committee appointed by the trustees. As Fort Thomas, on the adjoining Kentucky highlands, overlooks that large plant, the reorganization caused much comment in the foundry district." [4]

Evidently employers in Newport, Kentucky, challenging the power of the International Molders' Union of North America, placed more trust in their friends in Washington than in their friends in Frankfort. At the same time, the attitude of professional Army officers reinforced employers' faith in federal force. Major General Henry C. Corbin noted disapprovingly in 1903: "An insurrection may exist within a State—palpable and indisputable according to an ordinary observer— and the executive, who may be a party to the insurrection or in sympathy with it, may refuse to make the constitutional demands upon the Federal Government." [5] Corbin, a veteran of the Civil War, the troubled Plains from Kansas to New Mexico, the Spanish-American War, and the Coeur d'Alene strike of 1899, made this remark in the context of a Senate document that was unsympathetic to labor.

Labor's suspicions of Army reform extended also to the Pennsylvania State Constabulary, established in 1905 during Governor W. Pennypacker's administration. This experimental state police force was intended to make private armies obsolete. When first proposed, it appeared to meet the complaint of union men that in Pennsylvania deputy sheriffs were too often in the pay of employers and the complaint of employers that the state militiamen cooperated with strikers. In fact, several sources sympathetic to labor observed within half a dozen years of its creation that the new mounted force was efficient in performing its law enforcement duties. [6] But the "Pennsylvanian Cossacks" were primarily a strike police force and as such met with extensive union and socialist invective. [7] By 1911 the socialist J. H. Maurer, an early supporter of the scheme, was fighting hard for the abolition of the state police. He attacked the initially unobtrusive augmentation of the police power of a state, just as another socialist, Ernest Untermann, had complained that without notice from the press the militia bill of 1902–1903 had been pushed through Congress to strengthen the arm of federal repression. [8]

Law enforcement reform, of which U.S. Army reorganization is the chief example, was indeed partly aimed at ensuring social order in the United States, but there is no evidence that it was intended to help employers exclusively. It is, however, significant that employers fell back on federal strength. For this was a symptom of the failure of lower echelons in the law enforcement structure to give them unquestioning support. In terms of political influence, the employing class was on the retreat in the Progressive period in the face of Roosevelt's concept of a "Square Deal."

Left-wing criticism of American martial forces focused on the U.S. Army, reinforcing both the employers' assumption that Washington would back the capitalist and the associated idea that the state militia might well protect or support strikers. The distinction between a federal or "standing" army and a "people's" militia was as clear to socialists as it had been to the critics of the Constitution of 1787 and upholders of the first ten Amendments. It is true that in its first convention the Industrial Workers of the World adopted the resolution: "That any person joining the militia or accepting position under sheriffs and police powers or as members of detective agencies or employers' hirelings in times of industrial disturbance, shall be forever denied the privilege of membership of this organization." However, the IWW resolution of 1905 was passed only after criticism on the ground that control of the militia was both possible and important to the success of a revolution.[9]

The social democrats exhibited a similar tendency. Socialist Party of America leader and theoretician John Spargo in 1906 condemned the American military unreservedly. But in 1910 his more eminent comrade Morris Hillquit upheld the militia, as opposed to the oppressive standing army, as an instrument of democracy. When in its convention of 1912 the SPA adopted a resolution recommending that Socialists should try to win over to their side men in all the American armed forces, it recognized that employers no longer had the automatic sympathy of soldiers.[10]

Although most trade unionists were concerned with victory in strikes rather than with victory in the class struggle, their attitude to the military was similar to that of the socialists. Some trade unions were wary of the militia. For example, the Brotherhood of Painters, Decorators and Paper Hangers of America, the Journeymen Stone Cutters' Association of North America, and the National Union of the United Brewery Workmen of the United States all had in 1902 rules of various kinds prohibiting their members from belonging to the state militia. Yet, as noted in the previous chapter, trade unionists had at times received aid from the militiamen: State troops were said to be particularly prone to fraternize with railroad and streetcar strikers.[11]

The changing tactical position adopted by AFL president Samuel Gompers reflected the increasing tendency of militiamen to support, or at least refrain from harassing, strikers. Speaking on the afternoon of December 12, 1892, to an AFL convention suffering bitter memories of a year of suppressed strikes, he had condemned the militia as "a machine of monopolistic oppression against labor." [12] He had adopted a reserved tactical position, urging that trade unions should press for the election of officers by men and that, failing this, soldiers should not be allowed to become members of trade unions. Confronted after 1902 with the prospect of a larger and more efficient U.S. Army and with changing opinion in the militia ranks that made it more likely that militia officers would avoid antagonizing trade unionists, Gompers gave the state forces a less reserved approbation. On January 4, 1905, he addressed an open letter to W. L. Anthon of Dickinson College, Carlisle, Pennsylvania: "Now as to the matter of members of trade unions joining the State militia, . . . a man who is a wage-earner . . . has not only the right to become a citizen soldier, but that right must be unquestioned. The militia, i.e., the citizen soldiery of the several states in our country, supplies what might otherwise take its place—a large standing army. The difference between the citizen soldiery of the United States and the large standing armies of many European countries is the difference between a republic and a monarchy—it is the difference between liberty and tyranny." [13] Gompers rejoiced in the consequences of Root's failure to incorporate the militia in a standing army. In this respect, for him, the "Square Deal" had succeeded.

No amount of improvement in law enforcement was likely to succeed in creating a new atmosphere if the law itself was unjust or unjustly interpreted. In 1914 B. F. Moore, a legal expert advising the U.S. Commission on Industrial Relations, found that labor was discriminated against in law and by lawyers. He reached the following conclusions among others: "The implied power of the Constitutional clause giving the Governor authority to call out the militia to suppress violence is sufficient to override the clause of the Constitution positively guaranteeing personal rights" and: "Arbitrary action of the Executive in these cases [involving personal rights] has been justified by the judiciary on the grounds of expediency and necessity rather than the law." Moore's investigation had been confined, however, to areas afflicted by "serious labor disturbances" where the military authorities took exceptional liberties with the law.[14] A broader analysis shows that the law and lawyers were no more immune to change than any other section of society.

It will be recalled that in the 1840s Chief Justice Lemuel Shaw of Massachusetts created a controlling precedent by deciding that unions were not in themselves criminal conspiracies. Decisions in New Jersey and Pennsylvania in 1867 qualified the precedent when the courts decided it did not apply to unions attempting to establish the closed shop. In the 1880s and 1890s conspiracy prosecutions increased. But in the 1880s employers began to resort to the further tactic of obtaining injunctions from sympathetic judges, thus enjoining union leaders from engaging in activities calculated to injure the capitalists concerned. The historian Philip Foner has argued that corporation lawyers changed their emphasis from conspiracy prosecutions pure and simple to the obtaining of injunction writs because it was easier for them to influence a judge than a jury. Clarence Darrow, the labor movement's outstanding legal advisor, certainly believed by 1900 that the judicial system favored employers. In that year he attacked the conduct of the courts and advocated that "in every case where the act constitutes a criminal offence a jury should be empanelled to try the case." Darrow and the AFL disapproved of the situation whereby a judge might enjoin not only picketing, union meetings, inflammatory speeches, and intimidation, but also conspiracy in contemplation of any of these activities. They agitated for a law to prohibit the issuance of labor injunctions that made crimes of acts that in spheres other than industrial disputes would have been legal.[15]

It took a long time to obtain legislation against "government by injunction." Lawyers and legislators opposed to labor unions resisted it because it would have undermined one of their main premises, that unions depended on violence. Indeed, according to labor historian John Steuben, the issue of violence was the chief spur to legal minds bent on formulating legislation or legal precedent hostile to union aspirations. The debates about union picketing in the legislatures of Minnesota, New York, Massachusetts, and Illinois in 1863–1864 started a train of thought that produced extensive legislation by 1900. By then, statutes in twelve states prohibited violent picketing. An additional eleven states had, by 1900, some form of law against labor violence. Whereas most statutes and judicial decisions admitted the legality of picketing as such, some were stringent in their definition of violence.

People v. Wilzig, a New York court decision, in 1886 classified pla-
cards as a form of intimidation when displayed by pickets. The Mississippi statutes of 1898 provided for the imprisonment of any who
"implied" violence by parading a placard.[16]

Court decisions and laws concentrating on labor violence reflected
general currents in nineteenth-century public opinion, yet were particularly indicative of the positions taken by lawyers. James G. Jenkins,
in a case arising from the 1894 Northern Pacific strike, summed up
the prejudice of a railroad corporation lawyer turned judge in his
hackneyed observation that "a strike without violence would equal
the presentation of the tragedy of *Hamlet* with the part of Hamlet
omitted." According to U.S. Supreme Court Justice Samuel Freeman
Miller and the historian Gerald G. Eggert, bias was endemic in many
judges dealing with railroad injunction cases, because they had started
their careers as railroad corporation lawyers. In the industry-domi-
nated "Gilded Age," most judges and many legislative lawyers probably had a background as business attorneys, and bias in labor cases
and laws was inevitable.[17]

Although Gompers himself narrowly escaped imprisonment over the
injunction case involving the Buck's Stove and Range Company in
1908, labor's legal environment improved from the late nineteenth century onward. Laws against violent picketing proved to be inconse-
quential. Since the success of the vast majority of strikes did not depend on intimidation, the legislation had little effect except on public
opinion, which, after all, had helped to produce it in the first place.

We have already seen in Chapter 6 that injunctions restraining conspiracies to commit violent crimes had little practical effect on labor
disputes. They contributed to illusions of violence and helped to line
the pockets of private detectives whose least ambition was to see the
demise of labor unions. Labor injunctions, it is true, were offensive to
trade unionists, who were concerned with legitimacy and hated being
branded as would-be violent conspirators. But there were encouraging
signs on the horizon. In the first place, the advent of "government by
injunction" in the 1880s was, as Foner suggested, a reflection of the
reluctance of juries to convict strikers on flimsy evidence. In other
words, the employers' resort to an undemocratic legal procedure
showed that they were on the defensive. As for the long-drawn-out
battle for Congressional legislation against the labor injunction, it provided the AFL with endless opportunities for propaganda. The Clayton

Act of 1914 banned the issuance of injunctions forbidding actions that would have been legal outside the context of a strike, but this provision was undermined in the courts. The Norris-La Guardia Act of 1932, however, reaffirmed the 1914 provision and granted jury trial to defendants in contempt cases. By then, labor had repeatedly asserted its claim to legitimacy without, in fact, suffering crippling damage from injunction judges. Indeed, labor was becoming the executioner. President William Howard Taft was attacked as an "injunction judge" because of his court action in the Ann Arbor Railroad dispute of 1893, and CIR investigator Edwin E. Witte noted that by 1915 the "injunction record" of judges was an important electoral issue.[18]

Another circumstance redressing the social balance in favor of labor in the early twentieth century was the emergence of gifted or prominent lawyers able and willing to plead the workingman's case. Clarence Darrow, Louis Brandeis, Felix Frankfurter, and William Jennings Bryan all served labor's cause in the Progressive period. The heyday of the corporation lawyer was by no means over, but there was a diversification of background experience in the legal profession. Legal aid had been introduced in 1876. In 1896 the number of legal aid cases reached 15,000, and by 1916 it was over 117,000. Divorce work provided lawyers with a booming source of income in the Progressive years. Increasingly affluent labor unions retained their own counsel, ultimately producing that specialized breed, the labor lawyer. Progressive reformers on the state and federal levels set up new bureaucracies for the enforcement of laws protecting the interests of workers, farmers, and consumers, as well as businessmen. World War I further stimulated bureaucratic growth, and bureaucracy supported yet another type of lawyer, the government attorney. In the long run, such changes produced a fairer legal mind. This, as well as the developing idea of executive fair play, was one of the discernible trends of the reform period inaugurated by Theodore Roosevelt.[19]

Roosevelt's "Square Deal" concept was to be a legacy as well as a characteristic of his administration. Whatever contemporary employers, socialists, and labor unionists may have thought of U.S. Army reforms effected by Schofield and Root, the subsequent history of the use of federal force in labor disputes shows that fairness and restraint had arrived to stay. Further reforms aimed at impartiality also took root. New York and other states followed the example of Pennsylvania in establishing state police forces during and after World War I (though the corporation-appointed coal and iron police lingered on in Pennsylvania itself until 1931). Eleven states had state constabularies by 1929. Municipal police forces underwent changes designed to free them from political influence. From 1895 on, the selection of personnel began to occur on the basis of merit and civil service regulations, instead of political patronage. In the Progressive period, reforming police chiefs, such as August Vollmer of Berkeley, California, began to upgrade the professional standards required of officers. Such reforms may have been partly designed to keep labor sympathizers under the patronage of demagogic boss politicians from joining city police forces. Nevertheless, during the administration of President Woodrow Wilson, city policemen attempted to organize themselves with the help of the AFL, only to be demoralized by Governor Calvin Coolidge's use of soldiers in crushing the Boston police strike of 1919.[20]

In spite of the incipient changes in local and state police forces in the Progressive period, these forces failed to match the impartiality and efficiency of Presidentially authorized interventions. National Guardsmen and sheriffs continued to be political pawns, subject to unreliable constitutional procedures. The worst examples of partiality occurred in mining areas sharing the characteristics of the anthracite coalfield in 1902. Colorado, Michigan, Illinois, Tennessee, West Virginia, and Kentucky suffered from chronically unreliable law enforcement in their mining counties. In some cases the sheriffs and soldiers were controlled by workers instead of employers, but bias itself was slow to disappear. Against this background, the performance of the U.S. Army was, taken as a whole, an unexpected gift to lovers of order, justice, and freedom. The historian Charles Forcey has advanced convincing evidence in support of his contention that around 1912 the United States reached the "Crossroads of Liberalism": thenceforth liberals were to look to the federal government, not to the states, for the protection of American liberties.[21] In the case of law enforcement, this new liberal expectation was reasonable.

When Woodrow Wilson became President in 1913, he played an active and impartial role in some of the violent labor disputes occurring during his first administration. A year after taking office, he intervened in the grim struggle between the United Mine Workers of America and the Colorado Fuel and Iron Company, a corporation controlled and actively supervised by John D. Rockefeller, Jr. The strike to unionize Colorado's coal mines began in September 1913. A local sheriff revealed the partisanship involved in his remark: "I never arm both sides." Governor Elias Ammons soon called out the National Guard, and violence ensued when he instructed the soldiers to protect strikebreakers. Under pressure from businessmen, Ammons put General John C. Chase—the commander during the bitter 1903–1904 strike—once again in charge of peace-keeping operations. One of his officers, Lieutenant Karl E. "Jesus Christ" Linderfelt (who was reported to have declaimed on one occasion: "I am Jesus Christ, and my men on horses are Jesus Christs, and we have got to be obeyed"), authorized an attack on a tent colony at Ludlow that sheltered strikers and their families evicted from company houses. Some of the soldiers involved in the attack were company guards or adventurers; their professional standards were low. The tents caught fire. Two women and eleven young children were burned to death. At this point, the State Federation of Labor and the local miners took up arms, notifying President Wilson of their intention. Severe fighting occurred (the Ludlow toll being seventy-four dead in all) before federal troops arrived to restore order instantly.[22]

The Democratic President's military interventions in labor disputes in a firm and fair spirit conferred the blessing of bipartisan support on such actions. Wilson's policy was, indeed, an improvement on Roosevelt's in that he was less irrational toward the West. He exercised restraint toward metal miners in Arizona as well as coal miners in Colorado. On June 28, 1917, the IWW local in Bisbee, Arizona, called a strike in the area's copper mines. Copper was essential to the war effort, copper wiring being used for communications between trenches. Sheriff Harry Wheeler, a former Rough Rider, joined Governor Thomas Campbell in requesting federal troops. But the War Department's observer, Lieutenant Colonel James J. Hornbrook, reported that everything was peaceful, and the President refrained from action. Wheeler now deputized two thousand men and deported the Wobblies from Bisbee. This vigilante-style action brought criticism from the President, and the U.S. Army looked after the welfare of the deported men. It is possible that Wilson would have taken further remedial action, but for the strategic value of the copper mines and his enmity toward the IWW. As it was, he appointed a Mediation Commission, and was looked to by the revolutionary Big Bill Haywood as the only possible source of fair intervention.[23]

Much can be and has been justly said in criticism of the Wilson administration's disregard of civil liberties.[24] But in the sphere of labor relations pure and simple, the Democratic President continued in the style vigorously if imperfectly dictated by the Republican Theodore Roosevelt. By the end of Wilson's second term, it was generally expected of the President that he should take a lead in calming labor disturbances. When Wilson, preoccupied with affairs in Europe and his League of Nations proposal, refrained from intervening in the severe labor troubles in 1919, he was criticized for neglect of duty. Senator Henry Cabot Lodge of Massachusetts, Republican chairman of the Foreign Relations Committee, urged him to drop the League proposal and to concentrate on America's domestic problems.[25]

The lessons of the previous two decades were driven home once again during the attempts of the UMWA between 1919 and 1922 to recruit new members in the Border States and elsewhere. In May 1920 guards supplied to operators by the Baldwin-Felts Agency (which, like the Pinkerton Agency, took its loyalties to employers more seriously than most other detective agencies) challenged the sheriff of Mingo County, Sid Hatfield, and his deputies in a gun battle leaving ten dead men in its wake. In nearby Logan County, the operators controlled the sheriff, whose deputies were in their pay. In the early part of 1921, the miners took to arms. Since the state militia had proved ineffective in Logan County, Republican President Warren G. Harding acceded to the governor's request for federal troops. Harding's decision was beyond reproach because twenty-one men had already been killed. The arrival of 2,100 U.S. soldiers ended the disturbance immediately. In the summer of 1922, the President agreed to further requests for federal troops from the governors of West Virginia, Pennsylvania, Tennessee, Wyoming, Utah, New Mexico, Oklahoma, Kansas, and Washington. In spite of Harding's known hostility to organized labor, the miners in these states accepted the military in a peaceful spirit (there were no soldiers present at Herrin, Illinois, where twenty-one died in a gun battle). They were not demoralized by federal intervention, and the UMWA won a satisfactory nationwide agreement with the operators.[26]

Theodore Roosevelt tolerated labor unions but remained prejudiced toward labor unions in the West and toward the IWW; Woodrow Wilson tolerated labor unions in the West but did not uphold the rights of Wobblies. In 1934, Democratic President Franklin D. Roosevelt showed clearly that he respected the Constitutional rights of the Wobblies' successors on the extreme left, the Communists. The West Coast longshoremen's strike had, under the socialist leadership of Harry Bridges, tied up the port of San Francisco. At a time when the President was cruising aboard the U.S.S. *Houston* in the Pacific, great pressure was brought on him to intervene with federal force in San Francisco. But in the absence of evidence to confirm Bridges' alleged use of coercion, Roosevelt refrained from action. The principles of the "Square Deal" were alive and healthy in the "New Deal" period (1933–1941).[27]

The organization of labor was the first major protest movement in the twentieth century. It came to be rivaled and to a certain extent superseded in dramatic impact by the black movement. If one is to consider both movements within the same rubric, one should be on guard against assuming that the black protest movement and its relation to government and order were part of labor's historic heritage. For there was little communication or interchange of personnel between the two groups. Labor unionists in urban America thought of blacks as potential strikebreakers because, as the history of the Chicago teamsters' strike of 1905 shows, newly arrived blacks did at times assume this role. Blacks thought of white trade unionists as racists because ever since the 1890s organized labor, from Samuel Gompers down, had obstructed the entry of blacks into union membership. One of the first significant breakthroughs for black unionism in the twentieth century was the organization of the Brotherhood of Sleeping Car Porters in 1925 by A. Philip Randolph, an initiative of, by, and for black workers. It was not until the campaigns of Walter Reuther in the 1940s and the civil-rights movement of the 1960s that black inclusion in a multiracial labor movement was taken seriously. For these reasons, one should not accept lightly any theory suggesting that blacks learned from labor unionists how to cope with violent social conflicts.[28]

It does not follow, of course, that government did not learn from industrial riots how to cope with race riots. Furthermore, blacks were part of the same society as labor unionists and many of the problems they confronted in trying to better their conditions were similar. Yet even here, qualifications are in order. In terms of law enforcement, they presented a different problem and therefore encountered different responses. Whereas a labor union might present an organized threat to law and order, possibly carrying ideological or revolutionary implications, the black movement presented rather the specter of social destabilization, at once less menacing to the political system and less tractable. Another difference between labor and black movements was that blacks did not have to contend with the attentions of private detective agencies. The revival of the Ku Klux Klan in 1915 and the continued operation in the twentieth century of neovigilante groups and gangs comprised unequivocal opposition to black advancement rather than an attempt to fleece businessmen and hoodwink the media.

The labor and black experiences are, however, similar in that they both reflect and highlight strengths and weaknesses, variable and endemic, in the U.S. law enforcement system. Of particular note in this context are the impartiality or otherwise of federal interventions, the vexatious issue of gubernatorial versus mayoral responsibility for the preservation of order in cities, and the questions of shrieval weakness and police inadequacies.

A proper account of law enforcement and the black in the nineteenth century would concentrate (as many have) on the southern states: on the suppression of slave rebellions, the enactment of Black Codes immediately after Appomattox, the occupation of the South by federal soldiers during Radical Reconstruction, the terrorist activities of white night riders, and the eventual military enforcement of Jim Crow legislation and customs.[29] This history gave the blacks who migrated north—a million by 1910, half a million more by 1920—a set of attitudes. But it is generally recognized that blacks, who needed no convincing that their treatment hitherto was the single greatest indictment of American civilization, became more militant as a result of their experience in the extrasouthern factories and armies of World War I. By the summer of 1919, when America's heroes returned from the front, the black sections of several cities were poised to launch one of the most aggressive rebellions in black American history.[30]

The Chicago race riot started on July 27, 1919, when a teen-age black swimmer, Eugene Williams, strayed accidentally toward a white section of the beach and was stoned to death in Lake Michigan. A white policeman refused to arrest the white murderer who had thrown the fatal brick. This incident typified one of the Chicago blacks' grievances, that the police were biased against them, and sparked off the worst race riot of a violent year.[31]

Mayor William Hale "Big Bill" Thompson waited until the evening of July 30 before calling in the state militia. Assisted by rain and a drop in temperature, the militia brought the riot under control within two days, but in the uncontrolled period after Eugene Williams' death, thirty-seven people (fifteen whites and twenty-three blacks) were killed. The reasons for Thompson's delay in using the militia are reminiscent of the earlier labor history of the city. In the first place, Chicago's "Black Belt" had twice provided the crucial block vote that returned Thompson to office as mayor. Thompson waited until the blacks themselves demanded soldiers—he was afraid that any premature use of state troops would be interpreted as a hostile reaction by his most loyal group of supporters. To adapt one of Roosevelt's phrases, he was "truckling to the Negro vote." [32]

Furthermore, Thompson was in political rivalry with Illinois Governor Frank O. Lowden. The two men led opposed factions of the Republican Party, and each had Presidential aspirations. Lowden immediately mobilized the state militia in preparation for law enforcement in what he anticipated might be a major race riot in Chicago. Thompson refused at first to accept the help offered to him. The mayor's refusal of troops stemmed partly from political reasons—his fear of black retaliation at the polls and his ambition to show he could handle a race riot without outside help from his political rival. Indeed, Thompson was not the only politician to be accused in 1919 of advancing his career through the judicious handling of riots. During the Boston police strike of 1919, Governor Calvin Coolidge of Massachusetts, running for reelection and courting Presidential stature, was thought by some to have refrained from using state troops to stop looting until his action could be presented in the most favorable light.[33]

On the other hand, in delaying the introduction of troops Mayor Thompson did have reason to fear that intervention by forces under Lowden's control would be biased in favor of whites and therefore provocative. In the East St. Louis race riot of 1917, Governor Lowden had introduced state soldiers and showed little concern when, along with the local police, they sided openly with the whites instead of protecting the hard-pressed Negro population. In 1918 Lowden had incurred Thompson's displeasure by sending troops into Chicago on the supposition that a riot was about to occur. It did not occur, and while it is true that it might have but for the arrival of troops, it was not politically advisable for Lowden to take unilateral preemptive action in 1919.[34]

Charges of racial bias in connection with the Chicago riot abounded.

Although the militia, perhaps chastened by criticism arising from its role in East St. Louis, behaved with firmness and impartiality, the police had sided with the whites on several occasions during the riots. After the riot, the blacks' difficulties in obtaining compensation for property damage, and their conviction in disproportionate numbers on charges arising from the riot (in spite of the higher black casualty rate, suggesting there were more white than black criminals) indicated that, as in the case of so many labor union trials in the nineteenth century, the laws were being unequally applied.[35]

Charges of injustice arising from governmental responses to riots were by no means limited to Chicago. They were already being made in the aftermath of the Washington riot of July 19, 1919, and the few days following. Harlem's *Amsterdam News* noted that Washington had black patrolmen in the police force, but they had not been deployed in the riot. W. E. B. DuBois, editor of the radical civil-rights periodical *The Crisis,* agreed with the *News* that Washington's police were notoriously biased against blacks. Du Bois maintained that the police restored order only when the blacks started to get the upper hand in some of the street fighting. As in the case of Chicago's riots, the courts were particularly hard on blacks indicted in connection with the Washington disturbances, and this caused further resentment.[36]

In the aftermath of the Washington riot, the *New York Post* and the social reform periodical *Survey* revived the blacks' own demands for a federal anti-lynching law. This tactic resembled that of the labor injunction. On the one hand, it merely made two crimes out of one, for there was no way of making the crime of murder more criminal than it already was. But the real purpose was to involve the federal government in local situations, in the expectation that the statesmen of Washington would be relatively impartial. There were, however, two contemporary circumstances serving to dim this expectation. First. U.S. sailors and marines had been instrumental in starting the Washington riot following an alleged discourtesy toward the wife of a naval aviation serviceman. As in the Los Angeles "zoot suit" riots in World War II, members of the U.S. armed forces proved troublesome when not under the discipline of their officers (though the political scientist Arthur I. Waskow has remarked that "the distinction between the partiality of the Washington police and the relative impartiality of the federal troops once they intervened as an official unit was not lost on observers").[37]

A second factor that seemed to bode ill for the prospects of an impartial federal intervention was the attitude of President Wilson. During the East St. Louis riot, in which nine white people and thirty-nine
blacks were killed, the President, though fully appraised of the situation,
resisted all pressures from the newspapers and refused to intervene or
even comment. At a time when ex-President Theodore Roosevelt was
demanding "the fullest investigation into these murders" and threatening to punch Gompers for alleging that the East St. Louis blacks were
strikebreakers, Wilson's inactivity and silence were widely interpreted as
conspicuous confirmation of his racism.[38] In refusing to intervene, the
President may have been mindful of Cleveland's political setback in
overriding Altgeld in 1894 and cautious about rushing in to help
Lowden, a Republican governor with Presidential aspirations. The con-
sistency of his behavior toward blacks does suggest, however, that he
was prejudiced. Pleading League of Nations business and illness, he
failed to respond to a 30,000-strong petition appealing against the
severity of Negroes' sentences following the Washington riot.[39] Against
this discouraging background, the faith of *The Crisis* group and other
blacks in federal impartiality was testimony to the degree of obstinacy
they were encountering in nonfederal branches of the American police
system.

The history of organized labor has been one of sustained, organized
pressure, and labor riots have recurred fairly constantly not just in the
years subjected to special scrutiny in Chapter 2 (1890–1909), but
throughout the period from the 1860s to the 1930s. While race riots,
like labor riots, have spread to most parts of urban America, they have
occurred in concentrated bursts. In 1917–1918, 1943, and the mid-
1960s, they affected several cities at roughly the same time. But the
outbreaks have been relatively irregular over a period of several
decades. Perhaps for this reason among others, public officials responsible for law enforcement have been slow to learn from the history of
past race riots. However, the failure of these officials to apply the lessons of recent and contemporary labor history to the solution of police
problems arising from race disturbances also indicates the existence of
different layers of prejudice and the survival of inbuilt political and
Constitutional weaknesses.

The most serious race riot of 1943 began in Detroit on Sunday, June
20, and lasted for a week. Thirty-four people, twenty-five black and
nine white, were killed. As in the cases of the Los Angeles riot that

preceded it and the Harlem disturbance that followed on August 1 in the wake of the shooting of a black serviceman by a white policeman, poor relations between Negroes (Mexican-Americans in Los Angeles) and the police made the restoration of order difficult. The Detroit Chapter of the National Association for the Advancement of Colored People complained early in July 1943: "There is overwhelming evidence that the riot could have been stopped in Detroit at its inception Sunday night had the police wanted to stop it. So inefficient is the police force and so many of its members are from the deep South, with all their anti-Negro prejudices and Klan sympathies. . . ." [40]

As in the Los Angeles riots, off-duty sailors from the U.S. Navy played a prominent part in aggravating the 1943 street fighting in Detroit. Yet when federal troops arrived under the command of their officers, order was restored. Michigan's Governor Harry F. Kelly and Detroit's Mayor Edward J. Jeffries had been slow to resort to this help: The riots having started on Sunday, June 20, the troops did not arrive until Tuesday, June 22. Jeffries pleaded inexperience: "It will not take us that long next time [to obtain help]. . . . The responsible authorities at all three levels of government, City, State, and Federal, were greenhorns in this area of race riots, but we are greenhorns no longer. We are veterans. I admit we made some mistakes, but we will not make the same ones again." His critics alleged he was soft on law enforcement because of his sympathy for the Negroes. [41]

Charges of bias and political opportunism were levied yet again against an official responsible for law enforcement in 1957. On this occasion the federal courts ordered the desegregation of Central High School, Little Rock, Arkansas. Integration was to take place there, as elsewhere in Arkansas and the United States, in the aftermath of the Supreme Court's *Brown v. Board of Education* decision three years earlier, to the effect that separate educational facilities for blacks and whites meant inferior education for the former and a deprivation of Constitutionally guaranteed rights. When Orval Faubus, in a successful appeal for red-neck support for reelection to the state governorship, used National Guardsmen to keep the Central High School white, President Dwight D. Eisenhower introduced the authority of the Army to uphold the law as interpreted in U.S. courts. The first such use of federal troops in the South since Reconstruction was reminiscent of Cleveland's overruling of Altgeld in 1894 and was justified by precedents extending back to the Whiskey Rebellion of 1784. But the fact that Eisenhower and his local commanding officer, Colonel Edwin Walker, were reluctant integrationists enhanced the impression already prevailing outside conservative circles in the white South that federal intervention meant impartial law enforcement.[42]

During the urban race riots of the 1960s, perennial defects in law enforcement agencies were still in evidence. According to the Negro journalist Alex Haley, Captain Lloyd Sealy, sent to help calm Harlem after the assassination of El-Hajj Malik El-Shabazz (Malcolm X) on February 21, 1965, was "New York City's first Negro to command a precinct." The Watts County (Los Angeles) race riots of the same year were policed by handpicked, well-trained, and highly paid officers. Their leader was William H. Parker, whose father had been superintendent of the Homestake Mining Company, Lead, South Dakota, the largest gold mine in the United States in the Theodore Roosevelt years and the scene of a turbulent WFM strike in 1909. In spite of (or perhaps because of) this background, the Los Angeles police chief, though a highly professional officer in other respects, failed to appreciate the importance of impartiality. The Homestake dispute was something he could only "dimly remember" (he was seven years old at the time); that the lessons of labor history were lost on this man confronted with a 1960s racial conflict is indicated by his remarks deploring the liberal Supreme Court of Chief Justice Earl Warren and likening the actions of black Watts County rioters to those of "monkeys in a zoo." However well trained, Parker's policemen were white and unable to establish a reputation for impartiality in a predominantly black area.[43]

In contrast, the U.S. Army was desegregated as a result of executive orders issued by President Harry Truman and of the exigencies of the Korean War. Furthermore, the Army had maintained its expertise in handling civil disturbances. According to the *Report of the National Advisory Commission on Civil Disorders* (1968), the Army had "designated seven task forces, each of brigade size (approximately 2,000 men), to be immediately available for assignment to control civil disorders in the event federal troops are needed." The same source noted that "within hours" after the arrival of federal paratroops in Detroit on July 24, 1967, the hitherto "riot-torn area occupied by them was the quietest in the city." In the same year, the Department of Defense began to bring pressure on the National Guards of various states to recruit Negro soldiers, as the U.S. Army already had done.[44]

Race riots tested anew America's agencies and procedures for the preservation of order. Their history, like the story of labor violence, shows that some weaknesses in the system were remediable through changes in the law, in institutions and in public opinion. The history of major disturbances since the nineteenth century also suggests, however, that U.S. Constitutional provisions and state constitutions do not pin with sufficient clarity the ultimate responsibility for law enforcement on any one public official. In a federalist, pluralist democracy in which executive officials have to think about public opinion and votes, this imprecision has led to many fatal delays.

Chapter 10

Social Conflict
and Progressivism

REFORMERS OF THE U.S. ARMY AND OTHER LAW ENFORCEMENT AGEN-
cies between 1894 and 1916 often justified their measures by referring to the necessity of being able to handle labor violence. As we
have seen, the scope of the problem of labor, or class, violence was
not really physically definable in the Progressive period (1901–1916),
but the phenomenon was exaggerated for a variety of reasons and motives. The Progressives themselves, like the Army reformers, private
detectives, and others with interests at stake, tended to exaggerate industrial violence for reasons of their own. But it would be a mistake
to say simply that the Progressives exploited violence, using it
calculatingly to justify some of their proposals. Such a statement needs
to be qualified with the observation that genuine belief in a labor violence problem helped to motivate some Progressives, making them
particularly anxious to achieve social reforms.

To some extent, this idea is congruent with established historical
opinions on Progressivism. The connection between social conflict and
reform has been noted often enough. For example, the neo-Marxist
intellectual and Bolshevik leader V. I. Lenin argued that in capitalism's impending crisis, workers were becoming impoverished and
revolutionary in outlook. To fend them off, the capitalist class recruited
a bourgeois aristocracy of labor to its side, paying high wages to

skilled workers such as those in Gompers' AFL. To finance this policy, the businessmen launched imperialism, creaming off the wealth of weaker countries. Finally, the capitalists initiated or tolerated ameliorative reforms with altruism on their lips and self-preservation in their minds.[1]

Lenin thought this theory a good fit for American politics in 1912. Since his death in 1924, the idea that America's favored classes resorted to reform out of self-defense has found expression in several forms, for example in the historical works of Richard Hofstadter, Gabriel Kolko, Robert H. Wiebe, David P. Thelen, and Walter T. K. Nugent. However, it is clear in retrospect—as most of these historians would readily acknowledge—that the American workers were far from revolutionary in 1912. Furthermore, the widespread introduction of machinery in the United States and the resultant rise of the semiskilled worker diminished the wage gulf between unskilled and AFL workers. The analyses of Hofstadter and the other historians just listed are vulnerable to criticism because in a society as fluid as that of the United States, it is difficult to identify "middle," "ruling," or "upper" classes. Yet in spite of all this, we shall see below that the responses of diverse people to the specter of class violence and revolution were indeed an important factor, especially in the election year of 1912.[2]

If in the latter respect the evidence in this book upholds one of the main, broad interpretations of American reform, it also suggests that several qualifications and refinements are in order. First, the critical violence and class conflict that many Progressives perceived were imaginary. We have also seen in the preceding chapters that the stress placed on labor violence was the result, not solely of a collective desire to preserve the status of a middle or capitalist class, however defined, but of several different motivations such as the detective's desire to stay in business and the journalist's ambition to sell newspapers. We shall see below that several short-term pressures for reform just before 1912 arose in a picturesquely diverse rather than uniformly predatory way from labor's imagined proclivity for violence. Nor should one overlook, in the midst of theorizing, those reformers who regarded violence as the outcome of misery and sincerely wanted to diminish that misery.

Finally, it is clear that the Progressives' emphasis on violence, tactical or sincere, was instrumental in defeating the objective of social reform cherished by increasing numbers for so many different reasons.

The prospect of social conflict did goad some people to support reform, but it also produced a decisively strong reactionary spirit. Propaganda about violence failed to win massive support for reform in the Progressive period for the further reason that it had no charisma for the consumer, a powerful new force in politics. When women won the vote in 1920, the social-conflict-based reform tactic was doomed because it made no appeal to the self-interest of society's chief consumer, the housewife. Nevertheless, the issue of violence was to be raised once again with equally punitive consequences in the 1960s.

Although President Theodore Roosevelt made some conservatives nervous by speaking too often of social reforms, his main response to labor violence had been to suppress it as fairly as possible.[3] By 1910 the climate of political opinion was beginning to change, and many Americans came to see ameliorative reform rather than repression, however fair, as a way of solving the labor problem. In the period leading up to the Presidential campaign of 1912, social reformers pressed for particular pieces of legislation and for the establishment of a U.S. Commission on Industrial Relations with the purpose of establishing a blueprint for social change.

It seemed wise for social reformers to stress the issue of class conflict in the preelection days of 1912, because the discussion of violence, prevalent enough over the past decade, received sharp impetus from a number of short-term factors. These contributed to what the *Nation,* in June 1912, described as a "Vogue for Violence." That periodical deplored the violence that supporters of Theodore Roosevelt had threatened at the Republican Convention: "This tendency to substitute violence for reason and the argument of pike and gun for logic has had many recent manifestations not directly political. It seems to be getting the fashion to think in terms of force, not intelligence." [4]

Always charismatic, violence exercised a specially mesmeric influence on the intelligentsia for a short period, for diverse and coincidental reasons. For example, feminists who were entering their most militant phase created an attitude of tolerance toward other forms of militancy. Reflecting entirely different aspirations, social workers Henry Moscowitz and Lillian Wald deplored the 1912 "crime wave" in New York City and irrationally linked it with industrial violence.[5]

Nickelodeons (cheaper than dime novels) appealed to the illiterate or non-English-speaking poor. But the portrayal of violence in films did give it an intellectual currency. In 1902 the prototype of the modern, violent Western hero had appeared in Owen Wister's *The Virginian: A Horseman of the Plains.* The burgeoning film industry fastened onto crime as a theme and linked it with unionism. The French film *Sabotage* was translated as *Union Workers Spoil the Food.* Movies boosted the prestige of the detective. *The Capture of the Yegg Bank Burglars* (1904) was based on a talk by none other than W. A. Pinkerton.

Indigenous and foreign influences merged when city newspapers awoke to the eastern incursions of the IWW, and simultaneously French and German subjectivist literature came to America in translation. In 1912 and 1913 a number of pamphlets and books were published in the United States that dealt with syndicalism and treated the French idea of sabotage and the philosophy of the IWW as one. According to the historian Philip Foner, Emile Pouget's *Sabotage* and George Sorel's *Reflexions sur la violence* were in circulation in America following Haywood's visit to Europe in 1910. C. H. Kerr of Chicago published Arturo M. Giovannitti's translation of *Sabotage* in 1913. Sorel's *Reflexions* was published in New York in the following year in English translation.[6]

Anarchism, in a revived, more fashionable form, was another short-term influence contributing to a vogue for violence in the period of Progressive ferment. Hitherto, anarchists had been persecuted for their alleged violence. In the early 1890s, in the wake of the Haymarket bomb trial and an attempt by one of their number on the life of Homestead lockout protagonist H. C. Frick, anarchists found it difficult to gain a hearing. The assassination of McKinley was a further setback. Emma Goldman had to publish under an assumed name. She wrote to the editors of *Metropolitan Magazine* in December 1905: "It is true that I have gained an unpleasant notoriety which, however undeserved, may militate against me in a measure. . . ." But in that year Miss Goldman emerged once again under her own name, and in March 1906 the first issue of her anarchist magazine *Mother Earth* appeared. The anarchist cause gained further popularity in 1907 through the pages of Hutchins Hapgood's *The Spirit of Labor,* a book set in the Chicago of labor bosses "Skinny" Madden and Cornelius Shea and extolling, by contrast with their malpractices, the virtues of philosophical anarchism.[7]

Violent rebellion against society was the anarchist's ultimate license, and it is significant that the reputedly violent anarchists received more admiration and attention than the philosophical. The man who had attempted to kill Frick, Alexander Berkman, became for a while the darling of literary and social circles. He contributed to the journal published by his former mistress, Emma Goldman. *Mother Earth* was almost explicit in its advocacy of violence:

> The most important strikes during the last twenty years have been lost to labor. Defeat was due to lack of industrial organization, and the passivity and reliance on the "peaceful methods" advised by misleaders. "Don't alienate public opinion by law-breaking," is the pious advice to starving strikers. Yet "public sentiment" does not seem to be alienated by the violence of the masters. . . . Strikers, as a whole, are entirely too continent.[8]

It was a cause as well as a symptom of the vogue for violence that the social groups to which every radical intellectual aspired were enamored of the irrationalist creed. One of the groups most critical of American society during the Progressive period was the J. G. Phelps Stokes–William English Walling circle. Stokes bought an island off Stamford, Connecticut, and there he built houses for himself and his close friends Walling and Leroy Scott. Walling was an early critic of the conservative oligarchy of the Socialist Party (including, to their common embarrassment, Robert Hunter, who had married Stokes' sister, Caroline). He wrote a book on the Russian Revolution of 1905. Leroy Scott, the third inhabitant of Caritas Island, in the same year published *Walking Delegate,* a novel whose antihero was a union plug-ugly and whose hero sought to redeem his union through equally violent means.[9]

The list of house guests at Caritas Island illustrates the preoccupation of the influential "millionaire socialist" group with violence, real or imagined. It included the anarchists Emma Goldman and Leonard Abbott, Elizabeth Gurley Flynn and several other Wobblies, in addition to such front-runners and forerunners of radicalism as Maxim Gorky, socialist artist Rockwell Kent, and the slippery fugitive from justice M. A. Schmidt, the dynamiter for the IABSI said to have participated, later, in the *Los Angeles Times* explosion (after which William Burns and the police failed to trace him). Mrs. Stokes made a particular friend of Patrick Quinlan, later arrested for his activities in the IWW's Paterson strike.[10]

Less dedicated to socialism but instrumental in creating a middle- and upper-class interest in violence and protest was Mabel Dodge. To her successful New York salon she enticed, largely through Hutchins

Hapgood, the radicals hitherto regarded by society as social ogres. Mrs Dodge's own reaction to her protégés was mixed. Haywood she claimed to have tamed forever by showing him that a millionairess could be human; Goldman and Berkman she found intractable and a little too real in their violence. Nevertheless, she did not resist the temptation to have them confront society in her salon. Mrs. Dodge took credit also for having thought of the Paterson pageant, when the brutalities of that infamous strike were reenacted and brought home to New Yorkers at Madison Square Garden—whose Tower (erected by the redoubtable open-shop constructor W. H. McCord) that evening was surrounded on four sides by the letters "IWW" in bright red lights, ten feet tall.[11]

The satirist Carl Van Vechten captured the spirit in which the middle-class vogue was enacted: "When dulness, beating its tiresome wings, seemed to hover over the group, she [Mabel Dodge] had a habit of introducing new elements into the discussion, or new figures into the group itself, and one day . . . she transferred her interest to the laboring man, to unions, to strikes, to the IWW." Then it was that the six-foot-three-inch-tall Bill Haywood became the idol of the day, "crushing the heels of his huge boots into the Shirvan rug" as he spoke of violence while "débutantes knelt on the floor beside him." The atmosphere at Mabel Dodge's salon was not one of serious social concern: It was a mixture of rather desperate excitement and cynicism. But her experiment was publicized because, as Henry May put it, "the press were fascinated [and much invited]: New York had never heard of parties where women in evening dress not only smoked but discussed all sorts of things with roughnecks and Bohemians." [12]

Mrs. Dodge helped to make the middle class receptive to the vogue for violence. It was not that she sustained firm political beliefs. Her interest in radicalism developed suddenly with her affection for the young socialist John Reed. Nor did she travel widely in the United States to disseminate her newfound interests: Only Massachusetts and upstate New York diverted her from New York City or her European haunts. It was sufficient that she provided a clearinghouse for fashionable fads and imbued each fresh idea with the prestige of her acquaintanceship with such as Gertrude Stein, Isadora Duncan, Lincoln Steffens, Walter Lippmann, and others who left an imprint on the American mind.

The vogue for violence was not entirely a matter of pleasant, vicarious thrills. There was an underlying element of fear. On one level, the impressionable Mrs. Dodge was reluctant to enter a taxicab with Alexander Berkman. On a different level, hardheaded men responded to the threat of unrest. In January 1915 the efficacy of disorder in achieving reform was suggested in an editorial in *The New Republic,* the new magazine launched by political commentators Walter Weyl, Herbert Croly, and Walter Lippmann. The editorial described various industrial conditions, for example, labor espionage, terrorism, and unrest; averred that capitalists had displayed ignorance of such conditions in hearings before the CIR; and declared that riots were essential to educate the nation in the need for change.

> Last winter the IWW invaded the churches of New York. This winter the churches had organized to deal with unemployment. Last winter there were riots. This winter the head of the United States Steel Corporation is chairman of the committee to deal with unemployment. Of course there may be no causal connection. The committee which he heads is, however, not prepared to deal very drastically with the situation; certain city officials are very obstructive. There has been no unemployed demonstration this winter. Of course there may be no causal connection.[13]

Collectively, the various intellectual threads creating a vogue for violence among educated people had an impact on national political leaders. Croly tried hard to channel Roosevelt's sanguinary nationalism along Progressive lines, in the belief that this tactic would prevent conservatives from utilizing the contemporary irrationalist creed. In 1912 Colonel E. M. House, the future advisor to President Woodrow Wilson, anonymously published his propaganda novel *Philip Dru: Administrator,* proposing that "the seething, radical elements in the political cask today, under pressure of rising prices for the poor and greater privileges for the rich, [might] literally burst into one great conflict, the Second Civil War." House showed what could be done (in fiction, at least) for the less fortunate, through international adjustment and social amelioration.[14]

The vogue for violence seemed a gift to reformers. Many of them allowed the current mood to dictate their tactics. Social conflict was at the root of agitation for a federal commission on industrial relations and of reform politics generally in the months leading up to the Presidential election of 1912. Social reformers and politicians perceived, or at least talked of, a dangerous, radical threat to the social order.

Agitation for the federal commission was led by the *Survey* group.

Those associated with the social-work periodical naturally had experience of industrial conflict. Graham Taylor, for example, had been appointed to an abortive commission directed by Mayor Edward F. Dunne to investigate the Chicago riots of 1905. His close associate Edward Devine, editor of *Survey,* wrote after the McNamaras' confession that he feared a Sorelian philosophy of dynamite would sweep the United States.[15]

The self-constituted New York committee, which on December 30, 1911, urged President Taft to set up an industrial inquiry, confessed that it first met "at a time when the great bulk of comment provoked by the McNamara confessions was that of reproach, betrayal, and condemnation," but argued defiantly that investigation was the only answer to dynamite. Devine, Washington Gladden, and others who argued before the House Committee on Labor for the CIR repeated over and over again the dangers implied in the words "McNamara," "Lawrence," and "IWW." So did the pamphlets circulated by the pro-CIR lobby, the Committee on Industrial Relations. These were written by such men as William Borah and William Hughes (sponsors of the necessary congressional legislation), Roosevelt, Taft, and distinguished economists, such as J. B. Clark of Columbia University. Every congressman was written to by the organized social-reform lobby, usually in the language of crisis. Not many replied in the level-headed tone of Senator W. S. Heyburn of Idaho, that "the [labor] conflicts are merely a process of adjustment between people who must eventually engage in mutual enterprise." [16]

The tactic of using violence as propaganda for social reform was not confined to New York. On February 3, 1912, Jane Addams called to order a meeting at the City Club of Chicago with a view to lobbying for a federal industrial commission. Despite the argument of Mrs. Emmons Blaine against any emphasis on the McNamara case, it was evident to most of those present, who included the future CIR researchers Luke Grant, Robert Hoxie, and Harold Ickes, that violence was politically exploitable.[17]

Lobbying for a federal commission on industrial relations was complicated by the political upheaval taking place between 1910 and 1912. The Socialist Party was making a serious challenge for the ballots of the American voter. Both traditional parties were attempting to present their platforms and candidates as "Progressive."

It was in a spirit of pragmatism that Jane Addams, not always noted for her political adroitness, endorsed the idea of cajoling the major parties by using the dual threat of socialism and La Follette. La Follette was making a strong bid for the support of social reformers. Standard-bearer of the Progressive Republican League, he had announced his candidacy for the Republican nomination as early as June 17, 1911. Already Miss Addams had blessed the logic of one of La Follette's political and financial backers, Representative William Kent of California. Kent, who accepted Hiram Johnson's argument that it was not necessary to be a "regular Republican," estimated that only a strong Progressive rival would force the Democrats to choose a non-reactionary candidate of their own. Miss Addams approved of Kent's "words of wisdom" that "failing this fight [within the Republican Party for a Progressive challenger] and granting reactionaries on both sides, the people would naturally turn to the Socialists. This end is not one to be desired at the present time. I believe that a fight made for La Follette would force the Democrats to take up a positive character like Wilson." Close to "Fighting Bob" was the influential labor economist John Commons. In January 1912 Commons was suggesting "planks for the next platform" to the midwestern insurgent and passing on ideas from former Populists and interested intellectuals. But in February, Roosevelt belatedly declared his own candidacy for the Republican nomination, and this changed the complexion of things for La Follette.[18]

Big business leaders had a greater faith in Roosevelt. They were willing to accept reform measures from the former President, and indeed some of them had a bad conscience over labor. A few of these wished to atone for past deeds. John D. Rockefeller, Jr., started his own industrial inquiry. The McCormicks turned to social work. But George Perkins of United States Steel, who was eager to finance the Republican Party and, in 1912, the Progressive Party, advanced a strictly political appraisal of events. He was (in November 1910) concerned with the growth of the Socialist vote and the "rapidly approaching . . . crisis in this country on the question of the relation between capital and labor and business and the State."[19] La Follette was too radical for such men. Thus, when Roosevelt accepted the Progressive Party's nomination in 1912, he won better business backing than a third-party candidate could normally expect.

The "soundness" of Roosevelt from the viewpoint of reformers as well as businessmen was reinforced by the rhetoric he liked to employ.

The former President thought, with a touching faith in his own mission, that those less radical than he were dangerous reactionaries, those more radical, dangerous extremists, danger in each instance being the possibility of social disorder. He adhered to his position in a retrospective correspondence with Charles McCarthy (normally apolitical, McCarthy had rooted for Roosevelt in 1912, and the pair remained loyal to each other thereafter). In one letter, he expressed his view concisely:

> I am sure that the reaction in Wisconsin and, indeed, over the nation, is only temporary. As regards the nation, we have certainly suffered partly for the sins of some of the extremists. Reformers are the salt of the earth, and without salt one can't get a decent dinner; but a dinner composed exclusively of salt is not worth much! Here in New York some of the men who nominally stayed with us, like Amos Pinchot, really tried to turn the Progressive Party into an aid to the IWW, or a kind of parlor-anarchist association; and the public finally became convinced that we were altogether too much tainted with lunacy. But in Wisconsin it seems to me as though your University work, and such work as your own special bureau, have been so excellent as to deprive people of any sense of revolt.[20]

Immediately after the McNamara confessions, social reformers had only one political channel open to them, because President Taft was in office. It was he who had recommended the Federal Commission on Industrial Relations in a special message to the Sixty-second Congress on February 2, 1912. His terms of reference were broad and acceptable. The message stated that the trust issue had diverted attention from an equally important problem, class conflict. It further stated: "What is urgently needed today is a re-examination of our laws bearing upon the relations of employer and employee and a careful and discriminating scrutiny of the various plans which are being tried in several of our own states and in other countries." The pundits of comparative reform could bask in Presidential approval. But Taft had visibly lost his grip on the American consensus by 1912. He was of no use to the pragmatic reformer. His failure to nominate commissioners acceptable to Progressive reformers had further alienated their support, which therefore became available to the highest respectable bidder.[21]

In that the Democrats took on Woodrow Wilson, as Jane Addams and William Kent had intended, reformers' tactics apparently succeeded. In that Roosevelt took up the standard of social reform but went down to defeat, the same tactics were rewarded and punished, respectively. In a sense, reformers were quite irrelevant as lobbyists, in spite of their direct access to Roosevelt through McCarthy, Lippmann, and other intellectuals. Businessmen and politicians could see, unaided, that a conspicuous gesture would have to be made with respect to labor-capital conflict. If the actions of Perkins and Taft are not sufficient evidence of this, then the actions of Wilson are. As President, he consciously steered a leftward course in order to avail himself of the radical current, while at the same time keeping windward of revolution. On becoming President, he not only endorsed the CIR, but appointed John R. Commons, the mentor of contemporary social reformers, commissioner to represent the public.

When Wilson won the election of 1912, it seemed at first that social reformers would fail to benefit from their equivalent of the spoils of office, legislation. Yet the general concern over radicalism and conflict had, apparently, saved the day.

The United States Commission on Industrial Relations was a fact of political life during the first Wilson administration. Part of its significance lay in its existence independent of the Democratic and Republican parties but not alienated from them. In this way, the group was different from organized factions hitherto noted for their social reform agitation. Its Research Division, together with the legislative and administrative machinery that it proposed, offered a mechanism that was new (although foreshadowed in the states and in the philanthropic foundations) and recognized the realities of political power. Nothing attested to this more than the exodus from the Socialist Party of such astute young men as Leiserson, Witte, and Ickes, all active on behalf of the Research Division.

Second, the CIR had potential for success in that it represented a large government appropriation to finance the social research of university intellectuals. Support for the scheme came from all four political parties contesting the 1912 election.

Finally, the CIR was important to social reform because it had the opportunity of defining what legislative changes were needed and of drafting appropriate legislation. The Research Division was to undertake the drafting, in the light of what public hearings and discreet research uncovered. Americans had heard about the drawbacks of industrialism from Walt Whitman, Upton Sinclair, and a multitude in between. Now they were to hear what could be done. Change was to be put on an "efficient" basis, and politicians provided with a standard by which to judge their own success or failure.

The CIR was, as of 1912, neither guaranteed of success nor doomed to failure; it was up to its personnel to make the most of their opportunity. It was true that the reformers' lack of enthusiasm about Wilson in 1912 did not constitute an ideal start, but then, any practical reformer would eventually be glad to come to terms with political reality.

The question to be answered, then, concerns the ideas and achievements of the CIR reformers themselves. What did they accomplish? A review of the personnel, plans, and achievements of the CIR throws light on the question. And it emerges, on balance, that the intellectuals did not merit the trust placed in them, through the political parties, by the public.

Frank P. Walsh, chairman of the CIR, had overall responsibility for its activities. He concerned himself mainly with its public hearings because he thought that the commission's chief function was educational—to direct the public's attention to industrial grievances hitherto overlooked through indolence and to create a climate for reform by pointing to the misdeeds and violence of the oppressors, thereby redressing the balance in favor of the oppressed.

Charles McCarthy of the Research Division would at first seem to have been a man of more scholarly bent. His quarrels with Walsh and with Senator Robert M. La Follette, which were to be so damaging to the prospects for social reform, might seem to reflect their personalities alone, not his. McCarthy's was, however, a combative personality, and one that may have clouded his professional judgment. His friends Roosevelt and John D. Rockefeller, Jr. (bitter adversaries of La Follette and Walsh, respectively) admired his activities as coach to the Wisconsin football team. The trouble was, however, that McCarthy's sporting enthusiasm knew no bounds. He advised a nephew that he had never seen "a good man yet who did not fight everything out to the end" and that "the same spirit that makes a fellow a good athlete makes him a good student." [22] This outlook was not ideal in the director of what should have been a cooperative, academic investigation of violence.

McCarthy emphasized the necessity for impartial investigation. But as the researches of his team proceeded, it became clear that he was determined to prove the viability of his chosen method of reform. He was influenced by his experience as director of the experimental

Legislative Reference Bureau at Wisconsin. The idea behind the bureau was that capitalists and workers alike had an interest in efficiency, safety, and good working conditions. Therefore, they could afford to get together, without controversy, to draft enlightened laws. The Reference Bureau was meant to be the servant of the legislature. Ideally, the legislature would enact suggested reforms and set up joint commissions of employers and workers to see that they operated efficiently. This was the celebrated "Wisconsin Idea." McCarthy seemed at times to be converting the Research Division into an advertising agency of the Idea, and his single-mindedness led to the clash with Walsh.

The Wisconsin Idea, for all its stress on future harmony, was predicated upon a belief in existing conflict. Such a belief was central to the outlook of the mentor of McCarthy and the Research Division, the labor economist John R. Commons. He was already in the habit of visiting McCarthy to suggest ideas, supply drafts of bills, and call attention to students who might be of use and might benefit from research in the legislative reference department. Commons was also in touch with Robert M. La Follette and acted as an intermediary in the course of the troubled relationship between the senator and McCarthy. The professor was so influential that there was grumbling about the state university running the Wisconsin legislature.[23]

Commons had a long-standing interest in violence. In December 1906 he addressed the American Sociological Society on the subject of class conflict. Hitherto, he argued, workingmen's discontent had escaped through two safety valves, the frontier and politics. Now, the frontier had closed and civil-service reform could cut off the avenue of politics. Trustification and scientific management destroyed individuality and thereby fostered class consciousness. Immigration divided the lower-paid workers but united the better off. For such reasons as these, class consciousness was growing in the United States. When his address was republished in 1913, Commons added that the growth of the IWW justified his predictions. According to the Wisconsin economist, there was only one way out. He had little faith in third parties, but reform could be achieved through legislation. The working class was a permanent minority, but the middle class, comprising two-thirds of the population, could ensure the passage of the required legislation and, just as important, its enforcement. A policy based on such an analysis might ensure the permanence of reform, whereas previously the victories of the workers had been nibbled away.

Commons viewed his measures as essential if class conflict was to be averted.[24]

Commons personally directed inquiries into certain aspects of lawlessness, for example Margaret Stecker's inquiry into the recent molders' strike and Daniel O'Regan's into detective agencies. Information gleaned from such inquiries was supposed to lend force to the demand for ameliorative legislation and the law-enforcing commissions that Commons had already helped to set up. The labor economist exemplified another facet of the Wisconsin Idea, the borrowing of foreign solutions, when he directed Luke Grant's attention to conditions in Britain, France, Italy, Belgium, South Africa, and New Zealand. Commons had entrusted Grant (formerly labor editor of the *Chicago Record-Herald*) with an investigation of "Violence in Labor Disputes and Methods of Policing Industry." [25]

In directing Research Division investigators, McCarthy allowed Commons a free hand, for the two Wisconsin scholars thought much alike. McCarthy argued that, because of the exhaustion of natural resources in America, the social problems of England and Germany were about to afflict his own country. It was logical to suppose that German and English solutions (perhaps because of his Irish background, McCarthy preferred the former) might profitably be borrowed. Wisconsin, the playground of robber barons in the nineteenth century and the cradle of reform under La Follette, had found from experience that public hearings accomplished little, but investigations in support of good intentions were worthwhile. McCarthy urged that the solution to national problems was a "little reference department similar to mine," which might pick and choose among already tried foreign and local legislation and benefit in addition from a federal investigation of social conditions. McCarthy's protégés had already followed with eagerness earlier attempts to imitate the Wisconsin example on the national level, all of which foundered on the rocks of politics. In February 1913 Witte (who was secretary to Congressman John M. Nelson of Wisconsin) wrote to McCarthy's assistant William Leiserson: "In this session Owen and La Follette introduced [separate] legislative reference bureau bills in the Senate. Both bills appeared to have been drawn with the idea of giving particular persons jobs." [26]

In spite of their quarrels, the three leading figures of the CIR shared a belief in class conflict. At first they seemed to complement each other. Walsh provided the sensational publicity through his on-the-spot public hearings. Commons provided the ideas. McCarthy sent legislative proposals to Professor T. I. Parkinson of Columbia University to be drafted into legal form. In all, it was an efficient reform machine.

Under attack from the Wisconsin state legislature for his pluralism (though director of the Research Division, he still held on to his job at the state capitol), McCarthy countered in an enlightening manner. He argued that the federal inquiries that engaged his energies were of benefit to the Wisconsin Legislative Reference Library, to the state of Wisconsin, and to other states that sought to imitate the legislative innovations at Madison.

McCarthy went into detail. He summarized under nine main headings the ways in which Wisconsin benefited from his federal work. For example, the governor of Wisconsin had vetoed a bill that would have provided an appropriation for the investigation of various methods of sickness insurance. Selig Perlman of the University of Wisconsin had now undertaken the work at federal expense. Leiserson, formerly head of the Wisconsin employment offices and now in charge of the day-to-day business of the Federal Research Division (which had moved to Chicago for the convenience of the Wisconsin group), would be sure to place Wisconsin in the fore of his national drive for reforms in employment practices. The work of F. H. Bird, a former Wisconsin student, on the enforcement of the state's labor laws had already been of use to the Wisconsin commission. Anna Herkner of Maryland was looking into the enforcement of the Wisconsin child labor law. Another point made by McCarthy in his letter to his detractor was that Clara Richards and two other girls formerly employed by him in the state capitol were now in the reference library of the federal commission. They were making available to Wisconsin legislators a wealth of detail about comparative legislation.[27]

The Research Division provided able young men and women with an opportunity to develop their ideas in the working laboratory of life. Aspiring young intellectuals were uprooted from their classrooms, primed with ideas, deposited among trade unionists and slum dwellers, and paid to write up the resultant evidence and their conclusions. Edwin E. Witte is a good example. On October 31, 1914, Witte sent McCarthy reports on antitrust laws, trade-union law in Great Britain, and congressional action on the reform of the trade-union law. He had completed a section on violence and injunctions, which was to be part of the fourth projected Research Division report on labor injunctions.[28] Witte's reports were too late to be of use in the debates on the Clayton bill, passed on June 5, 1914, but he had become one of the nation's leading labor economists and a lifelong consultant on injunctions. Research Division personnel in due course produced authoritative works on collective bargaining, agriculture, education, welfare, and insurance.

An idea of the contribution of the Research Division to American social science may be gleaned from the personnel employed as investigators, special agents, statisticians, and research clerks. The roster includes the names of men who, after their training and experience with the division, became authorities in their various fields: George E. Barnett, Edwin E. Witte, David J. Saposs, Arthur E. Suffern, Ira B. Cross, Leo Wolman, Robert F. Hoxie, Selig Perlman, William Leiserson, Sumner Slichter, Paul F. Brissenden, George B. West, and Edgar Sydenstricker were among them.[29]

The written works of such men were influential, but in the 1930s some of them exercised a more direct influence. Ideas for the New Deal came in profusion from Harvard and Columbia, but the direct participation of former members of the Wisconsin group was not negligible. Witte contributed to several New Deal agencies and has a claim to be known as the father of social security in the United States. Harold Ickes became Secretary of the Interior and a name inseparable from the politics and policies of the 1930s. Sumner Slichter, who had moved to Harvard, lent his support to the Wagner bill. Leo Wolman served on the National Labor Board, while Leiserson inspired Roosevelt's unemployment insurance scheme and was chairman of the National Mediation Board by 1939; he and Witte were the architects of many bills designed to preserve the right of collective bargaining in the United States.[30]

The Wisconsin scheme stimulated some reform and started a number of young men and women on careers of distinction. Yet the Wisconsin tactics fell short of achieving the legislative goal established by the Research Division itself. The Progressive movement had, as it were, entrusted the pursuit of social reform to a group of intellectuals. These men and women, whether individually Democrat, Republican, formally Progressive or Socialist, proved to be collectively ineffective. In the measure that social reform had been one of its important objectives, the Progressive movement therefore faltered.

The Commission on Industrial Relations failed largely because of the stress that its members continued to place, in both public hearings and research, on class conflict. There were other impediments to its success. A shortage of cash seriously hampered the commission. Proposed national legislation, on unemployment and laws of benefit to labor, was beset by the constitutional problems of a federal political system. Nor was it the first time that reform had failed in America. If public support for legislative proposals quickly dwindled into apathy, this had in the past been the problem of reformers exploiting other short-term issues, such as the shortage of currency. Nevertheless, it is clear that the intellectuals' continued emphasis on violence between rich and poor was a significant step away from reform.

Violence was dangerous to reform for several reasons. First, it could distract as well as attract attention: International violence in the shape of the Great War eventually put the domestic "struggle" into its proper perspective. Second, violence as such could become the social problem in the eyes of many. Fear of revolution could produce reaction as well as liberalism; the emphasis on violence produced the Red Scare as well as the CIR. Third, within the CIR, valuable time was wasted in seeking documentation of social violence. Finally, this search assumed such importance that it led to quarrels among division personnel and to the disruption of their program. Such were the consequences, for American social reform, of the myth of industrial violence.

The prime bone of contention within the commission was not the cause of industrial violence or even its extent. A debate on either of these subjects would have been fruitful and constructive. Instead, there was an acrimonious, protracted, and time-consuming squabble over the failure of investigators to exhume the assumed evidence as to the existence of violence. There was constant demand for the services of Daniel O'Regan to investigate the widely accepted violence of private detectives. Commons complained about his failure to discover the slippery truth; O'Regan, overawed by the insistent wrath of his supervisors, Commons, Leiserson, Basil Manly, and McCarthy, prepared elaborate excuses about the apparent failure of his investigation—it never occurred to him that there was not much left to expose.[31]

Similarly, the search for violence was an important part of the misunderstanding in October 1914 between Charles McCarthy and Thomas I. Parkinson of Columbia University, director of the Legal and Legislative Department. All legal matters before the CIR were referred to

Parkinson, but Parkinson was not in charge of field workers assigned to his department. They reported to McCarthy and included some of the most able investigators: Witte and O'Regan, together with B. F. Moore (a lawyer and Columbia graduate), Patrick F. Gill (a former congressman from Missouri), Inis Weed (formerly dean of women at the University of Washington and a postgraduate student at Columbia), and Redmond Brennan (a lawyer from Missouri).[32] But Parkinson claimed that all his work and personnel came under the patronage of Walsh. His claim was a major frustration for McCarthy, who had hoped to work with Parkinson, since his own emphasis had so long rested on legislative reform with commission enforcement.

Parkinson complained that McCarthy was allowing Witte and Moore to duplicate his own and others' legal research. He had thought that the efforts of Witte, Moore, O'Regan, Gill, and Brennan were directed at unearthing instances of violence and legal malpractices associated with it, a task at which they were either negligent or incompetent. In accusing McCarthy of keeping them off fieldwork, Parkinson was in fact unjust. McCarthy had explicitly directed the work of Brennan, Gill, and Moore on questions about which he was as concerned as Parkinson. McCarthy wrote to the Columbia professor:

> Outside the work of the merest preliminary nature done by Moore, and which was necessary as an example to show concretely to the Commission in order to obtain their approval of what could be done in the future, every bit of energy has been bent on getting the illustrative material about which you ask. The country has been raked for it. The socialists have been asked for it; the IWW have been asked for it, literature has been raked for it and then investigators have been sent every place. You know well that this is a very difficult piece of work to do.

As Leiserson remarked subsequently, in a report to McCarthy on an attempt to patch up things with Parkinson, the Wisconsin man had looked further ahead to the question of bill drafting—it was his reform zeal, and not his lack of appetite for gory detail, that had led him to direct Witte to draft legislation, thereby stepping on Parkinson's sensitive legal toes.[33]

McCarthy was attempting to be conciliatory in November 1914. On the first of the month, with only three preliminary reports submitted, he drew up an outline of plans and progress by the Research Division. The report classified in nine sections the broad subjects of research and investigation. The very first of these sections concerned legal and legislative problems. Parkinson was thus accorded prominence if not preeminence by this arrangement, which satisfied McCarthy, too. Following sections largely concerned problems of violence; Walsh could not complain at this. McCarthy's own list of the causes of industrial unrest appeared modestly as the penultimate section. The whole document was a promising draft of what a unanimous final report might look like, except for one tactless procedure. The findings of the commissioners (summaries of the public hearings) were given an insignificant place at the foot of each section of the master plan.[34]

In Frank Walsh's opinion, the public hearings were the most important activity of the commission. As soon as funds began to run short in the fall of 1914, he had considered pruning the Research Division. McCarthy's attitude toward public hearings did not help, and this attitude soon became very clear. Walsh proposed to expose malpractices by the Rockefeller-owned Colorado Fuel and Iron Company, in particular the notorious "Ludlow Massacre." Walsh had decided to make a showpiece of his crusade against the Rockefellers. He even attacked the Rockefeller Foundation's own inquiry into industrial relations and picked a quarrel with Paul U. Kellogg, the new editor of *Survey,* in February 1915 for having failed to indict the foundation in a point-for-point comparison of the merits of the private and government inquiries. McCarthy's position was considerably weakened by his friendship with John D. Rockefeller, Jr., and Walsh dismissed him.[35]

Basil Manly was appointed to direct the efforts of the Research Division. But Commons knew that the end was in sight. He wrote to his former collaborator, Helen L. Sumner, on March 17, 1915: "We had quite a blow up in our Commission and they turned down McCarthy and me which means that practically all the staff that I had selected to write and work up the reports, recommendations and constructive program will have to go within a week or two." On May 11, 1915, Commons wrote to Miss Sumner (now working in Washington, D.C., on the reform of child labor conditions) that, as a result of disagreements within the CIR, he would submit an independent treatise. He advocated firmly, to the end, the paramount need for enforcing reform laws: "My greatest emphasis in my separate report will be on the administration of labor laws, and I am quite anxious to secure as early as possible publications which your bureau is getting out on administration of child labor laws." [36]

Commons' report was, finally, but one of three and did not draw on the originally anticipated depth of fulfilled research. His chosen Research Division team, who were intensely loyal to each other, felt that their views were never represented to the public. Referring to Walsh's attempt through his ally Manly to make his opinions appear to be the authentic conclusions of the commission, Witte wrote in October 1915: "One of the aspects of the history of the commission somebody I hope will bring out is that Manly's report is not really the staff's report, and that he had nothing to do with planning or directing research work." [37] One of the Research Division team, Inis Weed, wrote a book on industrial violence based on the collective findings but failed to find a publisher. The twenty thousand pages of Research Division reports yellowed through the years and never saw the light of day.

The CIR's emphasis on the danger of class revolt did more than remove an opportunity for constructive reform. It actually contributed to reaction. With the success of the war effort in 1918, the people of the United States gained in confidence. Not only were fresh American troops reported to be fighting well abroad, but the drafting of the National Guard forces, which had left the several states relatively under-policed, had prompted no domestic revolution (a point confidently noted in a U.S. government publication during the mobilization in 1941).[38] Now was the time to turn against internal foreign elements and against radicals. It was deemed safe to prosecute minorities, and it certainly seemed justifiable, since their violent intent had not been seriously questioned. The fighting that accompanied the Bolshevik success in Russia, beginning in the fall of 1917, confirmed the impression that socialists in the United States would use violence and should therefore be suppressed.

Far from questioning the threat of domestic revolutionary violence, a number of American social reformers fell in with the illiberal majority. A. Mitchell Palmer, who had wanted to curtail child labor, helped to engineer the federal contribution to the Red Scare. Commons, Leiserson, Jett Lauck (an early director of the Research Division), as well as several socialists, advanced dubious ethnic interpretations of American ills.[39] Radicals and ethnic minorities were persecuted not only because they challenged American institutions, but also because they were confidently seen to be violent and vulnerable.

Committed to impractical tactics, and to an overstated idea of class conflict, the prodigies of Wisconsin witnessed two decades of unre-

formed American life. It is true enough that partial reforms had
been made, by the entry of America into the Great War, in the fields
of child labor, hours of work in some industries and for women in
some areas, safety inspections, and workmen's accident compensation
in some states. Indeed, the historian Arthur A. Ekirch, Jr., has concluded that while Progressive America "lagged far behind" New
Zealand and some European countries, "the crusade for social justice"
in the Roosevelt-Wilson years succeeded in inculcating "a greater confidence that the social evils linked with modern industrial progress
could be conquered and permanent reforms achieved." [40] Yet, while
such qualifications should be borne in mind, a survey of Progressive
social reform reveals three things. First, it owed much to the thought
of previous decades—the Research Division was not flexible enough to
come up with legislative proposals of immediate appropriateness. Second, the legislative gains made under President Wilson in the field of
social reform owed more to old-fashioned agitation than to McCarthyist
tactics. Finally, the legislation affecting social matters was largely ineffective in the long run.

An examination of real and apparent reforms between 1913 and
1916 reveals the following. The establishment of a Department of Commerce and Labor in 1913 was a necessary preliminary to further
measures but owed little to the post-McNamara agitation. The limita-
tion on injunctions aimed at by the Clayton act in 1914 had been
long demanded by the AFL and was ineffective. The child labor bill
introduced by A. Mitchell Palmer was potentially revolutionary (it was
based on the Constitution's interstate commerce clause), and it enjoyed
the support of men associated with the CIR, such as Devine, Lovejoy,
and Felix Adler—but this, too, was a long-standing demand whose
veto by President Wilson could not imaginably have been forestalled by
Wisconsin intellectuals.

Perhaps the greatest social achievement of Wilson's Presidency
was the Seamen's Act of 1915. For years, the seamen's leader, Andrew
Furuseth, had been lobbying for a measure that would end the legally
sanctioned system of exploitation by shippers' agents in California.
The execrable living conditions of the ordinary seaman did not excite
the attention of Research Division investigators. It was neither this
nor the fear of mutiny that prompted the act of 1915. Rather, the public
was aroused by fear of shipwrecks involving passengers, that is, the
public themselves. Furuseth's friend, the anticapitalist agitator La

Follette, scorned by Roosevelt and McCarthy, was the chief architect of the act.[41]

Similarly, the Adamson Act of 1916, ostensibly regulating the hours of work on railroads to protect the health of the engineer, may be regarded in the light of consumer politics. The concessions of 1916 were motivated not by fear of revolution but by the Democrats' anxiety that the threatened general railroad strike could anger voters in an election year. The Adamson Act may also be considered as a response to public concern over fatal train crashes. A number of these had been the result of sleepiness among crews who had been on duty for protracted periods. President Roosevelt had pressed for legislation on this ground, and it may be argued that it was the queasiness of the middle class at the sight of its own blood—drawn in routine travel, not in revolution—that helped to prompt the legislation of 1916. The La Follette and Adamson bills became law because they favored the consumer as well as labor.[42]

As for the period of the Depression in the 1930s, the record of Research Division veterans appears less impressive when considered in the context of historian Otis L. Graham's finding that former Progressives were on the whole as likely to oppose the New Deal program of reform as to support it.[43]

The Commission on Industrial Relations, potentially a vehicle for social reform, came into being as a result of expectations of social upheaval. Its personnel did not question these expectations but placed their faith in violence as a stimulant to reform. Stressing violence to an extent that excluded sound investigation and precluded harmony among themselves, the federal inquirers allowed an opportunity to pass.

Chapter 11

Violence and Reform ———————

THE RHETORICAL EXPLOITATION OF VIOLENCE BY REFORMERS HAS NOT been confined to the Progressive period, nor have its consequences. Though threats of violence, subtle or crude, have occasionally won limited concessions for well-organized groups such as trade unionists or students, the clear lesson of twentieth-century American history is that rhetorical violence does not pay. Various reasons account for this. First, as we saw in the last chapter, threats of violence are not always strong or convincing enough to produce sustained pressure for reform. Second, to distort violence in the supposed interest of reform is to invite backlash. And third, the United States is a democracy with legitimate means of protest open to its citizens; consequently, the rhetoric of violence does not command the sympathy of a wide audience.

It is significant that the women's movement, which has made slow but steady gains since the 1830s and especially in the twentieth century, has relied very little on the rhetoric of physical violence, and that the Fair Deal, like Progressivism, was damaged by an anti-revolutionary rhetoric that got out of hand.[1] The present chapter will focus on two further twentieth-century attempts at social improvement, showing that the New Deal, the twentieth century's most successful reform movement, was not predicated upon violence, whereas the New Frontier–Great Society reform impulse of the 1960s echoed not only the violent rhetorical tactics of the Progressive period but also the failure of those tactics.

The notion that the New Deal was peaceful is challengeable, the idea that it was successful much-challenged. To consider first the hypothesis that New Deal rhetoric was not predicated upon violence, it is necessary to review critically the disorders that did occur in the 1930s and the responses to them. For there *were* incidents of collective violence in both rural and urban America in the 1930s. It is true that the great Missouri sharecropper demonstration of 1939 was nonviolent; furthermore, there were no great race riots, and the Ku Klux Klan had been discredited by sexual scandal and corruption in the 1920s, so extralegal intimidation of blacks was at a relatively low ebb. But it could still be argued that blacks received short shrift under the southern legal system. The Communist Party made an international cause célèbre of the case of the "Scottsboro boys," nine young blacks sentenced to death in 1931 for raping two white prostitutes on a freight train near Scottsboro, Alabama. The evidence against the boys was ultimately shown to be flimsy, which in turn showed (according to the Communists) how U.S. racists indulged regularly in judicial "murder." [2]

The radical novelist John Steinbeck portrayed the social violence of another part of rural America in *The Grapes of Wrath* (1939). "Okies," small farmers driven off their land in Oklahoma and adjoining states by dust, drought, and depression ran into a rough reception and retaliated in kind when they tried to obtain work and decent living conditions on the farms of the San Joaquin Valley in California. In cities throughout America, urban workers encountered similar opposition when they sought to organize. The accompanying industrial violence was scarcely less extensive than that of any of the preceding six decades.[3]

Nor was there any shortage of rhetoricians trying to make the most of the dissension that did occur in the 1930s. The American Liberty League, a well-organized coalition of conservatives established in 1934, sponsored speeches and publications by prominent public figures critical of the New Deal. Early in the election year 1936, former Democratic Presidential candidate Alfred E. Smith remarked at a league dinner: "There can be only the clear, pure, fresh air of free America, or the foul breath of communistic Russia." President Franklin D. Roosevelt returned his enemies' fire ("They are unanimous in their hatred for me—and I welcome their hatred"), though his rhetoric was usually of the *ad hominem* rather than class variety.[4]

Between 1936 and 1940, the La Follette Civil Liberties Committee investigated employers' interference with labor's "right to organize" as defined by the New Deal legislation. Its focus on violence is reminiscent of the preoccupations of the CIR investigation of 1912–1915. Furthermore, its advertisement of social discord fostered an embryonic backlash, especially after the fiasco of President Roosevelt's threat to pack the recalcitrant Supreme Court in 1937. The House Un-American Activities Committee, established in 1934 to investigate right-wing activities, turned its attention in June 1938, under the influence of Representative Martin Dies, to Communists and the threat of left-wing take-over in the United States. According to a report issued by the Dies Special Committee on Un-American Activities in January 1939, Communists were taking over the Congress of Industrial Organizations (which had split with the AFL in 1936) and were encouraging sit-down strikes in order to paralyze industry and produce revolution.[5]

The historian Jerold S. Auerbach has summed up the relationship between the La Follette committee, "class struggle," and reform in a passage that might well apply to the politics of Progressivism or of the 1960s:

> The committee, viewed from the perspective of its left-wing defenders or its right-wing assailants, demonstrated the popularity of the theme of class struggle during the New Deal decade. Few New Dealers found a haven in ideology, but many of them seemed to accept the premises of the Left when it suited their reformist instincts to do so. Class warfare, however, was a double-edged weapon. The New Deal and the La Follette Committee had wielded it adroitly, but by 1938 they were suffering from its painful counterthrusts. The committee, in particular, barely escaped dying by the sword it had lived by so successfully.[6]

Clearly, a case can be made for the view that New Dealers exploited the threat of revolution opportunistically and paid the price for their folly: Yet it is much weaker than that which can be advanced concerning the Progressives and reformers of the 1960s. Auerbach's suggestion that the New Dealers were relatively nonideological is true to the extent that they did not succumb to unrealistic rhetoric. Auerbach also draws our attention to the fact that while the La Follette committee (and by extension the group of politicians sympathetic with it) "barely escaped dying by the sword it has lived by so successfully," escape it did. The reaction against the New Deal in the 1930s was not nearly so pronounced as the backlash against social-reform Progressivism and the anti-poverty, civil-rights legislation of the 1960s.

Nervous conservatives did labor the significance of the interest taken in agrarian protest by the Socialist Party's leader Norman Thomas, by the Communists, and (in the case of the black Missouri sharecroppers in 1939) by the Trotskyists.[7] Yet no respected politician seriously suggested that the United States was about to experience a peasants' revolt. The Scottsboro boys were not portrayed as revolutionaries. Organized labor was, it is true, painted in lurid colors because of the resurgence of violence in the 1930s, and the penetration of some CIO unions by a small number of Communists. But the red-scaremongering tactic was stale, and the business spokesmen who used it were discredited by the Crash, Depression, and the New Deal congressional investigations. In retrospect, it may appear that the tactics of the Liberty Leaguers and other conservatives were doomed from the start; it becomes necessary to remind ourselves that they had no reason to lack confidence at the time, because they would have remembered how the rhetoric of violence and the Red Scare had so effectively put an end to social Progressivism in the last Democratic administration.

Liberal reformers had comparatively little use for the political rhetoric of violence in the 1930s because they had at their disposal the all-conquering propaganda issue, unemployment. More radical exponents of the class-conflict theme found that it was all too likely to suffer a sugary if lucrative death at the hands of Hollywood, Broadway, or government-sponsored arts projects. Steinbeck's *Grapes of Wrath,* for example, succeeded at the box office as one of Hollywood's family dramas. Some conservative businessmen did exaggerate the threat of revolution by force. The impact of their rhetoric was softened by its repetitious nature and the anti-business climate of opinion created by the La Follette hearings and the Senate's Nye investigations into the unfounded but influential allegation that American entry into World War I had been engineered by "merchants of death," a group of profiteering munitions capitalists. Furthermore, while it is sometimes maintained that big business did not cooperate with New Deal legislation, few historians would dispute the fact that the National Industrial Recovery Act of 1933 helped to prop up the ailing capitalist system: Many responsible businessmen realized they had cause to hesitate before inventing a "Red Specter," which might cripple a useful administration. As for private detective agencies, only a dwindling number of employers were still prepared to believe their self-interested reports of violent agitators at work in America's factories.

The effect of violent rhetoric on New Deal reform was limited by two additional factors. First, democracy and, to a lesser extent, capitalism were being challenged by a second totalitarian ideology, fascism, in the 1930s. In domestic as in international politics, there were two targets to attack; Hitler's and Mussolini's acolytes in America drew some of the fire that might otherwise have been directed exclusively at those aligned with Stalin. And second, rhetorical violence (such as it was) accompanied the New Deal but did not precede it. In 1933 Roosevelt took the nation by storm: In his first three months in office he and Congress set America on a new political course. Traditionally vocal groups like businessmen and left-wing agitators had already been taken by surprise by the Crash of 1929; Roosevelt's intensive activity took their breath away. This was significant for the fate of the New Deal: Since it was not predicated upon a threat of violence, it could not be hoisted with that particular petard.

It has nevertheless become fashionable to challenge the long-accepted idea that the New Deal was a success. In the 1930s and 1940s Roosevelt was already being criticized for going too far or going in the wrong direction. His detractors pointed out that it was World War II, not the New Deal, that reduced America's excessively high level of unemployment (there were still 10 million out of work in 1938, compared with 12 to 15 million in 1933; the problem had practically disappeared by 1943). FDR's conservative critics argued that his reliance on heavy public expenditure depressed business confidence and that social reform aimed at special groups did nothing to restore it.[8]

Those committed to government-sponsored social reform have, in contrast, complained that Roosevelt did not go far enough. Rexford G. Tugwell, who had headed a brief experiment in federally planned agriculture when the President put him at the head of the Resettlement Administration in 1935, expressed early if guarded reservations about the efficacy of New Deal social planning: He again lamented in 1957 that after Roosevelt's death in 1945 "forthright national planning" was "either not accepted or not fully so." In the 1960s and 1970s such "New Left" historians as Barton J. Bernstein have enumerated various shortcomings of the reforms of the 1930s: They have shown how relatively affluent farmers cornered funds designed to help poor share-croppers; how New Deal agencies discriminated against blacks in dire need of assistance; how nothing was done specifically for the people hardest hit by the Depression, such as blacks and Mexican-Americans; how big business throve on New Deal legislation ostensibly framed to help the small man; how the Tennessee Valley Authority assumed capitalistic mores, and how big labor—leading officials of the AFL and CIO giants—was bought off with encouraging legislation at the expense of the mass of industrial workers. The historian Paul Conkin concluded in his *FDR and the Origins of the Welfare State* (1967) that Roosevelt "did not have the substance, the wisdom, for great leadership." [9]

It is useful to assess the reform achievements of the Roosevelt administrations in comparative terms. Since reform is cumulative, it would, however, be impractical to make a straightforward comparison between his reforms and those of other Presidents: It would be as anachronistic to look for Roosevelt's view on the bussing issue as it would be to attempt to define Jefferson's opinion on fair employment opportunities for women. It is more helpful to ask how far the United States lay ahead of or behind other industrial countries in terms of social-reform legislation in the Progressive, New Deal, and New Frontier–Great Society periods respectively. To compare America with the most socially advanced countries is, of course, to apply a tough criterion, but the criterion is at least a consistent one and a useful control. A further objection to the international comparison is that reform impulses in Europe and America may not coincide. However, the "exceptionalism" of America has tended to diminish since nineteenth-century industrialization. For the purpose of present discussion, it is to be assumed that what the Italian historian Benedetto Croce referred to as Europe's "Liberal Age" (1871–1914) had its slightly retarded equivalent in America, that the New Deal was part of an international and broadly comparable response to a common international problem of economic depression and unemployment, and that the reforms attempted by Democratic administrations in the 1960s reflected and influenced the goals of contemporary social democrats in Britain and Germany.[10]

When Progressivism ended as a national reform movement in 1916, the United States lagged behind the leading industrial countries of Europe and, to a degree, the white-populated parts of the British Empire. On the eve of Progressivism, around 1900, Europe had already been ahead in some respects, for example the pioneering, if incomplete, social-insurance schemes launched by Prince Bismarck in Germany in the 1880s. Yet constructive discussion had already occurred in the 1830s, 1860s, and since, both on the state and the federal levels, concerning safety conditions, hours of labor, and kindred subjects of vital concern to working people. The United States was furthermore ahead of other countries in being so strongly committed to the provision of a free, universal, public education system up to and including secondary school level, and on the comprehensive principle.[11] Given such advantages in conjunction with their universal white male suffrage, Americans might have expected to be in the vanguard of social democracies by 1916.

Progressivism did provide the means for future social expenditure. Following the ratification of the Sixteenth (income tax) Amendment in 1913, Congress levied a 1 to 6 percent income tax to raise revenue lost by lowering tariffs. Furthermore, on the city and state levels reforms were adopted to provide free public leisure facilities (city parks) and to protect the safety of certain groups of workers and consumers. As we saw in the previous chapter, these measures had their limited counterparts in federal legislation. Also on the national level, young CIR researchers suggested lessons that might be learned from Britain, Germany, New Zealand, and other foreign parts. But at the end of the Progressive period of reform, the United States had no equivalent of the vitally important government-sponsored systems of health and other social insurance being organized by Lloyd George and European liberals such as Orlando and Clemenceau, whereas Belgium and other European countries were rapidly catching up in terms of provision for public education.[12] As we saw in Chapter 10, the specter of class violence had counterproductive effects in America in the Progressive period.

Social reform did not stand still in the period between the end of national Progressivism and the beginning of the New Deal. With military objectives primarily in mind, the Wilson government began to develop the resources of the Tennessee Valley in World War I, laying the foundation of the TVA in the 1930s. Republican Secretary of Commerce Herbert Hoover gave the blessing of bipartisan approval to federal civilian construction projects in the late 1920s by authorizing construction of Boulder Dam on the Colorado River in 1928. By this time, it was standard practice for Washington to subsidize highway construction, and the economist William Trufant Foster was advocating the benefits of calculated variations in public expenditure to even out fluctuations in the business and employment cycles. On the state level, the former Wisconsin student and CIR researcher William Leiserson had moved to Ohio and pioneered the "Ohio plan" for unemployment insurance. This differed from the Wisconsin plan in that it called for contributions from workers as well as from employers, and it laid the foundation for New Deal legislation. These developments do not, however, detract from the fact that the New Deal included more federally sponsored social reforms than any comparable period in American history.[13]

The distractions of foreign affairs and approach of World War II prevented most people from realizing that by 1938 the United States was the world's leading example of a welfare state. In some respects, it is true, America still lagged behind countries that had taken a lead in the "Liberal Age." For example, while the American Medical Association approved the private medical insurance scheme Blue Cross in 1933, its lobbyists defeated Senator Robert F. Wagner's plan for universal health insurance in 1940. In this aspect of reform, the United States appeared to follow weakly in the wake of such countries as New Zealand, whose Social Security Act of 1938 introduced an income-tax-financed, virtually free national health service as well as increased pensions and extended family allowances. According to the New Zealand social reformer and historian W. B. Sutch, the 1938 act "put New Zealand for a few years at the head of the Western world for the scope and liberality of its Social Security scheme." [14]

But medicare apart, the New Dealers did inaugurate social reform measures affecting millions of citizens. The U.S. Social Security Act of 1935 provided for old-age and unemployment insurance. While the federally adopted "Ohio plan" for unemployment insurance was attacked for being deflationary and more conservative than contemporary European schemes, Roosevelt was correct in asserting that workers' contributions made the system politically acceptable, and other countries ultimately switched to the American plan. The New Dealers backed up unemployment insurance with federal encouragement for employment exchange programs existing in or proposed by various states. In its efforts at social reconstruction through the TVA, the Works Progress Administration, and the Civilian Conservation Corps, the Roosevelt administration matched the expenditures of Germany and Russia without incurring their social costs and exceeded those of democratic countries. The Wagner Act of 1935 gave the United States a system for the redress of labor unionists' grievances far in advance of that in the main European industrial countries. The Fair Labor Standards Act of 1938, though perforated by numerous loopholes, gave respectability to the principle that humane working hours and a decent minimum wage were the prerogative of all workers, not just those privileged by labor union membership.[15]

New Left historians may well have supplied a valuable corrective to the dewy-eyed recollections of New Dealers and sympathetic historians. But if Roosevelt's caution and pragmatism resulted in some shortcomings, it should be stated unequivocally that the New Deal put America ahead of other comparable countries in terms of social reform for the first and only time in her history. Unemployment was worse in the United States than elsewhere, and affected every voter, male and female, either directly or indirectly: The government simply had to act.[16] While the New Deal's detractors are right in saying that its measures failed to reverse the downward economic spiral, Roosevelt's administrations did accomplish reform in the interest of social justice: a policy with short-term political objectives but long-term social consequences.

During the administrations of President Harry Truman (1945–1953), America lost the reform momentum that had put her in the lead among industrial democratic nations. It was in vain that Truman appealed to Congress for legislation to protect the more vulnerable members of society. His legislative plans for public housing, price controls, civil-rights legislation, and medicare (to name just a few of his proposals) came to nothing. While the President managed to hasten desegregation in the armed forces, it was only by using his executive authority: The temper of Congress in the 1940s is exemplified by the passage of the Taft-Hartley Law in 1947, which removed some of the benefits conferred on labor by the Wagner Act passed a dozen years earlier.

The reasons for the defeat of Truman's program echo the reasons for the defeat of the social-reform aspects of Progressivism. If the liberal rhetoric of violence used by Progressives, fired by the confidence of World War I victory, transformed itself into the Red Scare, it is arguable that the La Follette-style class-conflict rhetoric stressed by

Auerbach, encouraged by World War II victory, led to the confident anti-communism known as "McCarthyism." Following this train of thought, it may be suggested that the New Deal continued after 1945. It would therefore appear that La Follette was, after all, hoisted by his own petard when in 1946 he lost to Joseph R. McCarthy in the Wisconsin Republican primary election for the Senate seat held by La Follette and his father for the past forty years. This case is apparently strengthened by Richard M. Freeland's persuasive argument in *The Truman Doctrine and the Origins of McCarthyism* (1970) that President Truman himself exploited the communist issue in order to bludgeon Congress into supporting liberal policies.[17] It may be inferred from Freeland's evidence that the liberalism of the 1940s was impaled on its own sword.

Yet it would be wrong to suppose that McCarthyism was the logical outcome and poisoner of Truman's "Fair Deal," let alone the New Deal. McCarthy did not, in the Wisconsin primary of 1946, defeat La Follette on the issue of industrial violence and class conflict: It was only in 1950, in his now-infamous speech at Wheeling, West Virginia, that the ambitious midwestern demagogue "discovered" the issue of communism.[18] Nor should Truman's emphasis on socialist revolution be considered in the same light as the Progressives' similar concern thirty years earlier. To the Progressives, the Russian Revolution of 1917 simply confirmed their opinions concerning domestic turbulence: They were not yet in the position of having to exercise the responsibilities of a major power. In contrast, Truman was concerned almost exclusively with the problem of left-wing violence abroad, not at home.

The defeat of Truman's domestic social reforms is attributable to the breakup of Roosevelt's emergency-based Democratic coalition in Congress: Foreign emergencies had distracted attention from conservative gains in the 1938 congressional elections, but the strength of the conservative coalition of Republicans and southern Democrats could no longer be ignored after the 1946 midterm returns and it remained a potent factor in the Senate until the Democratic victories of 1958 and in the House until the debacle of Senator Barry Goldwater's Republican candidacy in 1964.[19] Truman's failure as a social reformer is further explicable in terms of the alienation of public opinion by the massive labor strikes of 1946 and of the President's increasing preoccupation after his election victory in 1948 (which gave him a personal mandate for reform) with the cold war. To a minor degree, the ventilation of class antagonisms in the 1930s bred the domestic illiberalism of the late 1940s and McCarthyism of 1950–1954, but its reaction to the disadvantage of reform does not compare with the effects of the Red Scare in the Progressive period or the backlash of the 1960s.

In the 1960s two Democratic Presidents called for thoroughgoing social reform. John F. Kennedy invited the American people, in his inaugural address in 1961, to overcome "the common enemies of man: tyranny, poverty, disease, and war itself." Lyndon B. Johnson made a similar demand for reform in his inaugural speech when he expressed a desire to be remembered as "the education President and the health President." Kennedy's slogan "New Frontier" and Johnson's "Great Society" as well as their rhetorical elaborations suggest that the social legislation of the period 1961–1969 should be measured against the yardsticks of novelty and effectiveness.[20]

A substantial part of the "New Frontier–Great Society" legislation was not innovative. Several laws upgraded or updated New Deal provisions to meet the demands of inflation and full employment or applied New Deal ideas to novel areas. For example, Kennedy made an effective appeal to Congress in February 1961 to raise the minimum wage from $1 to $1.25 per hour, and closed a few more loopholes in the minimum-wage laws. Kennedy's plan for area redevelopment and Johnson's Appalachian Regional Development Act (1965) echoed the social aims of the TVA scheme but lacked its business soundness. The idea of concentrating public resources on a geographically defined poverty area was an imaginative one. It had already inspired imitation in India and Colombia and had been ignored in Europe to the detriment of such slum cities as Naples and Glasgow. Many were inspired by the idea that the poor themselves should manage the funds diverted in their direction. This notion, which was indeed novel, fell into discredit because only a fraction of the intended money reached the poor and because the poor mismanaged the money when they got it. The program needed time to develop in a favorable political, economic, and legislative climate, which would have allowed educational reforms aimed at the poor to have their full effect. Time and stability might also have helped the Office of Economic Opportunity (established in 1964, a descendant of the New Deal's Civilian Conservation Corps), but the onset of inflation and conservatism ensured that the life cycle of these social reforms would be short.

Johnson's supporters in Congress did knock down for the first time some of the long-standing opposition to certain social-reform bills. Thus in 1965 the nation began to overtake the lead established by other countries by passing the Medicare-Social Security Act. According to the Associated Press, Medicare increased the hospital-patient population by 3 percent.[21] Its provisions made an appreciable difference to the welfare of the elderly. The Civil Rights Act of 1965 removed many forms of race discrimination and prepared the way for legislation in the next decade that prohibited sexual discrimination. Although addressed to ancient grievances, the directness of its attack on Jim Crow practices gave it a radical character, and Britain was later to follow the U.S. example by legislating against racial and sexual discrimination. The Johnson administration also achieved for the first time allocations of federal funds to education that were weighted in favor of the poor. For example, the Higher Education Act of 1965 set up federal scholarships for students in need, a new provision in terms of American history, though already anticipated in Britain.

Measured by the tough (but consistent) criterion of the best offered by other industrial democracies, the American welfare state of the 1960s was incomplete in several respects. While the federal government had established a framework for health, old-age, and unemployment insurance schemes, the schemes themselves were not compulsorily universal. Medicare was aimed at citizens aged sixty-five and over, and within that limited framework did not provide a comprehensive service for the octogenarian lady of restricted income who fell down and broke a limb.[22] In spite of its high level of medical expertise and technology, the United States still lacked a hospital system of uniform quality throughout the country. Special housing for the disabled or aged of unexceptional income remained outside the sphere of government responsibility. Piecemeal scholarships for the poor did not match the British provision whereby the government paid for the education of all university students, subject to a means test. Public crèches to enable mothers to pursue relatively uninterrupted careers remained a facility that the West's most powerful nation left to Communist countries such as Poland to exploit.[23]

This is not to deny that the United States is a socially progressive nation. The affluence of the country makes nonsense of some of the international legislative comparisons. For example, a much greater proportion of young people acquire higher education in America than in Britain because U.S. educational institutions are more widespread,

U.S. students are prepared to "work their way through college," part-time work is generally available for them, their parents are richer, and because graduates' subsequent salaries are sufficiently high to enable undergraduate debts to be paid off. Americans are therefore better educated than the British, on average. Yet in spite of such qualifications it remains true that, in terms of federal legislation aimed at strengthening the welfare state, America lost in the late 1960s the reform momentum that seemed so promising in the period 1960–1965, the kind of reform momentum that had given the United States a temporary lead in the field in the 1930s.

Several reasons may be advanced for the subsidence of reform in the late 1960s, but not all of them are convincing. There is no reason to suppose, for example, that congressional opposition and vested-interest lobbies such as the American Medical Association were exceptionally formidable and growing stronger in that decade. To argue that Kennedy lacked legislative expertise and Johnson imagination is to ignore the fact that JFK inspired his generation and that Johnson capitalized for a short while on the resultant mood in Congress. Still another explanation of the conservative backlash that put Nixon in the White House in 1969 is that the earlier legislation had been group welfare rather than general welfare in character: It was aimed at Appalachians, Negroes, Puerto Ricans, and Mexican-Americans, not at the American people. These groups were relatively worse off than other groups but collectively formed a minority of the poor. The majority of the poor, the white Americans, rebelled against the Democratic administration in 1968—but, as we shall see, the economic argument may not have been the prime cause of their rebellion. Finally, it may be argued that yet another period of Democratic reform was brought to a close by yet another Democratic war, Vietnam being the sequel of World War I, World War II, and the Korean War. Undoubtedly, the inflationary effects of the Vietnam War persuaded many voters of the need to cut back on public expenditure, and welfare appropriations suffered accordingly. On the other hand, the Indochina conflict distracted attention from some of the intrinsic shortcomings of Great Society legislation; its adverse effect on reform suggests that the advances of the 1960s were more fragile than those of the 1930s, which, like the Democratic Party itself, had survived a much more serious international holocaust.

One of the main reasons for the fragility of Democratic reforms in the 1960s was the susceptibility of liberal rhetoric in that decade to backlash politics. The liberal rhetoric reflected an ideology of black violence that was expressed in the early 1960s and is reminiscent, in the reactions it produced, of some aspects of white labor history. Black advocates of violence included Robert F. Williams, who was disciplined by the National Association for the Advancement of Colored People (NAACP) in 1959 for observing that it might be "necessary to stop lynching with lynching," Rap Brown, Stokely Carmichael, and the Black Panthers. El-Hajj Malik El-Shabazz (formerly Malcolm X of the "Black Muslims"), who commanded a certain following in the black ghettos and a wide audience in the white media, stated in 1965: "I *am* for violence if non-violence means we continue postponing a solution to the American black man's problem—just to *avoid* violence." [24]

It is interesting that while black rhetorical violence was directed at white people, the actual violence that occurred during the 1960s riots was directed more against white property and against fellow blacks (bearing in mind, of course, that many of the fatalities were, as always, *imposed on* the blacks by the predominantly white forces of "law and order"). This was partly because of the relative scarcity of whites in the large urban areas dominated by the black population; the race riots of 1919 had in contrast occurred when the black ghettos were mere enclaves in white society and when any disturbance was likely to result in interracial clashes. In spite of the extensive damage and casualties that occurred in the 1960s, therefore, it may be contended that white Americans were not endangered to a greater degree than they had been in earlier twentieth-century riots or in the days of the great slave insurrections, such as Nat Turner's rebellion in 1831, which accounted for fifty-seven white lives against a smaller population base than that of the United States in the 1960s.[25]

Against an unexceptional background, the black scare of the 1960s got under way. Malcolm X often and correctly noted it. He stressed the role of the media in distorting the threat of black violence against whites.[26] By the 1960s, television journalists had perfected techniques of on-the-spot reporting, so that violence was brought into the home with a freshness of impact unmatched in the media since the rise of yellow journalism in the 1890s. In the eyes of credulous viewers, extreme violence seemed the tactic of last resort of a minority group whose expectations were being frustrated by the permanent majority of voters in a democratic society. As in the Progressive period, when

Robert Hunter had defined the problem of poverty against an immigrant background, violence seemed the credible recourse of an embattled ethnic minority: a situation in marked contrast to that which obtained during the mass unemployment 1930s.

The illusion of revolutionary black violence was strengthened by a
foreign ingredient. It was clear by the 1960s that the U.S. government
would have to win the hearts of the Third World people on the levees
of the Mississippi River. Black leaders exploited this situation by identi-
fying their cause with the decolonization struggle taking place in Africa
and elsewhere. It therefore seemed natural to associate anti-imperial
ideology with the "Afro-American" struggle. North African revolutionary Frantz Fanon's observation that criminal banditry could be a step
on the road to revolutionary consciousness seemed applicable to drug-
store break-ins in Harlem. It was true that this idea appealed more to
the well-educated bourgeoisie of both races than to the black in the
street, who was no more enamored of Fanon than the "working-class
stiff" had been of Georges Sorel. But it was precisely in the middle-class
mind that the black scare had an important part of its genesis.[27]

In one respect, the black violence of the 1960s was less subject to
distortion than the labor violence of the Progressive period. The black
communities and their perceived enemies were not preyed on by private
detectives with a commercial interest in exaggerating revolutionary
potential. It is true that Fred P. Graham has accused the FBI of in-
flating its crime statistics in order to strengthen its case for congressional appropriations; other police forces may have exploited the tense
racial situation of the 1960s for similar reasons. Nevertheless, the law
enforcement officer on a regular salary lacks the incentive to distort
truth that afflicts the labor spy working on finite contracts. Black protest did not attract private-enterprise detectives because it did not seem
to pose a sufficient economic threat to the businessmen who would
have had to foot the bill. To this extent, the distortions of the 1960s
were less serious than those of the Progressive period. Indeed, the historian August Meier and sociologist Elliott Rudwick concluded in a
joint essay in 1969 that "the advocacy and use of violence as a deliberate program for solving the problems of racial discrimination remains thus far, at least, in the realm of fantasy." The fantasy, however,
did exist and was available for exploitation.[28]

Liberal reformers exploited the myth of exceptional anti-white personal violence in the 1960s. Indeed, advocates of the black cause had,

like labor leaders and reformers, spoken against a backdrop of potential violence for many decades. For example, W. E. B. Du Bois, a brilliant black intellectual and one of the founders of the NAACP, in 1920 predicted a second world war unless the black, brown, and yellow peoples' "oppression and humiliation and insult at the hands of the White World cease." Similarly, the moderate civil-rights advocate Ralph Bunche in 1940 warned that blacks were beginning to think in terms of a machine-gun solution to their problems.[29] As we saw in Chapter 9, politicians in Chicago and Detroit were accused of truckling to the black vote in 1919 and 1943; no doubt they hoped that white voters would support them as deliverers from potential black violence.

Malcolm X used to complain that interviewing journalists would not let him deviate from the subject of black-white violence, of which he was supposed to be a leading symbol. Like the journalists (many of whom worked for liberal papers and broadcasting corporations), leading reformers considered Malcolm X and others like him to be indispensable to their interests. Referring to the civil-rights "revolution," President John F. Kennedy said "our task, our obligation, is to make that revolution, that change, peaceful and constructive for all." By stressing the need for peace, Kennedy focused attention on the alternative to civil-rights reform. The Reverend Dr. Martin Luther King, Jr., founder of the Southern Christian Leadership Conference in 1957 and a practitioner of only the milder forms of extralegal, direct-action protest, also exploited the backdrop of potential violence by advocating the Gandhi principle of nonviolence. The assassinations of Kennedy and King in 1963 and 1968, respectively, though hardly revolutionary in character, reinforced the illusions of violence exploited by both men. Nor was the reformist exploitation of violence limited to liberal leaders. The gratuitous inclusion of the word "non-violent" in the title of the direct-action group the Student Non-violent Coordinating Committee (established in 1960) served the same purpose. Jerome H. Skolnick, director of the Task Force on Violent Aspects of Protest and Confrontation of the National Commission on the Causes and Prevention of Violence (1969), concluded: "This nation cannot have it both ways: either it will carry through a firm commitment to massive and widespread political and social reform, or it will develop into a society of garrison cities where order is enforced without due process of law and without the consent of the governed." [30]

Conservatives exploited the situation presented to them by the liberals' invocation of violent rhetoric. Though he was no match for the wily electioneer Lyndon Johnson, Republican Presidential candidate Barry Goldwater demonstrated in the campaign of 1964 the potential of the "southern strategy" (an appeal for the support of erstwhile Democrats alienated from their traditional party by its civil-rights stance) and of the "law and order" issue. In the Presidential election campaign of 1968, the Republicans' Richard Nixon made the most of the "law and order" issue, which, to judge from Nixon's victory and the postelectoral verdict of the psephologists, played a crucial part in winning the votes of the "silent majority." [31]

In his inaugural address, President Nixon showed a shrewd appreciation of the rhetorical nature of the law and order issue: "America has suffered from a fever of words; from inflated rhetoric that promises more than it can deliver; from angry rhetoric that fans discontents into hatreds; from bombastic rhetoric that postures instead of persuading." [32] With the exception of a few outbursts against student protestors by Vice-President Spiro Agnew, the law-and-order issue receded from national prominence. Nixon perceived that the issue would be of little use to him once in office: Though "crime on the streets" in fact continued unabated, the new President killed the phenomenon as a political problem simply by not mentioning it any more. Nor did he raise the expectations of the poor (if they had any left by 1969) through "inflated rhetoric." Though Nixon tried to show he was not a reactionary by, for example, extending welfare payments to unmarried mothers, reform legislation abruptly lost the momentum of the Johnson years, and in some cases—such as the ending of the anti-poverty program in 1973—went into mortal decline. President James E. (Jimmy) Carter's call, in the summer of 1977, for a new, work-related system of social security acknowledged the defeats of the 1970s even as it pointed a way to the 1980s. Social reformers paid, in the end, for their error in exploiting, during the ebullient sixties, the specter of anti-white black violence.

The backlash of 1968 differed in some ways from that of the Wilson and Truman years. As we have seen, Democratic politicians who called for reform were themselves partly responsible for red scares in 1912, 1919, and to a lesser extent in 1948, even if Republicans were glad to join in the chorus. But, perhaps because Nixon had served his political apprenticeship during the second term of Truman's Presidency, the

Republicans took the initiative in raising the black-scare law-and-order issue in the 1960s. It is possibly because the Democrats lost the initiative over the law-and-order issue to the Republicans that the political blacklists of 1917–1920 and 1947–1954 and the red scares associated with them were not repeated.[33] For twentieth-century Democrats, though "liberal" in their periodic tendency to pursue the welfare state, have been susceptible to and capable of illiberal repressiveness. Armored against criticism by their reformist ideals, jealous of the rivalry of left-wing parties, anxious to remain respectable and uncontaminated by association with the left, "liberals" have often been intolerant of agitators more radical than themselves. Yet they have been better acquainted than conservatives could be with those radicals, sharing a certain community of outlook with them. They have been both willing and able, therefore, to compile well-informed blacklists of potential "subversives." Nixon struck so quickly at the Democrats in 1968 that he preempted the use of any such tactics by the Democrats. Furthermore, the Republican administrations of the 1970s allowed freedom of access by individuals to government intelligence files concerning them. A traditional aspect of Democratic scaremongering was therefore absent from the politics of the period. Nixon had saved the Democrats from one of their excesses.

Red phobia was not, it is true, entirely missing from the politics of the 1960s and 1970s. There were those who perceived the influence of the Kremlin behind race riots and campus disturbances. In a press conference given by Governor Ronald Reagan of California in 1969, a reporter raised the question of student protests against U.S. involvement in the Vietnam War, a subject on which Reagan had frequently expressed strong views:

Q. What was the basis for your opinion that the monthly moratorium-day activities were actually planned behind the Iron Curtain?

A. Well, now, . . . I said shouldn't some of those who were sincerely interested in peace and who marched sincerely in the parade ask some very pertinent questions and I said, shouldn't they ask if meetings were not held in East Berlin at the peace conference last year in regard to this . . . I'm still asking the question, . . . and there might be a challenge to a free press to find out.[34]

Reagan's views on social order and communism helped him to run for the Republican Presidential nomination in 1976 so strongly that he almost ousted the incumbent President Ford. But anti-communist rhetoric was on the whole running at an average, not an exceptional, level in the 1970s, the tone of the decade being set (until the ascent of the moralistic Governor Jimmy Carter to the White House) by the "détente" that Nixon and Secretary of State Henry Kissinger sought with Russia and China.

The Republicans' appropriation of the law-and-order issue, the absence of blacklisting, and the low intensity of red scaremongering suggest that the history of Progressivism and Fair Dealism was not repeated exactly in the 1960s. Yet tradition asserted itself to the extent that the violent rhetoric of the 1960s was exploited by reformers of several hues. Intensive rivalry between, on the one hand, the old left of the New Deal liberal or communist varieties and, on the other hand, the "New Left" comprising civil-rights workers, students, poverty action groups, and peace movements not only comprised a weakness in itself, but provided the enemies of reform with a ready-made arsenal of invective. The "liberals'" strenuous condemnation of violence and radicalism proved as counterproductive in the 1960s as it had a half a century earlier, and the Great Society was left vulnerable to diminution by backlash.

Comparative history is strewn with pitfalls, and these must be negotiated before affirming that, with the exception of the New Dealers, American social reformers have been chronically tempted to scare the electorate, with resultant adverse effects on their programs. This case has been argued above by comparison with Europe. It has been assumed that such historians as Croce and the American William E. Leuchtenburg have been right to consider the postindustrialization reform cycle as international in character: A circumstance that makes legislative comparisons valid. But is it similarly legitimate to assume that the rhetoric of violence in European countries has been qualitatively comparable to that in the United States, yet less prone to sudden fluctuation, the tendency that (we have maintained) accounts for the varied fortunes of U.S. reform?

It may be argued that the violence-related rhetoric of the French right was qualitatively affected by that country's revolutionary instability in the nineteenth century. A. de Gobineau attacked the modern, centralized state because he thought it was the instrument of rational change; Georges Sorel was the progenitor of fascism; and Charles

Maurras sought to combat social decomposition through collectivity. Such radical, counterrevolutionary, and illiberal conservatism on a high intellectual plane is alien to the American political tradition and not comparable with it.

British violence-related ideology has had a closer bearing on the North American outlook. It provides a useful yardstick for comparison because, by and large, it has been a steady rather than a fluctuating concern of leaders and philosophers. One might argue that the British have been consistently occupied with the problem of law and order since the days of Welsh lawgiver Hywel Dda (910–950). The Tudors were concerned with order, a theme that has continued to bother the philosophers throughout the reputedly placid decades of British history.[35] Hobbes, Locke, and Burke were read on the subject on both sides of the Atlantic. Less phrenetically than their French contemporaries, yet more constantly than Americans, nineteenth-century British politicians were concerned about the possibility of revolution; the use of the law of conspiracy against trade unions, like the passing of the Combination Acts (1799, 1800), presupposed that trade unionists challenged the legitimate order. Such nineteenth-century attitudes cast their shadow over the 1920s and 1930s, finding substance in the Emergency Powers Acts (1920, 1939, 1940) and Trade Disputes Act (1927). Until the 1960s, concern with law and order in postindustrial Britain was qualitatively similar to that in America, but quantitatively less subject to sudden fluctuation.

With the approach of the general election of 1970, Britain was held for a short period in the grip of a law and order scare, but it owed nothing to social reformers in the Labour Party and little to disorder as such (in Britain, as elsewhere, students were demonstrating against racism, but allegations of widespread disorder were impossible to prove and the Tories dropped the issue a month before the 1970 election). Tory politicians who used the issue to attack the Harold Wilson government or advance their individual claims to the Conservative Party leadership were clearly influenced by U.S. politics in the 1960s. On the left of the party Lord Harlech, a former British ambassador to Washington and a faint prospect for the Tory leadership, in May 1969 argued that "a national housing partnership" had to be set up if Britain was not to be faced with the violence prevalent in American cities. On the right, Enoch Powell commented in a vein reminiscent of U.S. backlash logic on a report that two foreign students had been convicted for throwing petrol bombs in Ulster. The Conservative Member of Parliament observed in August 1969 that this was a phenomenon with kinship to events in the United States, Paris, and Berlin. Investigations were no good: They only discovered causes, which liberals turned into excuses for lawlessness and a rationale for reform. In March 1970 Quintin Hogg and the future Tory Premier Edward Heath made forceful policy speeches on law and order, an issue that the Tory leader Margaret Thatcher revived once again in 1977.[36]

It may be argued, then, that America by now so dominates the world, particularly the English-speaking world and its communications media, that it will in future be more difficult to make meaningful distinctions between rhetoric on each side of the Atlantic. Nevertheless, it seems safe to generalize that social reformers in Britain have suffered, until the advent of recent U.S. influence, constantly but involuntarily from the law and order issue, while in America such reformers have at irregular intervals steered their own talk in a dangerous direction.

Appendix

Enumeration of Deaths in 75 Strikes, 1890–1909

The following list was compiled from contemporary trade-union journals, city newspapers, and federal and state government reports.

Industry	Location	Date	Deaths
EXTRACTION—METALLIFEROUS			
Gold, lead, and silver	Coeur d'Alene, Idaho	1892	6
Silver	Cripple Creek, Colo.	1894	4
Silver	Leadville, Colo.	1896	5
Gold	Coeur d'Alene, Idaho	1899	5
Gold and silver	Telluride, Colo.	1901	3
Copper	Copper Flat, Nevada	1903	3
Silver	Cripple Creek, Colo.	1904	30
Gold	Dunneville, Colo.	1904	1
EXTRACTION—COAL (bituminous unless otherwise stated)			
Coke	Connellsville, Pa.	1891	8
	Gunnison Co., Colo.	1891	1
	Coal Creek, Tenn.	1892	4
General bituminous coal strike		1894	14
Anthracite	General and Lattimer, Pa.	1897	18
Central coalfield and Virden, Ill.		1898	9
	Little Rock, Ark.	1899	1
	Pana, Ill.	1899	7
	Carterville, Ill.	1899	6

Industry	Location	Date	Deaths
Anthracite	Pennsylvania	1900	3
	West Virginia	1901	3
	Kentucky	1901	2
Anthracite	Pennsylvania	1902	5
	West Virginia	1902	1
	Southern Colo.	1903	3
	West Virginia	1903	3
	Ala., Tenn., Ky.	1904	3
	West Virginia	1905	1
	Tennessee	1905	2
	Kentucky	1906	3
Anthracite	Pennsylvania	1906	9

TEXTILES, MANUFACTURING, AND MISCELLANEOUS

City water works	Detroit	1894	3
Silk workers	New York City	1902	1
Bookbinders	Akron, Ohio	1903	1
Glass workers	Rochester, N.Y.	1904	1
Shirtwaistmakers	New York City	1909	1

AGRICULTURE AND FOOD

Brewery workers	West Coast	1890	1
Cotton	Arkansas	1891	15
Meat packing	Chicago	1904	4

TRANSPORT
  (1) TEAMSTERS

Coal teamsters	Providence, R.I.	1903	1
	St. Louis	1904	1
	Chicago	1905	14

  (2) RAILROADS

General	General and Chicago	1894	10
Railroad conductors	Mobile and Ohio RR.	1903	1

  (3) STREETCARS

	Brooklyn, N.Y.	1895	1
	Cleveland, Ohio	1899	1
	St. Louis	1900	11
	Albany and Troy, N.Y.	1901	1
	Pawtucket, R.I.	1902	1
	Waterbury, Conn.	1903	1
	St. Louis	1903	4
	Sacramento, Cal.	1907	6

  (4) SAILORS

	San Francisco	1892	1
	West Coast	1893	5
	West Coast	1906	1

  (5) LONGSHOREMEN

Cotton	New Orleans	1894	1
Cotton	New Orleans	1895	5
Grain	Buffalo, N.Y.	1899	2
General	San Francisco	1901	5

CONSTRUCTION AND ALLIED TRADES

Housesmiths	New York City	1892	1
Marble workers	New York City	1898	1
General building	Chicago	1900	5
Construction	Croton Dam, N.Y.	1900	1

Industry	Location	Date	Deaths
STEEL AND ALLIED TRADES			
Iron molders	San Francisco	1890	1
Steel	Braddock and Pittsburgh, Pa.	1891	1
Steel	Homestead, Pa.	1892	10
Molders	Cleveland	1899	3
Iron molders	Cincinnati	1904	1
Metal polishers	Newark, Ohio	1905	3
Iron molders	Milwaukee, Wisc.	1906	1
Iron molders	Buffalo, N.Y.	1906	1
Car workers	McKees Rocks, Pa.	1909	9
STEEL ERECTION			
Ironworkers	Cleveland	1896	1
Ironworkers	General	1906	2
Ironworkers	General	1907	1
MACHINISTS			
Railroad machinists	Columbia, S.C.	1901	2
Machinists	Chicago	1901	1
		TOTAL	308

Notes

Abbreviations Used in the Notes

AFL	AFL-CIO Library, Washington
HIL	Hoover Institution Library, Stanford, Calif.
HL	Houghton Library, Harvard University, Cambridge, Mass.
JC	John Crerar Library, Chicago
LC	Library of Congress, Washington
LD	Legislative Division, National Archives, Washington
MHS	Massachusetts Historical Society, Boston
NA	National Archives, Washington
NL	Newberry Library, Chicago
NYPL	New York Public Library, New York City
SCCU	Butler Library, Columbia University, New York City
TI	Tamiment Institute Library, New York City
UM	University of Michigan Libraries, Ann Arbor
WL	State Historical Society, Madison, Wisc.
AMB	Anita McCormick Blaine Papers, WL
AMS	Algie M. Simons Papers, WL
BC	Bridgemen's Union Correspondence, UM
CIR	Commission on Industrial Relations materials, NA and WL
CM	Charles McCarthy Papers, WL
EEW	E. E. Witte Papers, WL

EG   Emma Goldman Papers, NYPL
ESt   Ethelbert Stewart Papers, NA
EVD   Eugene V. Debs Papers, TI
FW   Frank Walsh Papers, NYPL
GPRR   Gubernatorial Papers of Ronald Reagan, HIL
GT   Graham Taylor Papers, NL
HCL   Henry Cabot Lodge Papers, MHS
JI   Joseph Ishill Papers, HL
JL   Joseph Labadie Collection, UM
JRC   John R. Commons Papers, WL
LW   Lillian Wald Papers, NYPL
ME   Marc Eidlitz Papers, NYPL
MH   Morris Hillquit Papers, WL
NCF   National Civic Federation Papers, NYPL
SG/AFL   Samuel Gompers Letterbooks, AFL (now in LC)
SG/WL   Samuel Gompers Correspondence in AFL Papers, WL
SML   S. M. Lindsay Papers, SCCU
WD   Walter Drew Papers, UM
WEB   William E. Borah Papers, LC
WML   William M. Leiserson Papers, WL

Chapter 1: Introduction

1. Bernard Schwartz, *The Great Rights of Mankind: A History of the American Bill of Rights* (New York, 1977), p. 199.

2. For studies of vigilantism and white ethnic riots, see Richard M. Brown, *Strain of Violence: Historical Studies of American Violence and Vigilantism* (New York, 1975) and Michael Feldberg, *The Philadelphia Riots of 1844: A Study of Ethnic Conflict* (Westport, Conn., 1975).

3. On Revolutionary and antebellum ideology see, for example, Bernard Bailyn, *The Ideological Origins of the American Revolution* (Cambridge, Mass., 1967), David Brion Davis, *Homicide in American Fiction, 1798–1860: A Study in Social Values* (Ithaca, N.Y., 1957). On the genesis of the idea of the general-welfare state in the United States, see Sidney Fine, *Laissez-Faire and the General-Welfare State: A Study of Conflict in American Thought, 1885–1901* (Ann Arbor, 1956).

4. B. Rose, "Violence During Strikes—the Union Side," *Weekly Bulletin,* IV (August 1905), 5.

5. "Revival of Violence," *Nation,* XCM (1912), 580.

6. See Burns, *The Masked War: The Story of a Peril that Threatened the United States by the Man who Uncovered the Dynamite Conspirators and Sent them to Jail* (New York, 1913).

7. John R. Commons, *Labor and Administration* (New York, 1913), p. 72.

8. See Charles Forcey, *The Crossroads of Liberalism: Croly, Weyl, Lippmann, and the Progressive Era, 1900–1925* (New York, 1961).

Chapter 2: The Anatomy of a Myth

1. Edward Pessen, *Jacksonian America: Society, Personality, and Politics* (Homewood, Ill., 1969), p. 67.

2. John Steuben, *Strike Strategy* (New York, 1950), pp. 300–312.

3. Philip Taft and Philip Ross, "American Labor Violence: Its Causes, Character, and Outcome," in Hugh D. Graham and Ted R. Gurr, eds., *The History of Violence in America* (New York, 1969), p. 367.

4. John R. Commons *et al.*, eds., *A Documentary History of American Industrial Society*, 11 vols. (Cleveland, 1910–1911), V, 178. This passage selected for publication by Commons and his associates was, in fact, uncharacteristic of the normally sensible arguments advanced by Frances Wright. For this point I am indebted to Kathryn R. Phillips, whose essay "Frances Wright: Misplaced Recognition" will be published in the *Bulletin of the Scottish Society for the Study of Labour History* in 1978.

5. Maurice F. Neufeld, "Realms of Thought and Organized Labor in the Age of Jackson," *Labor History*, X (Winter 1969), 30.

6. Commons *et al.*, *Documentary History*, III, 377–378.

7. Philip S. Foner, *History of the Labor Movement in the United States*, 4 vols. (New York, 1947–1965), I, 354.

8. Brace, *Dangerous Classes of New York* (New York, 1872), p. 25.

9. Quoted in George Hardy, *Those Stormy Years* (London, 1956), p. 152.

10. Henry George, *Progress and Poverty* (50th Anniversary ed., New York, 1929), p. 10.

11. William Appleman Williams, *The Contours of American History* (Chicago, 1966), pp. 364–65.

12. Bellamy, *Looking Backward, 2000–1887* (New York, 1888), p. 18.

13. Behrends, *A Sermon on the Brooklyn Strike: The Pauline Doctrine of the Sword* (New York, 1895), pp. 3, 14.

14. Testimony of R. D. Layton in U.S. Senate, *Report of the Committee of the Senate upon the Relations between Labor and Capital, and Testimony taken by the Committee,* 4 vols. (Washington, 1885), I, pp. 13–14; "The Futility of Force," *Journal of the Knights of Labor,* XIII (August 1892), 2.

15. Charles Forcey, *The Crossroads of Liberalism* (New York, 1961), pp. 160–161, Inis Weed, The Industrial Causes of Violence . . . , 4 parts (n.p., n.d.), CIR/NA.

16. For example, Ray Stannard Baker, "Reign of Lawlessness," *McClure's,* XXIII (May 1904); Herbert Newton Casson, "Psychology of a Strike Riot," *Independent,* LIII (May 1901).

17. Isaac F. Marcosson, "The Fight for the Open Shop," *World's Work,* XI (1905), 6955.

18. Walter Drew in Minutes of the National Erectors' Association Executive Committee Meeting (New York, December 28, 1909), FW; Thomas Beet, "Methods of American Private Detective Agencies," *Appleton's Magazine,* VIII (1906), 439–445; John H. Craige, "Professional Strike Breaker," *Collier's,* IV (December 3, 1910), 20.

19. Runyon, *McClure's,* XXVIII (1906–1907), 379–385.

20. Christopher P. Connolly, "Protest by Dynamite," *Collier's* XLVIII (January 1912), 24.

21. Tichenor, *A Wave of Horror: A Comparative Picture of the Los Angeles Tragedy,* Rip Saw Series, No. 8 (St. Louis, 1911), p. 5.

22. Drew, *Closed Shop Unionism* (New York, 1910), p. 5.

23. Minutes NEA Executive (New York, January 9, May 16, 1911; Philadelphia, May 3, 1911), FW.

24. U.S. Senate, Committee on Education and Labor, *Violations of Free Speech and the Rights of Labor,* 76 Cong., 1 sess. (1939), Report No. 6, Part 6, *Labor Policies of Employers' Associations. The National Association of Manufacturers,* p. 7.

25. Colorado Mine Operators' Association, comp., *Criminal Record of the Western Federation of Miners: Coeur d'Alene to Cripple Creek, 1894–1904* (Colorado Springs, 1904); Western Federation of Miners, *Reply of the Western Federation of Miners to the "Red Book" of the Mine Operators' Association* (Denver, 1904).

26. National Foundry Association, *A Policy of Lawlessness* (Detroit, 1908).

27. Quoted in "A Report on Labor Disturbances in the State of Colorado, from 1880 to 1904, Inclusive," *Senate Document,* 58 Cong., 2 sess., no. 122 (1905), p. 49.

28. *Typographical Journal,* XXVI (September 1907), 314.

29. These generalizations are based on items in trade-union journals; for a listing of the individual editorials, see R. Jeffreys-Jones, "The

Problem of Industrial Violence in the United States, 1899–1909"
(Cambridge University, Ph.D., 1969), pp. 329–335.

30. Simons, "Violence and the Socialist Movement," *International Socialist Revue,* III (February 1903), 8.

31. Reviews clipped from *Independent* (December 28, 1911) and *New York Sun,* January 20, 1912, AMS.

32. *Pittsburgh Gazette,* December 31, 1911.

33. Clipping from *Living Age* (February 17, 1912), AMS.

34. Simons, "Socialism versus Anarchism," *Chicago Workers' Call,* September 21, 1901.

35. De Leon, *Socialism versus Anarchism* (New York, 1901).

36. Adams and Sumner, *Labor Problems* (New York, 1905), pp. 211–212.

37. Adams, "Violence in Labor Disputes," *Publications of the American Economic Association,* 3d ser., VII (1906), 184 n.

38. *Ibid.,* p. 179.

39. *Ibid.,* pp. 200, 201, 205.

40. Allen T. Davis, "The Campaign for the Industrial Relations Commission, 1911–1913," *Mid-America,* XLV (October 1963), 226; Philip Taft, *Organized Labor in American History* (New York, 1964), p. 227.

41. Davis, "Campaign," 226.

42. Stenographer's minutes, statements of William M. Leiserson, Edward T. Devine, and Charles McCarthy only, CIR (Washington, December 30, 1913), WML, p. 410.

43. Georges Sorel, *Reflections on Violence* (1908), trans. T. E. Hulme (London, 1915), p. 171.

44. See Luke Grant, Violence in Labor Disputes and Methods of Policing Industry (n.p., n.d.), CIR/NA, p. 28; Anon., "Violence of American Trade Unions," article reprinted from *The Nation,* n.d., in *Living Age,* CCLXXVI (February 1913), 312; Beet, "Methods," 445; AFL President Samuel Gompers' speech before the 1907 annual AFL convention, referred to in John F. McNamee, "Spies and Traitors," *Brotherhood of Locomotive Firemen's and Enginemen's Magazine,* XLVI (February 1909), 451; Robert W. Hunter, *Violence and the Labor Movement* (New York, 1914), p. 281; Sidney Howard, *The Labor Spy* (New York, 1924), p. 179.

45. Adams, "Violence," 207.

46. Fred P. Graham, "A Contemporary History of American Crime," in Hugh D. Graham and Ted R. Gurr, eds., *The History of Violence in America* (New York, 1969), p. 493.

47. McClure, "The Increase of Lawlessness in the United States," *McClure's,* XXIV (December 1904), 169.

48. B. Rose, "Violence During Strikes—the Union Side," *Weekly Bulletin,* IV (August 1905), 5.

49. Thompson, "Violence in Labor Conflicts," *Outlook,* LXXVIII (1904), 972.

50. Adams, "Violence," 187, 189, 191, 209.

51. Holmes, *Violence* (New York, 1920), p. xiv.

52. U.S. Senate, *Violations* (see note 24 above; known as the La Follette investigation after its chairman, Robert M. La Follette, Jr.), 76 Cong., 1 sess. (1939), Report No. 6, Part 3, *Industrial Munitions;* Howard, *Labor Spy* (New York, 1924); Levinson, *I Break Strikes!* (New York, 1935).

53. *New York Times,* March 25, 1942.

54. *United States News,* XXII (January 3, 1947), 27–31.

55. G. Higgins, Elinore Herrick, and Jack Barbash referred to in a review by John M. Corridan, *Social Order* (May 1951).

56. "Company Blasted by Union," *Detroit News,* December 2, 1948.

57. NLRB, for immediate release, March 1, 1960 (R-682), EEW.

58. Laski, *The American Democracy* (London, 1949), p. 200; Selig Perlman and Philip Taft, *Labor Movements, 1896–1932* (New York, 1955), p. 61.

59. Burke, *Reflections on the Revolution in France* (London, 1790); Glanmor Williams, ed., *Merthyr Politics* (Cardiff, 1966), p. 24; Archibald Alison, *History of Europe from the Commencement of the French Revolution,* 7th ed., 20 vols. (Edinburgh, 1847), I, p. xxiv.

60. Mill, *Principles of Political Economy,* in *Collected Works of John Stuart Mill,* ed. J. M. Robson (Toronto, 1965), II, pp. 396–398, III, pp. 929–934.

61. Sutherland, *The Gospel of Plunder and Murder* (London, 1913), pp. 96–97; W. Collison, *The Apostle of Free Labor* (London, 1913), p. 205; E. H. Phelps-Brown, *The Growth of British Industrial Relations* (London & New York, 1959), p. 322.

62. Phelps-Brown, *Growth,* p. 330; Dangerfield, *The Strange Death of Liberal England* (New York, 1935); Standish Meacham, " 'The Sense of Impending Clash': English Working-Class Unrest before the First World War," *American Historical Review,* LXXVII (December 1972), 1343, 1346–1348.

63. McClure, "Increase," 169.

64. Richard M. Brown, *Strain of Violence* (New York, 1975), p. 324.

65. See Richard Tilly, "Popular Disorders in Nineteenth-Century Germany: A Preliminary Survey," *Journal of Social History,* IV (Fall 1970), 34; Ted R. Gurr, *Rogues, Rebels, and Reformers* (Beverly Hills, 1976), pp. 56–64, 68–71.

66. Eric Hobsbawm, *Labouring Men* (London, 1968), pp. 1, 374.

67. French ratio based on figures in Phelps-Brown, *Growth,* p. 332.

68. Welsh ratio based on figures in Phelps-Brown, *Growth,* p. 322. Cf. David Williams, *A History of Modern Wales* (London, 1950), p. 244.

69. See Chapter 5 for the background to the leaflet. For the text, see Morris Friedman, *The Pinkerton Labor Spy* (New York, 1907), opposite page 130.

70. Graham, "Contemporary History," pp. 491, 493.

71. Ratios based on figures in Philip Taft and Philip Ross, "American Labor Violence: Its Causes, Character, and Outcome," in Graham and Gurr, *History of Violence,* pp. 289, 332 (the aggregates for 1877 and 1913, high as they were, being partial), in Steuben, *Strike Strategy,* pp. 300–312, and in the Appendix.

72. The last two columns in Table I are included to show that they contain insufficient data for any simple analysis. For guidance at this point, I am indebted to the statistician Mr. C. W. Derek Peare.

73. Reported in the *Machinists' Monthly Journal,* XVI (February 1904), 117.

74. For assurance concerning this point, I am once again indebted to Mr. Peare.

Chapter 3: The Making of U.S. Revolutionary Theory

1. Steffens, *Autobiography* (New York, 1931), pp. 285–291; Ireland, *The Personal Freedom of the Individual Citizen,* 2 parts (n.p., n.d.), part 1, p. 3.

2. J. M. Cooper, "The Army and Civil Disorder: Federal Military Intervention in American Labor Disputes, 1877–1900" (Wisconsin, Ph.D., 1971), pp. 40, 60, 61, 139, 140.

3. F. P. Graham, "A Contemporary History of American Crime," in H. D. Graham and T. R. Gurr, eds., *The History of Violence in America* (New York, 1969), pp. 490, 491; Franklin, "Social Workers and Labor Violence," *Survey,* XXIX (February 1913), 619.

4. Avelings, *The Working-Class Movement in America,* 2nd and enl. ed. (London, 1891), p. 238; Henry David, *The History of the Haymarket Affair* (New York, 1936), p. 534.

5. Avelings, *Working-Class,* p. 238.

6. Tucker-Labadie, June 5, 1886, JI.

7. Hunter, *Violence and the Labor Movement* (New York, 1914), p. 68.

8. Hunter, *Poverty,* ed. Peter d'A. Jones (New York, 1965, originally published in 1904), pp. vii–xi, 61.

9. Hunter, *Violence,* pp. 229, 230; Sorel, *Reflections on Violence,* trans. T. E. Hulme (New York, 1961), pp. 77, 112, 127, 186.

10. Hunter, *Violence,* Chapters 10 and 11.

11. Karl Marx, Frederick Engels, and Wilhelm Liebknecht against Louis B. Boudin (an essay by Hillquit, 1911), MH; Hunter, *Violence,* p. 324.

12. T. R. Gurr, *Rogues, Rebels, and Reformers: A Political History of Urban Crime and Conflict* (Beverly Hills, 1976), pp. 62, 63; Daniel Bell, *The End of Ideology,* rev. ed. (New York, 1965), p. 156; R. M. Brown, *Strain of Violence* (New York, 1975), pp. 324, 326; *Report of the National Advisory Commission on Civil Disorders* (New York, 1968), p. 115.

13. A. M. Schlesinger, Jr., *A Thousand Days: John F. Kennedy in the White House* (London, 1965), p. 113; Graham, "Contemporary History," p. 491.

14. E. J. Bacciocco, *The New Left in America* (Stanford, 1974), p. 187; Jack Woddis, *New Theories of Revolution: A Commentary on the Views of Frantz Fanon, Regis Debray and Herbert Marcuse* (London, 1972), p. 398; Bell, *End of Ideology,* p. 393f; Marshall McLuhan, *The Medium Is the Message* (Harmondsworth, 1967), pp. 18, 44, 117.

Chapter 4: Workers and Violence, 1886–1912

1. *New York World,* August 18, 1890; Powderly, "Powderly on Carnegie and Pinkertonism," *Journal of the Knights of Labor,* XIII (July 14, 1892), 1.

2. *New York Times,* August 31, 1896.

3. Haywood, "Socialism the Hope of the Working Class," *International Socialist Review,* XII (February 1912), 467.

4. C. P. Connolly, "Protest by Dynamite," *Collier's,* XLVIII (January 13, 1912), 9.

5. "Report on the Chicago Strike of June–July, 1894," *Senate Executive Document,* 53 Cong., 3 sess., no. 7 (1895), p. xlv.

6. *New York Times,* July 5, 1894.

7. U.S. Industrial Commission, *Reports . . . ,* 19 vols. (Washington, 1900–1902), XVII, *Labor Organizations,* p. 596; *Report on the Chicago Strike of June–July, 1894 by the United States Strike Commission* (Washington, 1894), p. 15.

8. Quoted in WFM, *Reply of the Western Federation of Miners to the "Red Book" of the Mine Operators' Association* (Denver, 1904), p. 29.

9. *Statesman,* clipping, June 28, 1906 in WEB.

10. Seidman, *Labor Czars* (New York, 1938), p. 11.

11. *New York Times,* October 16, 1892.

12. *Typographical Journal,* XXVII (September, 1905), 321–22; (Girard) *Appeal to Reason,* August 20, 1904.

13. *Tribune,* July 15, 1904.

14. *Typographical Journal,* XXVII (September, 1905), 321–22.

15. Henry Pelling, "Labor and Politics in Chicago," *Political Studies,* V (February 1957), 28.

16. *San Francisco Examiner,* September 26, 1893; *Coast Seamen's Journal,* VI (September 27, 1893), 8; John A. Commons and associates, *History of Labor in the United States,* 4 vols. (New York, 1918–1935), IV, 201.

17. Sellin and Wolfgang, *The Measurement of Delinquency* (New York, 1964), p. 31.

18. "A Scholarly 'Review'," *Coast Seamen's Journal,* V (September 14, 1892), 5.

19. *San Francisco Examiner,* September 26, 1893.

20. "Brickbats in the City of Brotherly Love," *Collier's,* XLVI (March 12, 1910), 12.

21. Mussey, "Trade-unions and Public Policy: Democracy or Dynamite?" *Atlantic,* CIX (April 1912), 442.

22. Franklin, "Social Workers and Labor Violence," *Survey,* XXIX (1913), 618.

23. *New York Times,* June 18, 1899.

24. "Some Errors of Trade Unions," *Independent,* LV (July 30, 1903), 1818.

25. Gompers, *Seventy Years of Life and Labor,* 2 vols. (New York, 1925), II, p. 180.

26. E. V. Debs, "The Martyred Apostles of Labor," *New Time* (February, 1899?), 80.

27. Cleveland, *Government in the Chicago Strike of 1894* (Princeton, 1913), p. 38.

28. *Typographical Journal,* XXXI (September 1907), 314; *New York Times,* November 20, 1915, quoted in Philip S. Foner, *The Case of Joe Hill* (New York, 1965), p. 103; "Samuel Parks Released," *Outlook,* LXXV (September 12, 1903), 98–99.

29. "Murder of Comrade Kelner," *Coast Seamen's Journal,* XIX (June 20, 1906), 6–7.

30. "Bloody Work at Morewood," *Journal of the Knights of Labor,* XI (April 9, 1891), 4; *New York Times,* July 6, 1896.

31. *Press,* July 2, 1892.

32. Fitch, *The Steel Workers* (New York, 1910), p. 101.

33. *Journal,* V (September 14, 1892), 5.

34. *Monthly Journal,* XXV, 507.

35. *Minutes of the Twelfth Annual Convention of the United Mine Workers of America,* 1901, p. 28, quoted in Philip Taft, *Organized Labor in American History* (New York, 1964), p. 175.

36. *Times,* September 20, 1902.

37. Roosevelt-Crane, October 22, 1902, in Elting E. Morrison, ed., *The Letters of Theodore Roosevelt,* 8 vols. (Cambridge, Mass., 1951–1954), p. 361.

38. For an assessment of the outcome of the strike, see Robert J. Cornell, "The Commission Decides," in *The Anthracite Coal Strike of 1902* (Washington, 1957).

39. United States Coal Strike Commission, Proceedings of the Anthracite Coal Strike Commission, 56 vols. (1902–1903), LC, I, pp. 1–2; Edward Pinkowski; *Lattimer Massacre* (Philadelphia, 1950), p. 11.

40. Anthracite Coal Strike Procs., XXXVI, p. 6022.

41. *Ibid.,* II, p. 136.

42. *Ibid.,* IV, pp. 415–416, 440–441, V, p. 469.

43. *Ibid.,* IV, pp. 430, 470.

44. *Ibid.,* IV, p. 430.

45. *Report on the Chicago Strike,* p. 152.

46. *Report of the Anthracite Coal Strike Commission* (Washington, 1903), pp. 500–501.

47. Anthracite Coal Strike Procs., IV, pp. 422, 426, 429, 437; V, pp. 476, 480.

48. Cf. "Problems to Be Solved," *American Federationist,* XVI (October 1909), 872; "Violence You Don't Read About," *Typographical Journal,* XXVII (September 1905), 303.

49. Anthracite Coal Strike Procs., IV, p. 438.

50. *Ibid.,* IV, p. 417.

51. *Ibid.,* V, p. 554.

52. *Ibid.,* II, p. 141.

53. "Violence Deprecated," *Locomotive Engineers' Monthly Journal,* XXXV (August 1901), 506; *Weekly Bulletin,* IV (September 1, 1905), 5; *Typographical Journal,* XXVII (September 1905), 321–322.

54. See, for example, "Unions and the Law," *Coast Seamen's Journal,* XX (June 19, 1907), 7.

55. *New York Times,* October 24, 1902.

56. Anthracite Coal Strike Procs., IV, p. 451.

57. *Ibid.,* V, p. 469.

58. *Ibid.,* IV, pp. 423–424, V, p. 469.

59. *Express,* June 17, 1893; *Conductor,* II (May 1896), 1; *Journal,* XXXV (August 1901), 506.

60. *San Francisco Examiner,* September 26, 1901; "Illustrating a Need," *Coast Seamen's Journal,* XV (October 2, 1901), 6.

61. John Mitchell, *Organized Labor* (Philadelphia, 1903), p. 385.

62. For example, *Mother Earth,* IV (September 1909), 194; Lincoln Steffens, *The Autobiography of Lincoln Steffens* (New York, 1931), p. 659.

63. *Teamster,* V (March 1908), 9. See also *Ibid.,* IV (March 1907).

64. *McClure's* (January 1903); "Crimes Against Non-union Workers," *Outlook,* LXXIII (January 17, 1903), 141; and see Chapter 2.

65. For a discussion of Gompers' attitude toward labor violence, see Chapter 5.

Chapter 5: Of Inner Circles and Masked War

1. *Denver News,* July 7, 1901.

2. "Colorado Miners' Strike," *Current Literature,* XXXVI (June 1904), 594–595; B. M. Rastall, *The Labor History of the Cripple Creek District* (Madison, 1908), pp. 71–72; S. H. Holbrook, *The Rocky Mountain Revolution* (New York, 1956), pp. 142–43; D. H. Grover, *Debaters and Dynamiters* (Corvallis, 1964), pp. 44–47.

3. "A Report on Labor Disturbances in the State of Colorado, from 1880 to 1904, Inclusive," *Senate document,* 58 Cong., 3 sess., no. 122 (January 27, 1905), pp. 190–191; F. P. Valiant, Colorado Strike (n.p., 1915), CIR/NA, p. 24; "Review of the Labor Troubles in the Metalliferous Mines of the Rocky Mountain Region," *Senate document,* 58 Cong., 2 sess., no. 86 (January 14, 1904), p. 4; M. Friedman, *The Pinkerton Labor Spy* (New York, 1907), pp. 81–82.

4. "Report on Labor Disturbances," p. 192; *New York Times,* December 5, 1903; *Denver News,* November 22, 1903; WFM, *Reply of the Western Federation of Miners to the "Red Book" of the Mine Operators' Association* (Denver, 1904), p. 16.

5. *Appeal to Reason,* October 15, 1906.

6. *Times,* November 23, 1903.

7. *Appeal to Reason,* October 15, 1906; *WFM,* Reply, pp. 1–2.

8. *New York Times,* June 11, 1904.

9. A. E. Horsley (alias Harry Orchard, alias Tom Hogan), *The Confessions and Autobiography of Harry Orchard* (New York, 1907), pp. 128–140, 196.

10. *Denver News,* July 7, 1904.

11. *Idaho Daily Statesman,* June 26, 1906.

12. Orchard, *Confessions,* pp. 127–128.

13. *Ibid.*, pp. 122, 126–140, 196.

14. *Official Proceedings of the Twelfth Annual Convention, Western Federation of Miners* (1904), p. 204.

15. "Developments in the Conspiracy," *Miners Magazine,* VII (May 1906), 5; Friedman, *Spy,* pp. 21–23, 30–34.

16. WFM *Proceedings* (1904), pp. 2, 18, 19, 185.

17. Charles Teller, "Labor War in Colorado," *Harper's Weekly,* XLVIII (1904), 641–643.

18. *Appeal to Reason,* October 13, 1906.

19. Cf. B. M. Rastall, *An Enquiry into the Cripple Creek Strike of 1893* (Colorado Springs, 1905), p. 6 and Rastall's *The Labor History of the Cripple Creek District* (Madison, 1908), pp. 63–64.

20. H. Cohen, "A Chapter from Chicago's History," *American Federationist,* VIII (September 1901), 344.

21. *Ryan et al.* v. *United States* (7th Circuit, U.S. Court of Appeals), 216 U.S. 13 (1914), 25, 27.

22. H. Seidman, *Labor Czars* (New York, 1938), p. 12; R. S. Baker, "Trust's New Tool—the Labor Boss," *McClure's,* XXII (November 1903), 31.

23. In ME.

24. H. F. Lofland, general manager of erection, American Bridge Company of New York—Walter Drew, September 23, 1907, WD.

25. *New York Tribune,* March 11, 1906.

26. Anon.—W. C. Post, March 18, 1907, WD.

27. *Review,* October 14, 1929.

28. Eidlitz & Hulse—Drew, May 1, 1907, WD.

29. Anon., Memoranda in re Thomas Slattery, October 15, 1913, WD.

30. Webb-McNamara, May 29, 1919, BC.

31. J. Pryor-Ryan, June 15, 1910, Webb-McNamara, June 28, 1910, H. Jones-McNamara, January 20, 1911, Ryan-McNamara, February 20, 1911, all in BC.

32. Drew—M. E. Hartigan, August 3, 1907, WD.

33. *New York Tribune,* November 30, December 8, 1905, March 25–28, May 10, 1906; Eidlitz & Hulse—Drew, May 1, 1907, WD.

34. Minutes of the National Erectors' Association General Meeting (March 28, 1911), FW.

35. "Blow Up Open Shop Houses," *Square Deal,* V (December 1909), 442.

36. *Ibid.; Ryan* v. *U.S.,* pp. 25, 27; Luke Grant, *The National Erectors' Association and the International Association of Bridge and Structural Ironworkers* (Washingon, 1915), p. 137.

37. Drew—C. L. McKenzie, May 22, 1907, WD.

38. Minutes of the NEA Executive Committee Meeting (March 1, 1907), FW.

39. Cohen-Drew, October 26, 1910, WD.

40. Minutes NEA Executive (June 19, 1908, July 9, 1909), FW; replies from NEA executive board members to Drew's proposals to consolidate his own detective bureau (1910), WD.

41. Charles McCarthy-Burns, February 10, 1915, CM; Minutes NEA Executive (December 28, 1909, October 25, 1910, January 9, 1911), FW; Minutes NEA General Meeting (March 28, 1911), FW; Drew-C. M. Cheney, May 1, 1911, FW.

42. Gompers to F. M. Ryan, May 8, 1911; SG/WL.

43. Drew, *Labor Unions* (n.p., n.d.), pp. 10–11; Drew, "Were the Acts of the McNamaras Individual or Representative?" *Los Angeles Times,* October 31, 1914.

44. *Report of the Proceedings of the Thirty-Second Annual Convention of the American Federation of Labor* (1912), p. 141.

45. Gompers-Ryan, June 16, 1909, SG/AFL.

46. Typewritten resolution or copy of the resolution, BC; *New Orleans Times-Democrat,* April 23, 1911.

47. Ryan-members of IABSI, circular letter, April 25, 1911, SG/ WL.

48. McManigal, *The National Dynamite Plot* (Los Angeles, 1913) p. 46; William J. Burns, "Unionism and Dynamite," *McClure's,* XXXVIII (February 1912), 364, 367; Kirby, "The Benefits of Industrial Combinations," *The Annals of the American Academy of Political Science,* XLII (July 1912), 123; *Chronicle,* April 24, 1911.

49. *Union,* December 9, 1911; Woehlke, "Terrorism in America," *Outlook,* C (February 6, 1912), 362; "Violence of American Trade Unions" (reprinted from *The Nation,* n.d.), *Living Age,* CCLXXVI (February 1913), 311.

50. David Fisher, "Home Colony: An American Experiment in Anarchism" (Edinburgh, M. Litt., 1971), pp. 136–137.

51. Edwin E. Witte, Injunctions and Acts of Violence in Labor Disputes (n.p., 1915), quoted in Inis Weed, The Industrial Causes of Violence . . . , 4 parts (n.d.), CIR/NA, part I, p. 57.

Chapter 6: Armed Guards

1. "Investigation of the Employment of Pinkerton Detectives in Connection with the Labor Troubles at Homestead, Pa.," *House Miscellaneous Document,* 52 Cong., 1 sess., no. 335 (1892), p. xiv; U.S. Senate, Committee on Education and Labor, *Violations of Free Speech*

and the Rights of Labor, 76 Cong., 1 sess. (1939), Report no. 6, Part 1, *Strikebreaking Services,* p. 7.

2. *Strikebreaking Services,* p. 14; *New York Times,* August 18, 1890, August 17, 1892; *New York World,* August 18, 1890; "Unity, and no Surrender!" *Journal of the Knights of Labor,* XI (August 1890), 2.

3. Petition of 142 union workingmen, citizens of Fort Wayne, Indiana, to House of Representatives, April 12, 1892, LD; "Investigation of the Employment of Pinkerton Detectives," pp. xiv, xv; "Investigation in Relation to the Employment for Private Purposes of Armed Bodies of Men, or Detectives, in Connection with Differences between Workmen and Employers," *Senate Report,* 52 Cong., 2 sess., no. 1280 (February 10, 1893), p. x.

4. *Richmond Times Dispatch,* June 17, 1903; *New York Herald,* n.d., quoted in *American Industries,* III (April 1905), 3.

5. *New York Herald,* n.d., quoted in *American Industries,* III (April 1905), 3; *New York Times,* March 3, 1905; W. Zumach, Report on Investigation of Detective Agencies (1914), CIR/WL, pp. 9, 10, 23.

6. Zumach, Report, p. 6; *New York Herald,* n.d., quoted in *American Industries,* III (April 1905), 3; *New York Tribune,* May 2, 1905; J. H. Craige, "Professional Strikebreaker," *Collier's,* XLVI (December 3, 1910), 20.

7. "Report on the Chicago Strike of June–July, 1894," *Senate Executive Document,* 53 Cong., 3 sess., no. 7 (1895), p. xliv; *New York Times,* May 5, 1905.

8. W. B. Bremer and P. Stewart, Report on the Strike of International Teamsters' Union against Montgomery Ward & Co. (1905), E St, pp. 189, 193 and appended figures.

9. *San Francisco Chronicle,* May 7, 1907; "Kellner Case Ended," *Coast Seamen's Journal,* XX (June 1907), 6.

10. *Report of the Bureau of Statistics of Labor for the State of Louisiana* (1902–1903), p. 31; *Richmond Times Dispatch,* June 17, 1903; *Appeal to Reason,* May 5, 1906.

11. *American Industries,* III (April 1905), 3; "Corporation Brutality in West Virginia," *The Weekly Bulletin of the Clothing Trades,* IV (September 1905), 4; Testimony of Jack Robinson of Chicago in "Peonage in Western Pennsylvania," *Hearings before the Committee on Labor of the House of Representatives,* 62 Cong., 1 sess. (1911), p. 6; *Michigan Union Advocate* (Detroit), September 1909.

12. "Slavery Practised," *The Amalgamated Journal,* X (August 1909), 1; *Pittsburgh Post,* July 21, 1909; *Strikebreaking Services,* p. 8; D. O'Regan, Conclusion Derived from Investigation of Armed Guards

up to September 1914, p. 3, Zumach, Report, *passim,* and Anon., List of Detectives (1914), both in CIR/WL.

13. G. Dilnot, *Great Detectives and Their Methods* (London, c. 1927), p. 217; F. Fligelman, Violence: Notes on Pinkerton's National Detective Agency (n.d.), CIR/WL, p. 21; F. R. Prassel, *The Western Peace Officer* (Norman, Oklahoma, 1972), pp. 29, 72; G. E. and E. H. Carte, *Police Reform in the United States: The Era of August Vollmer, 1905–1932* (Berkeley, 1975).

14. D. O'Regan, A Study of Detective Agencies that Supply Strikebreakers and Armed Guards in Time of Industrial Disputes (1914), CIR/NA, p. 1.

15. J. B. Hogg, "Public Reaction to Pinkertonism and the Labor Question," *Pennsylvania History,* XI (1944), 180; *Strikebreaking Services,* p. 15; *New York Times,* May 25, 29, 1894; *Pittsburgh Post,* May 24, 25, 1894; *Annual Report of the Secretary of Internal Affairs of the Commonwealth of Pennsylvania,* part 3, *Industrial Statistics* (1894), pp. 20–30; "Committee," signed by A. Campbell and others for Local Assembly 5539, K of L, memorandum/petition to Allen, June 2, 1894, LD; *Seventeenth Annual Report of the State Bureau of Labor Statistics Concerning Coal in Illinois* (1898), p. 7.

16. *Strikebreaking Services,* pp. 15, 17; Drew-John R. Commons, November 9, 1914, CM.

17. Dunn's National Detective Agency-McGill Manufacturing Co., August 6, 1920, JL.

18. *Report of the Committee of the Senate upon the Relations between Labor and Capital,* 4 vols. (Washington, D.C., 1885), I, p. 811.

19. E. V. Debs-A. Lee, October 10, 1918, EVD; "Alabama," *United Mine Workers Journal,* XIX (September 3, 1908), 4.

20. Proceedings of the GMA of Chicago (3 vols., 1886–1894), JC, II (1892–1893), p. 26, III (1894), pp. 106, 232; Walling, "Can Labor Unions be Destroyed?" *World's Work,* VIII (May 1904), 4757.

21. *Bulletin of the National Metal Trades Association;* Inis Weed, Preliminary Report on Violence (1916), CIR/NA, p. 96.

22. Lloyd, *Men, the Workers* (New York, 1909), p. 151; *Open Shop,* inside back cover; *American Industries* (May 1906).

23. E. L. Cole, reported in the *New York Call,* November 6, 1909; F. E. Sheldon, *Souvenir History of the Strike of the Ladies' Waist Makers' Union* (New York, c. 1910), p. 6.

24. Gompers, "Organized Labor," *United Mine Workers Journal,* I (April 1891), 1.

25. Bliss, *New Encyclopedia of Social Reform* (New York, 1910), p. 1167.

26. L. Grant, Violence in Labor Disputes and Methods of Policing

Industry (n.d.), CIR/WL, p. 80; U.S. Industrial Commission, *Final Report* (Washington, 1902), p. 891; *Final Report of the Commission on Industrial Relations* (Washington, 1915), p. 143; Damon Runyon, "The Song of the Strike-Breakers," in *The Tents of Trouble* (New York, 1911).

27. Hunter, *Violence and the Labor Movement* (New York, 1914), pp. 316, 324; *New York Times,* August 18, 1899; *Detroit Sentinel,* January 7, 1899; "Labelle Company's Disgrace," *Amalgamated Journal,* XI (November 1909), 1; U.S. Senate, Committee on Education and Labor, *Violations of the Free Speech and the Rights of Labor,* 77 Cong., 1 sess. (1941), Report No. 151, Part IV, *Labor Policies of Employers' Associations. The "Little Steel" Strike and Citizens' Committees,* p. 39; "A Stirring Account of the Chicago Strike," *Weekly Bulletin,* IV (December 1904), 1.

28. Lewis, *The Rise of the Slum Proletarian* (Chicago, 1907), p. 200; Mussey, "Trade Unions and Public Policy: Democracy or Dynamite?" *Atlantic Monthly,* CIX (1912), 443.

29. "Investigation of the Employment of Pinkerton Detectives," p. 35; "Unity, and No Surrender!" *Journal of the Knights of Labor,* XI (August 1890), 1.

30. Zumach, Report, p. 1; Grant, Violence, p. 6.

31. O'Regan-B. M. Manly, June 29, 1914, CIR/NA.

32. Zumach, Report, pp. 14–16.

33. Harold Seidman, *Labor Czars: A History of Labor Racketeering* (New York, 1938), pp. 45, 46; S. H. Holbrook, *The Rocky Mountain Revolution* (New York, 1956), pp. 147–150.

34. S. Gompers, F. Morrison, and A. Furuseth-members 55 Cong., January 6, 1898, Victor resolution of February 18, 1898, and E. F. Parker, president, Peoria Printing and Stationery Company, Peoria, Illinois-Senator A. J. Hopkins of Illinois, February 2, 1904, all in LD.

35. Witte, Summary of the Report on Injunctions in Labor Disputes (1915), CIR/NA, p. 1, "The Labor Injunction—A Red Flag," *American Labor Legislation Review,* XVIII (September 1928), 316, and "Value of Injunctions in Labor Disputes," *Journal of Political Economy,* XXXII (1924), 335, 336, 338, 343, 354.

36. Bremer and Stewart, Report, p. 171.

37. Zumach, Report, pp. 19, 21.

38. "Peonage in Western Pennsylvania"; "Limiting Federal Injunction," *Hearings Before a Subcommittee of the Senate Committee on the Judiciary on S. Res. 92,* 63 Cong., 1 sess. (1913), vol. I; Inis Weed, The Industrial Causes of Violence, 4 parts (n.d.), CIR/NA, part 3, p. 32.

39. *Twelfth Biennial Report of the Bureau of Labor, Industries and*

Commerce of the State of Minnesota (1909–1910), p. 50; *Rocky Mountain News,* December 18, 1903; *Michigan Union Advocate,* May 13, 1904; "The Culprit's Cry of 'Stop Thief!' " *American Federationist,* XI (January 1904), 35.

Chapter 7: Labor Spies

1. W. L. O'Neill, *Divorce in the Progressive Era* (New Haven, 1967), p. 20. For interwar reactions to "divorce work," see "The Gutting of Couffignal" in *The Big Knockover and Other Stories* (Harmondsworth, 1969), p. 25, and other stories by the former Pinkerton agent, S. Dashiell Hammett, and *The Lady in the Lake* (Harmondsworth, 1971), p. 10, by Raymond Chandler.

2. R. W. Rowan, *The Pinkertons: A Detective Dynasty* (London, 1931), pp. 13, 14, 246, 248; G. Dilnot, *Great Detectives and Their Methods* (London, c. 1927), p. 217.

3. *Glasgow Sentinel,* March 6, 1869 in H. G. Gutman, ed., "Five Letters of Immigrant Workers from Scotland to the United States," *Labor History,* IX (Fall 1968), 388–391; W. G. Broehl, *The Molly Maguires* (Cambridge, Mass., 1964).

4. Gutman, "Five Letters," 388.

5. G. F. O'Neil in S. A. Lavine, *Allan Pinkerton, America's First Private Eye* (London, 1965), p. vii.

6. A. J. F. Behrends, *A Sermon on the Brooklyn Strike* (New York, 1895), p. 8; "Investigation of the Employment of Pinkerton Detectives in Connection with the Labor Troubles at Homestead, Pa.," *House Miscellaneous Document,* 52 Cong., 1 sess., no. 335 (1892), p. xiv; Morris Friedman, *The Pinkerton Labor Spy* (New York, 1907), p. 4.

7. Friedman, *Pinkerton,* pp. 7, 22, 23, 178; *Idaho Daily Statesman,* June 20, 1906.

8. Friedman, *Pinkerton,* pp. 53, 54; Siringo, *Two Evil Isms: Pinkertonian and Anarchism; by a Cowboy Detective who Knows, as he Spent Twenty-Two Years in the Inner Circle of Pinkerton's National Detective Agency* (Chicago, 1915), title and p. 94.

9. Drew-Rossiter, March 9, 1907, WD; Scott-Furnas, August 4, 1920, JL.

10. Leo Huberman, *The Labor Spy Racket,* 2nd. ed. (New York, 1966), pp. 6, 15–17, 197; J. S. Auerbach, *Labor and Liberty: The La Follette Committee and the New Deal* (Indianapolis, 1966), pp. 99 n. 7, 112.

11. S. A. Doyle-Gompers, April 3, 1911, and M. Boyle-AFL, May 3, 1911, both in SG/WL.

12. *Proceedings of the Twenty-sixth Annual Convention of the Massachusetts State Board of the AFL* (1911), pp. 92, 93.

13. U.S. Senate, *Violations of Free Speech and the Rights of Labor,* 76 Cong., 1 sess. (1939), Report no. 6, Part VI, *Labor Policies of Employers' Associations. The National Association of Manufacturers,* p. 12; P. A. Zizelman-General Manager, Weltman Bros., New York City, July 14, 1905, JL.

14. Gompers speech to 1907 AFL convention quoted in J. F. McNamee, "Spies and Traitors," *Brotherhood of Locomotive Firemen and Engineers' Magazine,* XLVI (February 1909), 451; Adams, "Violence in Labor Disputes," *Publications of the American Economic Association,* 3rd Series, VII (1906), 180; Inis Weed, The Industrial Causes of Violence, 4 parts (n.d.), CIR/NA, part 3, p. 1; Jean E. Spielman, *The Stool Pigeon and the Open Shop Movement* (Minneapolis, 1923), p. 16; S. C. Howard, *The Labor Spy* (New York, 1924), p. 1.

15. Huberman, *Spy Racket,* pp. 6, 7, 193.

16. *Railroad Trainmen's Journal,* VIII (June 1891), 377.

17. *New York Times,* March 25, 1942.

18. Howard, *Labor Spy,* p. 65.

19. O'Regan, A Study of Detective Agencies that Supply Strike-Breakers and Armed Guards in Time of Industrial Disputes (1914), CIR/NA, p. 2.

20. Weed, Industrial Causes of Violence, part 1, pp. 15, 17; Burns-McCarthy, February 16, 1915, CM.

21. Foster-F. Mann, Mann & Co., New York, July 30, 1920, JL.

22. Murphy-J. H. McGill, president, J. M. McGill Manufacturing Co., Valparaiso, Indiana, August 16, 1920, JL; Cohen-W. Drew, October 26, 1910, WD.

23. Keleher-P. J. Furnas, General Food Products Co., New York City, July 22, 1920, JL.

24. W. D. Haywood, *A Detective* (n.p., n.d.), JL; McNamee, "Spies and Traitors," 449, 450, 452.

25. "The Brother in the Secret Service," *Railroad Trainmen's Journal,* XXIII (June 1906), 643; L. Grant, Violence in Labor Disputes and Methods of Policing Industry (n.d.), CIR/NA, p. 103.

26. S. A. Doyle-Gompers, April 3, 1911, M. Boyle-AFL, May 2, 1911, Frayne-Gompers, April 13, 1911, all in SG/WL; Zumach, untitled report on Burns' supervision (1914), CIR/WL.

27. Wein-Ray, September 17, 1901, NA.

28. Max Lowenthal, *The Federal Bureau of Investigation* (New York, 1950), p. 7.

29. C. McCarthy-Burns, February 10, 1915, and Burns-McCarthy, February 16, 1915, in CM.

30. Burns, *The Masked War* (New York, 1913), p. 209; Grant, Violence in Labor Disputes, p. 6.

Chapter 8: Truckling to the Labor Vote:
Theodore Roosevelt's Presidential Departure

1. Bernard Bailyn, *The Ideological Origins of the American Revolution* (Cambridge, Mass., 1967), p. 312.

2. H. B. Butler-Porter, April 30, 1899, in "Coeur d'Alene Mining Troubles . . . Correspondence regarding the Miners' Riots in the State of Idaho not included in Report of Brig. Gen. H. C. Merriam," *Senate Document,* 56 Cong., 1 sess., no. 142 (February 5, 1900), p. 54.

3. *Congressional Record,* 56 Cong., 1 sess., App. p. 669; *Who's Who in America* (Chicago, 1906–1907). Cf. B. M. Rich, *The Presidents and Civil Disorder* (Washington, 1941), pp. 114–120.

4. "Brickbats in the City of Brotherly Love," *Collier's,* XLIV (March 12, 1910), 11; *Final Report of the Commission on Industrial Relations* (Washington, 1915), p. 147; Grant, Violence in Labor Disputes and Methods of Policing Industry (n.d.), CIR/NA, p. 30; "Police Promotions; examination questions," *The Chief: Journal of the [New York City] Civil Service* (n.d.), NYPL, 2.

5. "A Report on Labor Disturbances in the State of Colorado, from 1880 to 1904, inclusive," *Senate Document,* 58 Cong., 3 sess., no. 122 (January 27, 1905), pp. 171, 249; B. M. Rastall, *The Labor History of the Cripple Creek District* (Madison, 1908), p. 152; *New York Times,* June 1, 1900; *Nashville American,* November 7, 1901, quoted in J. Ireland, *The Personal Freedom of the Individual Citizen,* 2 parts (n.p., n.d.), part 1, p. 19.

6. "Investigation of the Employment of Pinkerton Detectives in Connection with the Labor Troubles at Homestead, Pa.," *House Report,* 52 Cong., 2 sess., no. 2447 (February 7, 1893), p. xi and investigation of the same title, being *House Miscellaneous Document,* 52 Cong., 1 sess., no. 335 (1892), pp. 57, 58; *New York Times,* July 6, 1892; R. D. Smith, "Phases of the McKee's Rocks Strike," *Survey,* XXIII (October 2, 1909), 41.

7. *San Francisco Examiner,* September 30, October 1, 1901.

8. "Report on Labor Disturbances in the State of Colorado," p. 178; S. Gompers, *Seventy Years of Life and Labor,* 2 vols. (New York, 1925), II, p. 174; *Congressional Record,* 52 Cong., 1 sess., App. p. 285.

9. *New York Times,* October 28, 1894; *New Orleans Times-Democrat,* March 20, 1895; *St. Louis Republic,* May 27, 1900; *San Francisco Examiner,* September 26, 1901.

10. "Review of the Labor Troubles in the Metalliferous Mines of the Rocky Mountain Region," *Senate Document,* 58 Cong., 2 sess., no. 86 (January 13, 1904), p. 7.

11. *New York Times,* August 18, 1897; V. Hicken, "The Virden and Pana Mine Wars of 1898," *Journal of the Illinois State Historical Society,* LII (Summer 1959), 274; *Seventeenth Annual Report of the State Bureau of Labor Statistics Concerning Coal in Illinois, 1898,* p. 6; "The Crime of Competition," *Railroad Trainmen's Journal,* XV (November 1898), 921.

12. *Kansas City Star,* May 9, 1900; *St. Louis Globe-Democrat,* May 9, 10, 22, 23, 26, 29, 30, June 1, 1900; *St. Louis Republic,* May 10, 24, 1900; *New York Times,* May 25, 30, 1900; "Sizzling Bullets," *United Mine Workers' Journal,* XI (May 24, 1900), 1; Lincoln Steffens, *The Shame of the Cities* (New York, 1904), pp. 38, 104.

13. *St. Louis Republic,* May 26, 28, 1900; *Kansas City Star,* June 11, 1900.

14. *New York Times,* May 14, June 12, 1900.

15. G. G. Eggert, "Richard Olney" (University of Michigan, Ph.D., 1960), p. 420.

16. H. Wish, "The Pullman Strike," *Journal of the Illinois State Historical Society,* XXXII (September 1939), 303.

17. *New York Times,* March 14, 1895; *New Orleans Times-Democrat,* March 13, 1895.

18. "Coeur d'Alene Labor Troubles," *House Report,* 56 Cong., 1 sess., no. 1999 (June 5, 1900), pp. 1, 6; *Boise Idaho Daily Statesman,* April 30, 1899; Report of Congressman C. H. Grosvenor (Ohio) from the House Committee on Rules, January 8, 1900, *Congressional Record,* 56 Cong., 1 sess., 691; "Coeur d'Alene Mining Troubles," *Senate Document,* 56 Cong., 1 sess., no. 142 (February 5, 1900), pp. 63, 64.

19. Grosvenor report, p. 691; "The Imprisoned Men at Wardner," *American Federationist,* VI (July 1899), 105; W. D. Haywood, "Socialism the Hope of the Working Class," *International Socialist Review,* XII (February 1912), 467; "Labor Troubles in Idaho," *Senate Document,* 56 Cong., 1 sess., no. 42 (December 14, 1899), p. 3.

20. *New York Times,* May 20, 1899; Root-Steunenberg, September 28, 1899, in "Coeur d'Alene Labor Troubles," p. 17; *Congressional Record,* 56 Cong., 1 sess., 185, 234 (December 11, 12, 1899), 1155 (January 23, 1900), 3207, 3258 (March 23, 1900), 6074 (May 25, 1900). Cf. Rich, *Presidents,* p. 118.

21. G. W. Chessman, *Governor Theodore Roosevelt: The Albany*

Apprenticeship, 1898–1900 (Cambridge, Mass., 1965), pp. 202, 214.

22. *Times,* May 5, 1899; *Express,* May 10, 1899; T. Roosevelt, *Autobiography* (New York, 1914), p. 280.

23. *New York Times,* April 17, 20, 1900; Roosevelt-F. N. Goddard, in Roosevelt, *Autobiography,* p. 326.

24. Roosevelt-J. B. Bishop, October 13, 1902 in E. E. Morison, ed., *The Letters of Theodore Roosevelt,* 8 vols. (Cambridge, Mass., 1951), III, p. 349; Roosevelt, *Autobiography,* p. 291.

25. C. E. Graves (assist. sec. Republic Iron and Steel Co.)-Senator A. J. Hopkins of Illinois (Rep.), January 26, 1904, NA; Roosevelt-Grover Cleveland (October 5, 1902), and others, Morison, ed., *Letters,* III, pp. 323, 339, 341, 343, 362; Roosevelt, *Addresses and Presidential Messages of Theodore Roosevelt, 1902–1904* (New York, 1904), p. 288.

26. G. Korson, "A History of the UMWA," *United Mine Workers' Journal* (December 1, 1965), 4, 5; Stewart Culin, *A Trooper's Narrative of Service in the Anthracite Coal Strike, 1902* (Philadelphia, 1903), p. 69.

27. United States Coal Strike Commission, Proceedings of the Anthracite Coal Strike Commission, 56 vols. (Washington, 1902–1903), NA, II, pp. 150–151; *New York Times,* October 15, 1902.

28. Simons, *Capital and Labor* (Chicago, c. 1903), p. 54; *New York Times,* August 8, 1902.

29. Anthracite Proceedings, II, p. 140; Culin, *Trooper,* p. 64.

30. "Lattimer Tragedy-Wilkesbarre Farce," *American Federationist,* V (March 1898), 11–13; *New York Times,* September 11, 12, 1897; *New York World,* September 11, 1897; Edward Pinkowski, *Lattimer Massacre* (Philadelphia, 1950), pp. 8, 9, 11.

31. "The Hazleton Slaughter," *Locomotive Firemen's Magazine,* XXIII (November 1897), 372–74; "Lattimer Tragedy," 12, 13; *Pittsburgh Press,* September 11, 1897; *New York World,* September 11, 12, 1897; Means, "Miners' Strike and the Law," *Nation,* LXV (July 22, 1897), 63; *New York Times,* September 13, 14, 1897.

32. *New York Times,* February 8, March 10, 1898; "Guilty, Proven; but Acquitted," *American Federationist,* V (April 1898), 37; "Lattimer Tragedy," 13; Pinkowski, *Lattimer,* pp. 33, 34, 38; Wilson in *Monthly Journal of the International Association of Machinists,* X (March 1898), 134.

33. *New York Times,* September 13, 1897; Pinkowski, *Lattimer,* p. 20; "Hazleton Slaughter," 272, 273.

34. Anthracite Proceedings, IV, p. 1423, XXIV, pp. 4637, 4639; *New York Times,* October 14, 23, 1902; Culin, *Trooper,* p. 64.

35. Culin, *Trooper,* p. 30; Anthracite Proceedings, IV, pp. 439–440.

36. Roosevelt-Crane, October 22, 1902 in Morison, ed., *Letters, III,* p. 361; Anthracite Proceedings, XXIX, pp. 4639, 4642.

37. Roosevelt, *Autobiography,* p. 481; Roosevelt-Robert Bacon, October 7, 1902, in Morison, ed., *Letters,* III, p. 344.

38. W. B. Bremer and P. Stewart, Report on Strike of the International Teamsters' Union against Montgomery Ward & Co. (April 6, 1905), ESt, p. 171.

39. *New York Times,* May 11, 1905; Bremer and Stewart, Report, p. 242; G. J. Knott in *Typographical Journal,* XXVII (September 1905), 321.

40. *Western Clarion,* January 25, 1906, quoted in the *Idaho Daily Statesman* (Boise), June 28, 1906, and *Statesman* of June 25, 1906, clippings, WEB.

41. See H. F. Pringle, *Theodore Roosevelt* (London, 1934), p. 452.

42. Roosevelt-A. R. Cowles, May 15, 1886, in H. L. Hurwitz, *Theodore Roosevelt and Labor in New York State, 1880–1900* (New York, 1943), pp. 110–111. See London's *Call of the Wild* (New York, 1903) and *Iron Heel* (New York, 1907).

43. F. M. Kleiler, "White House Intervention in Labor Disputes," *Political Science Quarterly,* LXI (June 1953), 232–233; *New York Times,* December 8, 1903; F. L. Mott, *American Journalism,* rev. ed. (New York, 1950), pp. 567–569.

44. "Colorado's Carnival of Crime," *Current Literature,* XXXVII (August 1904), 104–105; *Rocky Mountain News* (Denver) July 7, 1904.

45. "Colorado's Carnival," 105; *Houston Post,* June 7, 1904; Western Federation of Miners, *Reply of the Western Federation of Miners to the "Red Book" of the Mine Operators' Association* (Denver, 1904). pp. 7, 16. Cf. Rich, *Presidents,* pp. 121–135.

Chapter 9: Government and Order

1. Theodore Roosevelt, *The New Nationalism* (Englewood Cliffs, N.J., 1961), pp. 101, 157.

2. *Journal* quoted in "Statement of the Western Federation of Miners," *Senate Document,* 58 Cong., 2 sess., no. 163 (February 20, 1904), p. 39. Cf. J. M. Cooper, "The Army and Civil Disorder: Federal Military Intervention in American Labor Disputes, 1877–1900" (University of Wisconsin, Ph.D., 1971), pp. 60, 61, 139, 140, 149, 359.

3. John Swinton, *A Momentous Question: The Respective Attitudes of Labor and Capital* (Philadelphia, 1895), p. 220; unidentified

newspaper clipping dated Washington, D.C., October 11, 1895 (?), EVD; *New York Times,* July 7, 1894; George E. Mowry, *The Era of Theodore Roosevelt* (New York, 1962), p. 125.

4. *Nashville American,* November 5, 1901; *Louisville Courier-Journal,* November 23, 1904.

5. "Federal Aid in Domestic Disturbances, 1787–1903," *Senate Document,* 57 Cong., 2 sess. (March 2, 1903), p. 258.

6. See, for example, R. D. Smith, "Phases of the McKee's Rocks Strike," *Survey,* XXIII (October 2, 1909), 41 and *Peonage in Pennsylvania: Hearings before the Committee on Labor of the House of Representatives pursuant to H. Res. No. 90,* Cong., 1 sess. (August 1, 1911), 8.

7. See the *Toledo Union Leader,* November 12, 1909, and Mary H. Jones, *The Autobiography of Mother Jones,* ed. Mary F. Parton (Chicago, 1925), p. 60.

8. Inis Weed, The Industrial Causes of Violence (n.d.), CIR/NA, Part 2, p. 46; Untermann, "The Militia Bill," *Wayland's Monthly,* XXXIX (July 1903), 1.

9. IWW Convention *Proceedings,* 1905, pp. 269, 274, 275.

10. Spargo, *Socialism* (New York, 1906), pp. 153, 154; Hillquit, *Socialism in Theory and Practice* (New York, 1910), p. 302; SPA Convention *Proceedings,* 1912, p. 85.

11. U.S. Industrial Commission, Vol. XVII, *Reports on Labor Organization, Labor Disputes, and Arbitration* (Washington, 1901), pp. 151, 168, 276; U.S. Strike Commission, *Report on the Chicago Strike of June–July, 1894* (Washington, 1894), p. 41.

12. AFL Convention *Proceedings,* 1892, p. 12.

13. Copy of the letter as stated in Anon. (possibly Ralph M. Easley, secretary of the National Civic Federation), Socialism as an Incubus on the American Labor Movement (n.p., n.d.), NCF.

14. Moore, Martial Law, Writ of Habeas Corpus and Constitutionally Guaranteed Personal Liberties (March 9, 1914), CIR/NA, p. 1.

15. B. F. Helfand, "Labor and the Courts: The Common Law Doctrine of Criminal Conspiracy and Its Application in the Buck's Stove Case," *Labor History,* XVIII (Winter 1977), 91; Foner, *History of the Labor Movement in the United States,* 4 vols. (New York, 1947–1965), II, p. 26; "Report of a Hearing before the Committee on the Judiciary of the House of Representatives March 23, 1900, on the bill 'To limit the meaning of the word "conspiracy" . . . ,' " *Senate Document,* 56 Cong., 2 sess., no. 58 (March 23, 1900), p. 8.

16. Steuben, *Strike Strategy* (New York, 1950), p. 183; U.S. Industrial Commission, Vol. V, *Report on Labor Legislation* (Washington, 1901), pp. 6, 72; *Sixteenth Annual Report of the Commissioner*

of Labor (Washington, 1901), pp. 991–1032; Leon F. Miner, Picketing (Ann Arbor, 1909), UM, p. 19.

17. Miner, Picketing, pp. 10, 11; Eggert, *Railroad Labor Disputes* (Ann Arbor, 1967), pp. 234, 235.

18. Unspecified work by Witte cited in Weed, Industrial Causes, Part 1, p. 62.

19. A. P. Blaustein and C. O. Porter, *The American Lawyer* (Chicago, 1954), p. 82; W. L. O'Neill, *Divorce in the Progressive Era* (New Haven, 1967), pp. 20, 22–23 n., 26.

20. *Encyclopaedia Britannica,* 14th ed. (London, 1929), Vol. XVIII, p. 160; G. E. and E. H. Carte, *Police Reform in the United States: The Era of August Vollmer, 1905–1932* (Berkeley, 1975); R. Lyons, "The Boston Police Strike of 1919," *New England Quarterly,* XX (June 1947).

21. Forcey, *The Crossroads of Liberalism* (London, 1967).

22. Weed, Industrial Causes, Part 4, p. 18; Graham Adams, Jr., *Age of Industrial Violence, 1910–1915* (New York, 1966), pp. 158, 159; P. Taft and P. Ross, "American Labor Violence," in H. D. Graham and T. R. Gurr, eds., *Violence in America* (New York, 1969), p. 332.

23. Taft and Ross, "Labor Violence," p. 335; Melvyn Dubofsky, *We Shall Be All; A History of the IWW* (New York, 1969), p. 388.

24. See Dubofsky, *We Shall Be All;* William Preston, Jr., *Aliens and Dissenters: Federal Suppression of Radicals, 1903–1933* (Cambridge, 1963); Donald Johnson, *The Challenge to American Freedoms: World War I and the Rise of the American Civil Liberties Union* (Lexington, Ky., 1963).

25. Lodge-L. A. Coolidge, May 31, August 9, 1919, HCL.

26. Taft and Ross, "Labor Violence," pp. 337–339.

27. Irving Bernstein, *Turbulent Years* (Boston, 1969), pp. 287–289.

28. See B. Mandel, "Samuel Gompers and the Negro Workers, 1886–1914," *Journal of Negro History,* XL (January 1955); Jervis Anderson, *A. Philip Randolph* (New York, 1974); Victor Reuther, *The Brothers Reuther and the Story of the UAW* (Boston, 1976).

29. See, for example, J. H. Franklin, *The Militant South, 1800–1861* (Cambridge, Mass., 1956); C. Vann Woodward, *The Strange Career of Jim Crow* (New York, 1955).

30. N. A. Wynn, *The Afro-American and the Second World War* (London, 1976), pp. 6–10.

31. W. M. Tuttle, Jr., *Race Riot: Chicago in the Red Summer of 1919* (New York, 1972), pp. 6, 33.

32. A. I. Waskow, *From Race Riot to Sit-In: 1919 and the 1960s* (New York, 1966), pp. 38, 43; Tuttle, *Race Riot,* p. 203.

33. Tuttle, *Race Riot*, p. 206; D. R. McCoy, *Calvin Coolidge* (New York, 1967), pp. 92, 441 n. 17.

34. E. M. Rudwick, *Race Riot East St. Louis* (Carbondale, 1964), p. 74; Tuttle, *Race Riot*, p. 203.

35. Waskow, *Race Riot to Sit-In*, p. 45.

36. *Ibid.*, pp. 33, 34.

37. *Ibid.*, 23, 36; Wynn, *Afro-American*, p. 72.

38. Rudwick, *Race Riot*, pp. 4, 133.

39. Waskow, *Race Riot to Sit-In*, p. 73.

40. A. M. Lee and N. D. Humphrey, *Race Riot* (New York, 1943), p. 73; Wynn, *Afro-American*, p. 69.

41. Lee and Humphrey, *Race Riot*, pp. 74, 75.

42. William Manchester, *The Glory and the Dream* (London, 1975), pp. 799–809; B. M. Rich, *The Presidents and Civil Disorder* (Washington, 1941), pp. 2–20.

43. Haley, "Foreword," in *The Autobiography of Malcolm X* (Harmondsworth, England, 1968), p. 61; W. H. Parker-Jeffreys-Jones, February 2, 1966; *New York Times*, August 14, 1965; W. C. Benfer, "The Story of the Homestake Lockout," *International Socialist Review*, X (March 1910), 782–783.

44. *Report of the NACCD* (New York, 1968), pp. 100, 499, 507.

Chapter 10: Social Conflict and Progressivism

1. V. I. Lenin, "Imperialism: The Highest Stage of Capitalism (1916)" in *The Essentials of Lenin*, 2 vols. (London, 1947), I, p. 723.

2. Lenin, "The Results and Significance of the U.S. Presidential Elections," *Pravda*, November 9, 1912, in *Collected Works*, 41 vols. (Moscow, 1963), XVIII, pp. 402–404; Hofstadter, *The Age of Reform* (New York, 1955); Kolko, *The Triumph of Conservatism* (Chicago, 1967); Wiebe, *The Search for Order* (New York, 1967); Thelen, "Social Tensions and the Origins of Progressivism," *Journal of American Studies*, LVI (September 1969); Nugent, *From Centennial to World War* (Indianapolis, 1977).

3. See G. E. Mowry, *The Era of Theodore Roosevelt* (New York, 1958), chapters 6 and 7.

4. "Revival of Violence," *Nation*, XCIV (1912), 580.

5. Moscowitz-Wald, August 19, 1912, LW.

6. J. G. Brooks, *American Syndicalism* (New York, 1913); W. E. Trautman, *Direct Action and Sabotage* (Pittsburgh, 1912); J. Spargo, *Syndicalism* (New York, 1913); Foner, *History of the Labor Movement in the United States*, 4 vols. (New York, 1947–1965), IV, p. 159.

7. Goldman-editors *Metropolitan,* December 4, 1905, EG.

8. *Mother Earth,* IV (1904), 194–195.

9. Interview with J. M. Whitcomb (collector of Rose Pastor Stokes papers), August 19, 1969; Whitcomb-Jeffreys-Jones, February 20, 1970; W. E. Walling, *Russia's Message: The True World Impact of the Revolution* (New York, 1908); Scott, *Walking Delegate* (New York, 1905).

10. Stokes guest book and Whitcomb correspondence with Kent, RPS (kindly supplied prior to deposit at Yale University by J. M. Whitcomb). See also R. B. Stokes, *The Woman Who Wouldn't* (New York, 1916); R. Kent, *This Is My Own* (New York, 1940).

11. Mabel Dodge Luhan, *Intimate Memories,* 4 vols. (New York, 1933–1937), III, *Movers and Shakers,* pp. 46, 47, 57, 186, 203; Minutes Iron League Erectors' Association (New York, November 16, 1909), FW.

12. Vechten, *Peter Whiffle* (New York, 1926), pp. 125, 126, 135, 136; May, *The End of American Innocence* (Chicago, 1959), p. 312.

13. "So-called Industrial Peace," *New Republic,* I (1915), 6. Charles Forcey, *The Crossroads of Liberalism* (New York, 1967), pp. 3–6, 29.

14. E. M. House, *Philip Dru: Administrator* (New York, 1912), dust jacket to first edition.

15. Manuscripts relative to Chicago teamsters' strike of 1905, GT; E. T. Devine, "Industrial Dispute or Revolution?" *Survey,* XXVI (1911), 835–837.

16. Committee on Industrial Relations, *A Communication to the Honorable William Howard Taft, President of the United States, Urging the Creation of a Federal Commission on Industrial Relations* (n.p., 1911); *Hearings before the Committee on Labor of the House of Representatives on the Bill HR 21094 to Create an Industrial Commission,* 62 Cong., 2 sess. (1912), pp. 5, 18, 19; Heyburn-J. Kurtz, February 26, 1912, SML.

17. Minutes of the Chicago meeting, AMB.

18. Addams-A. M. Blaine, May 15, 1911, enclosing Kent-Addams, May 11, 1911, which had in turn enclosed a copy of Kent-V. C. Lawson (of the *Chicago Daily News*), May 10, 1911, AMB; Commons-La Follette, January 15, 1912, JRC.

19. Kolko, *Triumph,* p. 192.

20. Roosevelt-McCarthy, January 29, 1915, CM.

21. Taft, *Message to Congress: Industrial Relations* (New York, 1912), pp. 3, 5; A. T. Davis, "The Campaign for the Industrial Relations Commission, 1911–1913," *Mid-American,* XLV (October 1963), 223–225.

22. E. E. Witte, Diary, November 1, 1909, EEW; McCarthy-C. F. McCarthy, December 15, 1914, February 19, 1915, CM.

23. Commons, *Myself* (Madison, 1964), pp. 108–110, 151, 166.

24. Commons, *Labor and Administration* (New York, 1913), pp. v, 71–84.

25. Stecker, Appendix-Violence (n.d.), O'Regan, Rough Draft of a Proposed Federal Act to Regulate Detective Agencies (1914), and Grant, Violence in Labor Disputes (n.d.), all in CIR/WL.

26. USCIR Minutes (Washington, December 30, 1913), pp. 403–416, and Witte-Leiserson, February 7, 1913, both in WML.

27. McCarthy-M. S. Dudgeon, December 9, 1914, CM.

28. Witte-McCarthy, October 31, 1914, CM.

29. H. G. Lee-McCarthy, enclosing Divisions of the Broad Subjects of Research, November 1, 1914, and List of Payments to Research Division Employees to 31 January 1915, both in CM.

30. Leiserson-E. D. Thomas, May 9, 1939, WML.

31. Leiserson-McCarthy, November 30, 1914, CM; O'Regan-B. M. Manly, June 29, 1914, CIR/NA.

32. J. A. Fitch, "Field Investigation of the Industrial Relations Commission," *Survey*, XXXIII (1915), 578.

33. McCarthy-Parkinson, October 26, 1914, and Leiserson-McCarthy, November 22, 1914, both in CM.

34. Divisions of the Broad Subjects of Research, November 1, 1914, CM.

35. McCarthy-W. J. Lauck, October 6, 1914, CM; Kellogg-Walsh, February 5, 1915, FW.

36. Commons-Sumner, March 17, May 11, 1915, JRC.

37. Witte-Leiserson, October 10, 1915, WML.

38. "Use of Federal Troops in Labor Disputes," *Monthly Labor Review* (published by the U.S. Bureau of Labor Statistics), LIII (1941), 561–571.

39. See J. R. Commons, *Races and Immigrants in America* (New York, 1907); W. M. Leiserson, *Adjusting Immigrant and Industry* (New York, 1924); J. W. Jenks and W. J. Lauck, *The Immigration Problem* (New York, 1911); Ira Kipnis, *The American Socialist Movement, 1897–1912* (New York, 1952).

40. Ekirch, *Progressivism in America* (New York, 1974), pp. 88, 89.

41. See B. C. and F. La Follette, *Robert M. La Follette* (New York, 1953), chapter 37.

42. J. F. Stover, *American Railroads* (Chicago, 1961), pp. 168, 169; T. Roosevelt-Senator W. B. Allison, February 26, 1907, and Roosevelt-Interstate Commerce Commission, March 15, 1907, in E. E. Morison, ed., *The Letters of Theodore Roosevelt,* 8 vols. (Cambridge, Mass., 1952), V, pp. 600, 623.

43. Graham, *An Encore for Reform: The Old Progressives and the New Deal* (New York, 1967).

Chapter 11: Violence and Reform

1. See R. M. Freeland, *The Truman Doctrine and the Origins of McCarthyism* (New York, 1974).

2. See D. T. Carter, *Scottsboro* (New York, 1971).

3. See Chapter 2.

4. George Wolfskill, *The Revolt of the Conservatives* (Boston, 1962), pp. 110, 189.

5. William Gellerman, *Martin Dies* (New York, 1972), pp. 65, 145.

6. Auerbach, *Labor and Liberty: The La Follette Committee and the New Deal* (Indianapolis, 1966), p. 175.

7. Louis Cantor, *A Prologue to the Protest Movement: The Missouri Sharecropper Roadside Demonstration of 1939* (Durham, N.C., 1969), p. 125.

8. T. C. Cochran, *Great Depression and World War Two, 1929–1945* (Glenview, Ill., 1968), pp. 56, 78.

9. Tugwell, *The Democratic Roosevelt* (Garden City, 1957), p. 9; Bernstein in Bernstein, ed., *Towards a New Past* (London, 1970), pp. 267–282; Conkin, *FDR* (New York, 1967), p. 21.

10. Benedetto Croce, *History of Europe in the Nineteenth Century,* trans. Henry Furst (London, 1934), p. 266.

11. See Oscar Handlin, *John Dewey's Challenge to Education* (New York, 1959), and T. R. Sizer, *Secondary Schools at the Turn of the Century* (New Haven, 1964).

12. Croce, *History,* pp. 292, 293.

13. H. G. Warren, *Herbert Hoover and the Great Depression* (New York, 1959), pp. 64f., 72f.; E. E. Robinson and V. D. Barnet, *Herbert Hoover* (Stanford, 1975), p. 154; Joseph Dorfman, *The Economic Mind in American Civilization,* 5 Vols. (New York, 1959), IV, pp. 347–351, V, pp. 623, 624.

14. D. S. Hirshfield, *The Lost Reform: The Campaign for Compulsory Health Insurance in the United States from 1932 to 1943* (Cambridge, Mass., 1970); Keith Sinclair, *A History of New Zealand,* rev. ed. (Harmondsworth, England, 1969), p. 270; Sutch, *The Quest for Security in New Zealand 1840 to 1966* (Wellington, N.Z., 1966), p. 236.

15. W. E. Leuchtenburg, *Franklin D. Roosevelt and the New Deal* (New York, 1963), p. 133 and passim; D. M. Nelson, "The Development of Unemployment Insurance in the United States" (Wisconsin, Ph.D., 1974), pp. 540, 575–577.

16. W. E. Leuchtenburg, "The Great Depression," in *The Com-*

parative Approach to American History, C. Vann Woodward, ed. (New York, 1968), p. 296.

17. Freeland, *Truman Doctrine,* p. 150 and passim.

18. R. H. Rovere, *Senator Joe McCarthy* (Cleveland, 1960), p. 4.

19. I am grateful to Dr. James V. Compton of San Francisco State College for instruction on this point.

20. H. S. Commager, ed., *Documents of American History,* 7th ed. (New York, 1963), p. 689; William Manchester, *The Glory and the Dream: A Narrative History of America, 1932–1972* (London, 1975), p. 1041.

21. Manchester, *Glory,* p. 1042.

22. As evidenced by the experience of the author's landlady in Belmont, Massachusetts, 1972.

23. Author's observation during visit to Wroclaw, Poland, in 1970.

24. A. Meier and E. Rudwick, "Black Violence in the 20th Century: A Study in Rhetoric and Retaliation," in H. D. Graham and T. R. Gurr, eds., *The History of Violence in America* (New York, 1969), p. 399; *The Autobiography of Malcolm X* (Harmondsworth, 1968), p. 484.

25. Meier and Rudwick, "Black Violence," p. 406; Herbert Aptheker, *American Negro Slave Revolts* (New York, 1943), p. 298.

26. *Autobiography of Malcolm X,* pp. 340, 349, 477.

27. Fanon, *The Wretched of the Earth,* trans. Constance Farrington (Harmondsworth, 1967), pp. 40, 41; I. L. Gendzier, *Frantz Fanon* (London, 1973), pp. 263, 264; J. H. Skolnick, *The Politics of Protest* (New York, 1969), pp. 138, 144, 145.

28. F. P. Graham, "A Contemporary History of American Crime," in H. D. Graham and T. R. Gurr, *The History of Violence in America* (New York, 1969), p. 495; Meier and Rudwick, "Black Violence," p. 411.

29. Meier and Rudwick, "Black Violence," p. 401.

30. Manchester, *Glory,* p. 981; S. E. Morison, H. S. Commager, and W. E. Leuchtenburg, *A Concise History of the American Republic* (New York, 1977), p. 697; Skolnick, *Politics,* p. 346.

31. Morison and others, *Concise History,* p. 746.

32. *Ibid.*

33. Cf. Freeland, *Truman Doctrine,* p. 360.

34. Typescript of press conference, December 2, 1969, GPRR.

35. On the placid reputation, see Committee of the Society of Conservative Lawyers, *Public Order* (London, 1970), p. 3.

36. *The Times* (London), May 6, 1968, March 9, 17, 1970, August 29, 1977; *Daily Telegraph* (London), February 2, 1970.

A Guide to Further Reading

The reader wishing to acquire more detailed knowledge of the topics dealt with in this book will find help in a number of studies. There is an extensive bibliography in R. Jeffreys-Jones, "The Problem of Industrial Violence in the United States, 1899–1909" (Cambridge, Ph.D., 1969; available from EP Microform, Wakefield, England). M. F. Neufeld's *Representative Bibliography of American Labor History* (Ithaca, N.Y., 1964) has been and still is supplemented annually in the periodical *Labor History*. The intricacies of revolutionary rhetoric in the 1880s and 1960s, respectively, may be approached through Henry David's *History of the Haymarket Affair,* 2nd ed. (New York, 1958), and E. J. Bacciocco, *The New Left in America: From Reform to Revolution* (Stanford, 1974), while Robert Hunter's *Violence and the Labor Movement* (New York, 1914) is suggestive of some of the ideological undercurrents of the Progressive movement. J. M. Cooper's "The Army and Civil Disorder: Federal Military Intervention in American Labor Disputes, 1877–1900" (Wisconsin, Ph.D., 1971; available from University Microfilms, Ann Arbor, Michigan) contains the argument that expansionist U.S. Army officers exploited class conflict without believing in it; Cooper's bibliography may be usefully referred to in conjunction with the footnotes in Robert Reinders' "Militia and Public Order in Nineteenth Century America," *Journal of American Studies,* 11 (April 1977). J. S. Auerbach deals with the political significance of the La Follette Committee as well as with its findings in *Labor and Liberty: The La Follette Committee and the New Deal* (Indianapolis, 1966). Problems of social and reform history are among those placed in an international perspective in C. Vann Woodward, ed., *The Comparative Approach to American History* (New York, 1968).

Several aspects of social violence ignored or fleetingly referred to in this book are treated in H. D. Graham and T. R. Gurr, eds., *The History of Violence in America* (New York, 1969); for example, Sheldon Hackney examines homicide-suicide ratios and psychological-cultural factors in his essay on "Southern Violence." Pauline Maier discusses the relationship between preindustrial crowd disorders and revolutionary change in her book *From Resistance to Revolution: Colonial Radicals and the Development of American Opposition to Britain, 1765–1776* (New York, 1972). R. M. Brown has collated quantitative information on vigilante and black-white violence in *Strain of Violence: Historical Studies of American Violence and Vigilantism* (New York, 1975), in which he advances the view that some of America's violence was "positive" in character.

A. D. Grimshaw's *Racial Violence in the United States* (Chicago, 1969) is an interdisciplinary anthology of essays on the history and nature of black-white violence. The "Selected Bibliography" in August Meier, Elliot Rudwick, and F. L. Broderick, *Black Protest Thought in the Twentieth Century*, 2nd. ed. (Indianapolis, 1971), supplies references on violent black rhetoric. John Higham's *Strangers in the Land; Patterns of American Nativism, 1860–1925* (New Brunswick, N.J., 1955) is an attempt to explain ethnic tensions in terms of native-American crises of confidence and contains a "Bibliographical Note." In *Work, Culture, and Society in Industrializing America* (New York, 1976), H. G. Gutman explores the idea that ethnic disorders have been caused by repeated agrarian influxes into America's industrial cities.

Index

About the Author

Rhodri Jeffreys-Jones was born in Carmathen, Wales, and received his B.A. degree at the University College of Wales, Aberystwyth. He received his Ph.D. degree at the University of Cambridge, England, and is now lecturer in history at the University of Edinburgh, Scotland.